THE ROAD MAP OF THE WAY.

T. Noyes-Lewis

THE
SUN
AND THE
SERPENT

HAMISH MILLER

AND

PAUL BROADHURST

Pendragon Press
Cornwall

First published in 1989 by
Pendragon Press, Launceston, Cornwall

Paperback edition 1990
Second imprint 1991
Third edition 1994
This edition 1998

ISBN 0 9515183 1 3

Design by Evan Jones

Typeset, printed and bound by
Penwell Print Ltd., Callington, Cornwall

*This book is dedicated
to all those who, with the wind in their hair
and love in their hearts, have sought, and continue to
seek, the ways of the Earth Spirit.*

Note to the Fifth Edition

Since this book was first published in 1989, it has generated a considerable amount of correspondence from around the world. This has overwhelmingly supported the evidence in the following pages that there are, flowing through the surface of the Earth, bio-magnetic arteries of natural energy which were recognised by our ancestors. These are discernable by dowsing and also have a profound spiritual dimension.

Many people have felt inspired to visit the places documented and to approach them with a reverence that befits humanity's role as guardians of these ancient sanctuaries. Some of these, once neglected, are again attracting the attentions of sincere pilgrims following ancient paths.

THE SUN AND THE SERPENT is essentially the journal of a quest that took place over a certain period of time. For this reason it would be inappropriate to include the changes to the landscape that have occurred during the last five years or so, and the mass of information that has been forthcoming from readers. A few slight changes have been made, and some colour photographs are also included to enable the reader to connect more readily with the strange magic of these places. The book is a diary, an account of an adventure taking place in a familiar, but secret, landscape; the Earth beneath our feet. It is the intention of the authors and publishers to help revive an interest in the idea of pilgrimage and encourage a sensitivity to Nature and the great wisdom it reveals.

For the last few years, a similar project has been under way following the European St Michael Line (see pages 126-7). The discoveries made during this quest are now being assimilated, and interested readers are invited to write to the publishers who will notify them of publication in due course.

CONTENTS

COLOUR PHOTOGRAPHS

by Paul Broadhurst

LIST OF ILLUSTRATIONS

Photography by Paul Broadhurst
Maps and Plans by Hamish Miller

INTRODUCTION

JOHN MICHELL

I T WAS, I THINK, in 1966 that I first went to Glastonbury, in the company of Harry Fainlight, the poet and great Wandering Jew of that period. We had no very definite reason for going there, but it had something to do with William Blake, William Stukeley, Alfred Watkins, Wellesley Tudor Pole, Joseph of Arimathea, strange lights in the sky, new insights, new music, and our conviction that the world was about to flip over on its axis so that heresy would become orthodoxy and an entirely new world-order would shortly be revealed. We were in favour of that process, and meant to help it along.

Harry had lived in New York and was an ally of Allen Ginsberg, another Blakean. They had both been stirred by Blake's address to the Jews, where he informed them that all their priestly traditions had come to them from the Druids, and that the heavenly Jerusalem would descend to earth in England. Blake's authority for these statements was the eighteenth century antiquarian and Druid revivalist, William Stukeley.

Stukeley's vision, as set out in his book *Abury, a Temple of the British Druids*, is the foundation of modern Druidism, and it also produced the British Israelite movement by which Harry at the time was strongly influenced. He had succeeded, to a far greater extent than I had at that time, in freeing himself from the rationalistic dogma of college education, and eventually he achieved a state of perception so cruelly acute and lucid that it killed him.

On our way to Glastonbury from London we stopped at Avebury, which Stukeley had called a serpent temple. We went by hitch-hiking, carrying sleeping bags. At Avebury we first went to the church, noticed the serpent-killing bishop carved on the font, and thought it a good place to conceal our packs and sleeping bags while we explored the stones. When we came back the church was locked, so we spent a cold night under hay in a local shed.

Glastonbury, when finally we reached it, was quite different from how it is today. The New Age had not yet dawned there. There was no Gothic Image bookshop, no art galleries, no health foods, no weird-looking people on the streets. Surly publicans were not yet displaying 'No Hippy' placards. Instead, the signs on their doors said 'No Gypsies'.

At the Abbey Café, Benedict Street, an eggs, beans and chips sort of place, we talked about UFOs until a nervous lorry driver told us to stop. After he had left we continued, and thus we made friends with the owner, Gino Schiraldi from Italy. He was a natural mystic and anti-clerical, and the subject of UFOs appealed to him because it was neither materialistic nor religious. Later he wrote the most prophetic of Glastonbury books, *The Phenomena of Avalon*. Gino and his wife, Nancy, asked us to stay in their house, giving us a base from which to explore the mysteries of Glastonbury.

In her book *Avalon of the Heart*, first published in 1934, Dion Fortune, who lived below Glastonbury Tor where Geoffrey Ashe now lives, gives a picture of Glastonbury early this century when the Avalonians were active. The people she thus named were a collection of artists and mystics who came individually to Glastonbury, intending in their various ways to promote a spiritual revival there. They were exciting times. Alice Buckton had bought the Chalice Well property and made it a centre of arts and crafts; plays and operas were performed in the Assembly Rooms, and on the site of the old abbey Frederick Bligh Bond's excavations, guided by psychic messages from the former monks, were revealing the architectural glories of the past. It seemed to many at that time that Glastonbury was beginning to fulfil its natural destiny as England's Jerusalem.

By the time Harry and I got there, all that was long past. The only surviving relic of the Avalonians was the Chalice Well, preserved by the initiative of the mystical writer, Wellesley Tudor Pole. The garden around it was smaller than it is today, but just as lovely. A kind old lady sat in a wooden hut at the entrance, selling tickets, crabapple jelly and little booklets of a spiritual nature. One of the titles was *Michael, Prince of Heaven* by a number of contributors including Wellesley Tudor Pole. It was largely about pilgrimage. Tudor Pole spoke of Michael the Archangel as the light-bearer of a coming New Age and called for a revival of pilgrimages to his hilltop sanctuaries, from Glastonbury through the West Country to St Michael's Mount at the far end of Cornwall. He implied that the Chalice Well garden should serve as a resting place for pilgrims on the St Michael route.

At that time I was writing the first of my published books, *The Flying Saucer Vision*. It followed up the idea, first put forward by C.G. Jung in his 1959 book on flying saucers, that the strange lights and other phenomena of the post-War period were portents of a radical change in human consciousness coinciding with the dawn of the Aquarian Age. A theme in my book was the connection between 'unidentified flying objects' and ancient sites, as evidenced both in folklore and in contemporary experience. UFOs were constantly being sighted over St Michael's tower on Glastonbury Tor. Mark Palmer, Maldwyn Thomas and their group were then travelling with horses and carts on pilgrimages across England. They often camped near the Tor, and while I was with them we used to watch the nightly manoeuvrings of lights in the sky. Jung's prophecy of aerial portents being followed by a change in consciousness was evidently being fulfilled.

Travelling west from Glastonbury towards Taunton, we came across a great mound of a hill, the Mump at Burrowbridge, also topped by a ruined church of St Michael. The road makes directly for it and then skirts its base in a curve. From the summit of the Mump, Glastonbury Tor is visible in the distance about 12 miles away. The spiritual link between these two hills is obvious. They appear in some way to be in communication, and not merely between themselves but as points in a more extensive chain of communication, conveying a type of spirit which the early Christians in Britain associated with St Michael. Visions of Michael, as reported at St Michael's Mount in the fourth century, are traditionally in the form of glowing apparitions, and this suggested a possible connection between the Michael spirit and the strange lights which we had seen floating over Glastonbury Tor.

As well as both being dedicated to St Michael, the Tor and the Mump have another feature in common, their orientation. The axis of the Mump is directed towards the Tor, where the line is continued by the old pilgrims' path along the ridge of the Tor to St Michael's tower. This line drew attention to itself and demanded further investigation, so I extended it further east, and the result confirmed its significance. The line went straight to the great stones at the entrance to the megalithic temple at Avebury. In the other direction, westward, it pointed towards St Michael's Mount by way of other prominent Michael sanctuaries.

The accuracy of this alignment, precisely between the entrance to Avebury and the summits of the Tor and Mump, was later confirmed through geodetic calculations by Robert Forrest. Also on the line, a few miles east of Avebury, he located the church at Ogbourne St George (St George, according to Rudolf Steiner and Tudor Pole, representing an earthly aspect of St Michael), and his calculations showed that the western end of the line was not St Michael's Mount, which it bypasses a short distance to the north, but a point on the coast beside Land's End, the extreme western tip of Cornwall. From there it runs across country to the bulge of East Anglia, virtually the extreme eastern point of England. Almost half-way up the line is the great temple of Avebury.

In his book on Avebury, first published in 1743, William Stukeley was inspired to identify it as a winged serpent temple. The serpent was formed by the two curved avenues of standing stones which met within the Avebury circle. At the eastern end of the serpent was its head, represented by two concentric stone rings which Stukeley called the Sanctuary. It stood on a ridge of Hackpen Hill, a name which Stukeley translated as Serpent's Head. He interpreted the overall design as an alchemical symbol of sacred energy, created by the Druid priests as a means of attracting divine influences and sanctifying the whole countryside.

Other associations between the serpent, as a symbol of the earth spirit, and the Avebury landscape are mentioned in Michael Dames' very perceptive book of 1977, *The Avebury Cycle*. It seems natural to extend the serpent imagery to the St Michael Line which has Avebury as its mid-point. On an early visit to Glastonbury I painted a large mural across a wall of Gino's Abbey Café, showing the line as the spine of a giant earth figure, a reference to Blake's Albion, with its eye at Eye in Suffolk, other *chakra* points at Avebury and Glastonbury and its feet at Land's End. Twirling round the spine were serpents symbolising its vital energies.

The only reason for mentioning this crude effort is that it was the first illustration of the St Michael Line, and even at that early stage in its conception it had attracted to itself the imagery of the serpent. This appeared spontaneously and I sought for no particular meaning in it. In this book the same symbolism reappears in connection with the St Michael Line across England, but this time it is shown that it does indeed have meaning. Paul Broadhurst and Hamish Miller have opened a new dimension to studies of the St Michael Line. *The Sun and the Serpent* is one of the strangest, most stirring books I have ever read, and it may prove through its implications to be one of the most important. For if the authors are correct in what they affirm, they have uncovered in the English landscape the most remarkable of ancient secrets.

If the authors are correct . . . That is obviously the first thing one wants to know on reading this amazing book. Are they deceiving us, or deluding themselves, and can their findings be checked and reproduced by other people?

The first part of this question is easy to answer. I have known Paul and Hamish long enough and well enough to be absolutely confident in saying that they are entirely honest and straight-forward. Everyone I have met who also knows them says just the same. They are without guile and quite incapable of wilfully misleading anyone. Could they themselves, then, have been misled? Dowsing is an intuitive practice and therefore to some extent subjective. Beginners soon learn how easy it is for results to be conditioned by one's own, and even by other people's, thoughts and wishes. Hamish, however, is not a beginner. He is an experienced, self-critical dowser, much respected by the dowsing fraternity, and he is professionally alert to the constant possibility of delusion. The fact that he is confident enough to stake his reputation on the findings reported in this book is impressive to those who know the worth of that reputation. Paul's good name is also at stake here. He is well aware of this, and he has watched Hamish narrowly on their journeys along the St Michael Line, needing to be sure in his own mind that the dowsing results were genuine. Often, unknown to Hamish, he set him tests, taking him on unfamiliar roads to see where he would pick up the line of energy. Always the spot found was on the continuation of the line as previously established. I too have seen Hamish at work on a section of the St Michael Line, and was impressed by his certainty. On that occasion, other dowsers, who had acquired the 'feel' of the energy line being followed, were able independently to confirm his results.

This brings us to the question of whether other, neutral dowsers, outside the influence of our authors, will be able to detect the energies of the St Michael Line as and where Hamish Miller has done. Science likes experiments to be repeatable, and if the phenomenon here described is to have scientific standing, other people also must find it. With that in mind, and to facilitate detailed investigation of their claims, the authors offer to provide interested readers with local maps, marked with the lines of current which they have found (see page 211).

From what has been said above, there is surely a case *prima facie* for taking this book at face value and allowing that there may be an energy pattern in connection with the St Michael Line. Some readers will probably not be inclined to accept that without further evidence. Others will hear in it the ring of truth and find that it coincides with their intuition. Whatever one's attitude, there is plenty to enjoy in these pages. In the entire literature of antiquarian ramblings there has never been one like this! How lucky we are in England to inhabit such a diverse, mysterious, symbolically rich landscape.

Finally we must come down to brass tacks and ask the hard question. It is, of course, about meaning. Granted that the straight pole of the St Michael Line, from the furthest western to the furthest eastern point in England, is entwined by serpentine earth energies, what are we supposed to think or do about it? Since I have been asked to write this Introduction, I presume that I am allowed, even required, to contribute some personal notions. Here they are, then.

We are living through a period of revelation. In response to the dire necessities of this apocalyptic time, answering the demand for real knowledge and wisdom, our minds and senses are receiving messages from nature—from Gaia as the Lovelockians have it. Jung predicted this in his Flying Saucer book. In the thirty years since he wrote it, the portents he foresaw have grown ever more numerous and insistent. The UFO phenomenon has solidified from mere lights and rumours, now leaving its physical marks every summer in the form of energized 'crop circles' in the fields around Avebury, Warminster and other ancient parts of Wiltshire. Here again the question of meaning arises; and it arises also in connection with modern discoveries of aligned sacred sites ('leys') throughout the world, of temples orientated astrologically to receive light and energies from certain heavenly bodies, of the mystical science of geomancy and of the cosmological patterns and formulae which sustained ancient civilizations. Revelations abound. Individually, and in terms of modern rationalistic conventions, they appear meaningless. But together they amount to a statement, given directly by nature; a statement that our present way of understanding and treating the earth is wrong, that we inhabit a living planet and we must give it the respect due to any living creature. From that follows a quite different perception of our relationship to nature, leading to the rediscovery of the ancient spiritual sciences.

We do not know why serpentine energies spiral around the course of the line of St Michael sites from the far west to the far eastern end of England. Others before us have recognized the phenomenon, and they have made their sanctuaries and pilgrimage routes in relation to the earth energies. The ancients, as Plato reminds us, were simple people. They did not ask reasons from nature, but accepted things as they were, so that if a certain rock was known for giving dreams and true oracles, they listened to it. Plato also emphasizes that everything, all human science, knowledge and wisdom, originates in divine revelation. Those of us who, from a rational point of view, have assessed the likelihood of human survival under the present regime of thought reckon it a lost cause. Yet the rational point of view gives no prospect of revelation, and thus prevents us from seeing what has been going on in recent years. The signs of an approaching climax of revelation are rapidly increasing, and this book is one of them. It was not written by the authors' own decision or for their own benefit. They were impelled to do it by those forces in nature which are now active in disclosing knowledge, long hidden, to a generation that desperately needs it and is now ready to accept it.

Be ye therefore wise as serpents
and gentle as doves

Matthew 10:16

STRANGE ALCHEMY

Is not that Sun thy husband and the Moon thy glimmering veil?
Are not the Stars of heaven thy children? art thou not Babylon?
Art thou Nature, Mother of all?

William Blake

MAYDAY, AVEBURY, 2000 BC. Under a glittering starlit sky, the shadowy landscape waits. A diaphanous mist rises from the ground, swathing the old stones in low, swirling clouds. Groups of ethereal figures silently glide through the twilight world of megaliths and sculpted earth, illuminated by the thin light of a crescent moon. They gather at special places; Silbury, Windmill Hill, The Sanctuary.

Since the last new moon, pilgrims have trod the ancient ways to this place. From the far corners of the land they have followed in the footsteps of the gods, who, according to tradition, marked out the old sacred paths in the earliest days, blessing them with a divine significance. After visiting the shrines and centres of their ancestors, they approach the great temple with a sense of timeless continuity. The countryside has become alive, its arteries pulsing with human energy dedicated to the coming celestial event. Every heart, every mind is directed towards the temple, and to the fiery orb of the Sun, hidden from sight by the body of the Earth as it dances its eternal spiral through space.

There is a profound hush over the land. Everything happens in silence. Crowds of pilgrims assemble around the old stones, pouring from groves and hilltop camps to surround the sacred circle. A great energy begins to build, uniting everyone with its vibrant, numinous spirit. Senses are sharpened, everyday perceptions transcended. A wild joy begins to take hold of the people, their spirits uplifted by the promise of revelations to come.

The heavens grow light. Blue velvet turns to transparent azure; a bright pigment of pink is washed across the sky as the orb of the Sun approaches the horizon. Still in silence, those assembled at The Sanctuary proceed down the giant serpentine avenue of stones. The time is right. They move along as if carried by a powerful current of energy that bathes them in an irresistable magnetism, drawing them to the sacred centre. Vast stones, alive in the changing light, wait to welcome them.

At the Henge they pass between two enormous monoliths that mark the boundary, and are joined by others flowing in from different directions. A small group gathers around the Obelisk. The atmosphere intensifies as all eyes are turned towards the reddening sky, the landscape becoming vivid in the reflected glow. As if all assembled are but one great being, arms spontaneously outstretch towards the coming Sun. The tension is reaching a crescendo.

There is a flash on the horizon. In the distance, yellow flames leap skyward and tiny figures can be glimpsed silhouetted against a flickering fire burning on a hill to the north-east. Then the Sun rises in splendour directly behind it, its first rays striking the faces of the people in the Henge, their eyes filled with an overwhelming, ineffable joy. A collective gasp of awe is involuntarily uttered, breaking the silence.

Simultaneously, behind them to the south-west, another fire is kindled. It explodes into life just before the first shaft of sunlight moves across the countryside to touch it. Far down into the west, a great chain of fires is sparked across the land, each one in succession, drawing the light from the Sun as if by some powerful alchemical resonance. The other sacred centres spread their fire across the landscape forming a straight line from coast to coast; an alignment illuminated and echoed by the rays of the Sun God as he returns on the first day of summer to stimulate and excite the elements of the Earth Goddess. The cycle is complete. The Goddess is fertilized by the God. The fruits of their seed will flourish.

But there is more. The fusion creates an enchantment over the land. Energies and forces within the body of the Goddess react to this cosmic coupling after months of frigidity and purification when life was suspended by winter. Her secret centres are suffused with ecstasy, the channels and currents that link them cleansed and revitalized. The power that animates the countryside flows again in rhythmical pulses as the heart of the solar system pumps vitality into its veins and arteries. The creatures of the Earth, seen and unseen, rejoice. Bathed in the afterglow of reunion, they celebrate in innocent enthusiasm the restoration of earthly harmony.

Chapter One

A MEMORY STIRS

MANY PEOPLE TODAY have heard something about the St Michael Line, certainly the most famous ley line in Britain. Even if they are not quite sure exactly what a 'ley line' is, they are intrigued by the associations that come to mind. Images of some immensely ancient science of landscape engineering tantalize the brain, replete with a forgotten wisdom of bewildering sophistication. Is there any truth behind claims that the earth was once covered in such a network of alignments spreading across country, comprising earthworks, megaliths and stone circles, whose purpose seems on the one hand to be utterly obscure, yet on the other appears to stir ancient memories within the collective psyche?

Certain academics will suggest it is all wishful thinking, a product of the over-active imaginations of those with a romantic turn of mind; that ancient peoples were far too primitive and preoccupied with food and shelter to concern themselves with such grandiose schemes. Others will point to the demonstrable accuracy of stone circles and their correlation with celestial bodies as proof that some arcane understanding did exist. There is also the tangible evidence; the unarguable fact that enormous effort went into the creation of great lines in the landscape, stone temples which have survived thousands of years, and a great diversity of prehistoric enigmas wherever one looks. The discriminating observer, perhaps, may suspect that modern science is itself undergoing a learning process, that there are greater things in heaven and earth than have yet been conceived by the fashionable philosophy of the time. Fashions change, and what was once considered plain common sense may well be overtaken by fresh inventions, discoveries and revelations which can radically affect the way that people view the universe around them. The present time is just such a period of revolutionary insights, perhaps triggered by the realization that our poisoned planet may soon begin to respond to centuries of relentless abuse. There is a natural tendency to look back to previous times, when a more harmonious relationship existed between the Earth and its creatures, a feeling that the people of the past ordered their lives to a cosmology based on a deeper understanding that is alien to mechanistic concepts. There seems to be an undeniable intuition that deep mysteries lie hidden in the landscape, and that the vanished civilizations that gave us Stonehenge, Avebury and a baffling array of earth and stone structures throughout the land were guided by a purpose that was profound indeed.

This book is an exploration into the forgotten territory of natural energies which our ancestors undoubtedly understood. On the face of it, taking a single phenomenon such as the St Michael Line can never give us more than a glimpse of the intention behind such an extraordinary concept. Yet it leads into a world where everything is truly interdependent, where the Earth is acknowledged as a part of a greater whole, a philosophy which, while rooted in a spiritual understanding, is also pragmatic and practical. The old temples were built to enhance the environment, not to create disharmony, and so a technology of natural forces was employed, the same forces which create life and vitalize the countryside. The St Michael Line seems to have had a particular significance in all this. The remarkable continuity of sites that mark its path and the powerful residual knowledge that has in the past been so central to the growth of succeeding religions may have an important message for us in the world today.

The surprising ease with which the concept is accepted by many people is striking. It is also a paradox. Faced with implications which must inevitably lead to a complete reappraisal of ancient civilizations, it seems curious that the idea appeals to such a diversity of individuals irrespective of cultural background. The only explanation appears to be that a deep memory is surfacing in the collective mind, echoing across countless centuries to a world which desperately needs to re-establish its links with nature to prevent the final catastrophe.

The rediscovery of this alignment of sacred sites that stretches from coast to coast was made by the mystical scholar John Michell in the 1960s. It had been introduced into the popular consciousness through his classic exposition of the ley phenomenon *The View Over Atlantis*, a book of considerable charm and erudition which laid the foundation for much of the current research into ancient landscape traditions and their significance. It appeared to touch a nerve connected to some previously unacknowledged memory-bank, stimulating a generation of people to look at the Earth with new eyes, focussed on the revelation that it was not merely a lump of dead rock with a molten core and an abundance of water, a place where life thrives by accident, but a living being, with its creatures and plants the individual cells. Since then, science has itself adopted this previously heretical idea, and it is currently fashionable to talk of GAIA (the concept of the Earth as a living entity) as a breakthrough in our understanding of how the planet, or biosphere, works. These ideas reflect an attitude, however, that was the universal core of all ancient cultures and religions, which possessed far greater knowledge than ourselves about the nature of existence. Perhaps it is now possible for us to look to the preserved fragments of this wisdom, enshrined in their great works of earth and stone, and learn from the vision of lost unity that reveals itself. Is there a chance that we could rediscover in this forgotten ethos elements of natural laws which could help to resolve our critical dilemma, brought about by a strangely naive but arrogant view of how the world works? Such an idea appears superficially to be wildly over-optimistic. Yet certain ideas, especially when they issue from the depths of the human psyche, have an immense potential for radical transformation. It may be that the time is rapidly approaching when the ways of the remote past can be married to those of the modern world, the result of such a union taking us forward to a new vision that surpasses both. A new awareness could certainly cause a shift which may have profound consequences for humanity and the Earth, for according to the mystical teachings of past ages, it is the image you hold in your mind that is the one which will come to pass.

THE ST MICHAEL ALIGNMENT

On a clear day in the late 1960s, John Michell stood on the summit of Glastonbury Tor looking out across the flat landscape of the Somerset levels. From this lofty pinnacle, crowned by St Michael's tower, he could see in the distance the distinctive shape of a prehistoric mound known as Burrowbridge Mump, surmounted by a ruined church, and known locally as King Alfred's Fort. The church was also dedicated to St Michael.

Some years before he had come across the work of a Herefordshire businessman and pioneer photographer by the name of Alfred Watkins. A keen observer of the countryside and an expert on local folklore, Watkins had spent years riding on horseback through the Bredwardine Hills, and was known and greeted by everyone he passed in a landscape that had changed little over the centuries. The rural life was still ordered by the cycle of the seasons and the speed by which horse-driven carts travelled along country roads.

Watkins had made an extraordinary discovery. In the early 1920s he had looked out across the landscape and experienced a revelation. By some process independent of the rational mind, he had glimpsed a vision of the countryside that had been totally forgotten, an image so powerful that it was to transform existing attitudes to prehistoric cultures in a remarkable way. As he later recounted to his son, Allen, 'The whole thing came to me in a flash'.

What he saw spread out across the landscape in front of him was an astonishing network of lines linking all manner of ancient sites; earthen mounds and encampments, old stones, churches built on pre-Christian sites, holy wells, moats and ponds, crossroads. Precise alignments of the remnants of antiquity covered the land, radiating out to include mountainous peaks and hills where beacons had once been lit. A web of intersecting lines was woven over the face of the Earth, laid out by some remote prehistoric culture and preserved for thousands of years by the natural evolution of sacred sites. This vision was to change his life, as well as the perceptions of many to come.

Delving into etymology, he found that certain names occurred frequently on such alignments, and believed that they were all linked by words denoting light. Amongst them were the words Cole (Welsh *coel*, light or splendour), and Ley, meaning a cleared glade (related to the Saxon *leye*, an obsolete word for fire). This led to him calling these lines across the landscape 'leys', and he spent the rest of his life exploring the phenomenon, writing books, and along with members of 'The Old Straight Track Club', attending outings to sites of antiquity where they spent their weekends plotting alignments on maps and in the field. Towards the end of his life he began to suspect that leys were not simply the trading routes of prehistory as he had once thought, but concealed a deeper significance.

John Michell had also felt that there was some profound knowledge behind the existence of leys. Wherever one travelled in the district surrounding the Somerset levels, the enigmatic shape of Glastonbury Tor hung on the horizon. There was a mood of mystery about the old sacred hill that seemed to cast a spell over anyone who approached it, and there was talk of consciousness shifts and psychic experiences, of all manner of visions and revelations. The features of the legendary landscape around the Isle of Avalon seemed to possess a powerful energy that affected the mind, giving glimpses of hidden realities.

Standing on the summit, he observed that the axis of the curiously-shaped Tor seemed to point directly towards the projecting mound of the Mump. An image began to form. It was of a great line stretching across country, from the Mump a few miles away in the south-west over the low-lying landscape of the levels to the Tor, where it ran along the spine of the elongated conical hill and extended across country to pass through the remains of the great megalithic temple complex at Avebury. Such a powerful impression seemed to have a reality beyond mere imaginative fancy, and it was soon discovered that when this line was transferred to a map, other intriguing features of this alignment could be observed. St Michael's church at Othery stood very close to the dead straight line between Glastonbury and the Mump, and after passing through Stoke St Michael Church

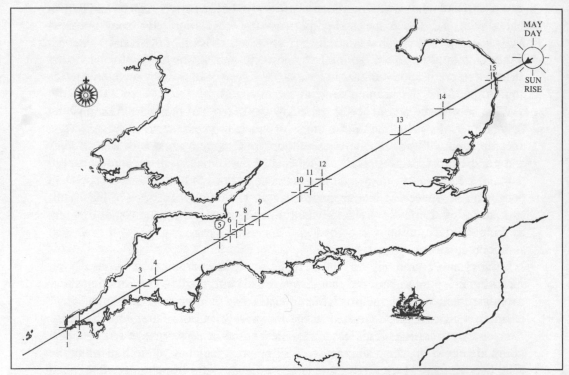

The St Michael alignment of sacred sites across southern Britain, which stretches from the furthest western tip of Cornwall to the extreme eastern part of East Anglia: 1. Carn Lês Boel; 2. St Michael's Mount; 3. Cheesewring; 4. St Michael's Church, Brentor; 5. St Michael's Church, Trull; 6. Burrowbridge Mump; 7. St Michael's Church, Othery; 8. Glastonbury; 9. Stoke St Michael Church; 10. Avebury; 11. Ogbourne St George; 12. St Michael's Church, Clifton Hampden; 13. Royston; 14. Bury St Edmunds; 15. St Margaret's Church, Hopton.

and the southern entrance at Avebury Henge, the line continued on through Ogbourne St George church and then to St Michael's church at Clifton Hampden. Further research showed that the line could be extended right across southern Britain, and down in the west, ran very close to St Michael's church, Brentor, St Michael's chapel at Roche Rock and the great island sanctuary of St Michael's Mount. On the edge of Bodmin Moor, it passed through the imposing weathered rock-pile known as the Cheesewring, a place thought in the past to be a Druid idol. At St Michael's church, Trull, close to Taunton, a nearby hill was the legendary site of the dragon's death, an image repeated on the ancient worn font in Avebury church where an early bishop tramples on a dragon and stabs it with his crozier, both apparently using the same symbolism as St Michael subduing the dragon. Projected eastwards, the alignment extended through the great medieval religious foundation at Bury St Edmunds to the east coast at a point between Lowestoft and Great Yarmouth.

This striking discovery of what has become known as the St Michael Line cannot fail to impress an age where great works of engineering are looked upon as pinnacles of scientific achievement. Those who may be tempted to dismiss the idea as a remarkable coincidence are faced with other evidence of a grand design, to an extent that it becomes exceedingly difficult to ignore. Recent computer calculations by statistician Robert Forrest show that a large section of the line is very accurate indeed, and that it is perfectly straight from Ogbourne St George church, through the southern entrance at Avebury, the St Michael churches on Glastonbury Tor and Burrow Mump and the Cheesewring. Over such a distance, the curvature of the earth is negligible, involving only a few feet, so that the precise alignment can be plotted on Ordnance Survey maps without complex corrections which could confuse the issue. The 'key section' from Ogbourne St George to Burrow Mump is so accurate that a dead-straight line joining them passes just three metres to the south of the centre of St Michael's chapel on the Tor. Those who may sense in all this some mysterious purpose could, perhaps, be forgiven for wondering exactly how such terrestrial engineering was apparently undertaken in remote prehistory when it is assumed that there was no way of looking over the horizon.

Robert Forrest also found in his researches that if the alignment is treated as a 'corridor' or 'route' rather than a dead-straight line, then the coincidences multiply. If a tolerance of 500 metres is allowed either side of the line, extended across its entire length, then no less than 63 churches fall within the boundary. Of these, 10 churches are dedicated to St Michael or St George and 23 to St Mary. This introduces another aspect, which appears to indicate that the St Michael Line could also be a St Mary Line. However, perhaps it is not so strange when one considers that St Mary is commonly understood to be the Christianized Earth Goddess of pagan times.

The precise reason for the existence of this line of dragon sites across southern England is currently beyond our comprehension, although this book does attempt to answer some of the central questions as to its function, pointing to a science of natural energies that had considerable significance in the ancient world and which

may yet have profound implications for the future. Crucial to the philosophy that
created such an Herculean attempt at a natural technology is a view of the
universe as a single system, a living entity which includes the Earth as an integral
part. This is indicated by perhaps the most intriguing property of the St Michael
Line, the fact that it appears to be constructed on an axis that aligns with the centre
of our solar system at crucial times of the ancient calendar.

Beltane (May Day) and Llughnasad (Lammas) were the high spots of the
ancient world, when beacon fires were kindled on the hills and people across the
land celebrated the return of Bel, the Sun God, with his power to fertilize the land
with the energizing vitality of spring, and later thanked him and his consort, the
Earth Goddess, for their bountiful harvest. On these occasions, around which the
whole year revolved, wild orgiastic festivities took place at the old sacred places,
not out of the crude licentious lust reviled by Victorian vicars, but rather as an act
of sympathetic magic to draw the fructifying cosmic energies into the Earth.

Standing on, for example, St Michael's Mount at Beltane would have been a
memorable experience. Great fires would have illuminated the sky to the east,
continuing like a string of incandescent jewels across country to Avebury, the
'mother-circle' of ancient Britain. There, at dawn, large numbers of people from
the whole of southern England assembled each year to welcome the return of the
Sun God. Pilgrims from as far away as the Land's End in Cornwall and the area
around Bury St Edmunds in Suffolk travelled along prehistoric upland routes that
led directly to Avebury. The remains of these ancient trackways still exist and
offer a poignant connection with the past for those who wish to follow in the
footsteps of forgotten peoples. The Icknield Way, its stony surface worn smooth
by countless feet, runs from Hertfordshire to join with the ancient Ridgeway, a 90
mile long track from Buckinghamshire that terminates in Wiltshire, passing by
churches and shrines which occupy sites of prehistoric sanctity. Another ancient
track runs from the far western tip of Cornwall to join the Ridgeway at Avebury,
a pilgrim route of great antiquity which is currently being reinstated as 'the Sunset
Trail' by a former Cornish Grand Bard, Mr Hugh Miners. This upland route
passes through some of the finest scenery in Britain, and its revival for the use of
modern travellers could offer a moving experience for those following the path of
ancient peoples who would have passed that way heading for Avebury and the
May celebrations.

Even in Victorian England, Mayday rituals were enacted with religious
devotion in all parts of the land, with every village honouring its May Queen as
children danced around gaily-decorated maypoles. Echoes of the importance of
these festivals to previous countryfolk can still be heard at the beginning of May
as evocative music emanates from town and village, stirring a potent ancestral
memory. Two famous rites are still performed in Cornwall, with the powerfully
pagan Padstow 'Obby 'Oss and the more prim Helston Furry Dance continuing a
tradition that leads back to prehistoric times. In the former, the wildly frenetic
'Oss dances through the narrow streets with a fearsome dragon-like mask, whilst
at Helston, St George and the Dragon are in evidence amongst the flounces and
frocks, top hats and tails of a more sedate ritual.

The return of the Sun-God at Beltane was celebrated with festivities, revelry and the lighting of fires throughout the land, many situated on prominent sites on or near the St Michael Line. The alignment created a cosmic orientation determined by the Sun itself, which, at dawn, would coincide with the line of sacred sites. A person looking towards the great line of fires that glowed on hills and mounds would suddenly see the greatest fire in the solar system rise directly behind them in a momentous act of celestial union. In continuance of such an apparently wondrous cosmology, as the Sun wheeled its way to its midsummer extreme and then retraced its route across the heavens, observers at the sacred places could again look east to behold the corresponding summer solar display, when the sun again aligned, this time to mark Llughnasad, the time of bountiful fruits.

The dragon-like 'Obby 'Oss cavorts through the narrow streets of the Cornish town of Padstow, a Mayday fertility ritual that has continued uninterrupted since pre-Christian times.

The accuracy of this solar interplay is difficult to define today, mainly due to the precession of the equinoxes, where the Earth has slightly shifted its axis through the ages, and to the fact that we do not have a precise date for the original setting out of the line. We may well be talking about a time that is far more remote than generally recognized. It is also true that the precision of this sunrise alignment is affected by the angle of elevation; ideally, an observer's eye must be level with the horizon when looking towards the north-east or the moment of the Sun's appearance will be affected by the respective positions of horizon and point of observation. The observer's situation at different points along the line also alters the sunrise alignment; thus, according to Robert Forrest, someone looking towards Avebury from the south-west would note that the sunrise alignment at

Avebury currently occurs on May 7th and August 5th, and at Bury St Edmunds on May 2nd and August 10th. The corresponding sunsets, which may have had an equally important significance, can be observed from Avebury on February 3rd and November 9th, both very close to the other major fire festivals of Imbolc (February 1st) and Samhain (November 1st). It would also seem that the convention of using May 1st for Beltane, August 1st for Llughnasad etc, is more for the convenience of modern calendars than an accurate reflection of the fire festivals of previous times. The crucial times were measured by the movements of the heavenly bodies, not by mundane calculation, the proof of which is apparent to anyone who cares to study a little astro-archaeology, and the way that megalithic monuments (Stonehenge being the foremost example) correspond to the passage of Sun, Moon, stars and planets across the skies. Thus, perhaps more accurate dates for the four major fire festivals are currently:

SPRING (Beltane) Sun at 15 degrees Taurus (5-8 May)
SUMMER (Llughnasad) Sun at 15 degrees Leo (2-7 August)
AUTUMN (Samhain) Sun at 15 degrees Scorpio (5-7 November)
WINTER (Imbolc) Sun at 15 degrees Aquarius (2-7 February)

Whilst no correction has been made for the earth changes that have taken place over vast epochs of time, it can be seen that there does indeed seem to be some crucial solar involvement with the countrywide axis of the St Michael Line, of which ancient people, so concerned with celestial events, could hardly have been unaware.

DOWSING THE ST MICHAEL LINE

In the 1950s the reclusive mystic, writer and artist Ithell Colquhoun wrote a book that contained one of the first indications that there existed the phenomenon we now call the St Michael Line. *The Living Stones* referred to a line of magnetic energy that extended from the east coast to the tip of Cornwall, passing very close to Lamorna Cove where she lived. She hinted that it was a line of a pre-Christian force which, in modern terms, could be thought of as the Michael-force, and connections were made with the Knights of the Round Table and their enigmatic brothers-in-spirit, the Knights Templar, who apparently understood its significance and incorporated it into their teachings. As both physical and spiritual guardians of the pilgrim routes, the Templars exercised a special responsibility over the old pathways, and they were charged with the protection of pilgrims as one of their main functions at their formation at Jerusalem in 1118. Later they were to become so powerful throughout Europe that they threatened the established Church, which felt it necessary to exterminate them in the most brutal manner. Today they are credited with a deep understanding of natural energies, sacred geometry and architecture and the initiation of Rosicrucian and Masonic traditions.

This reference in Ithell Colquhoun's book was one of the first signs that some sort of renaissance might be occurring in connection with the St Michael Line. A decade later John Michell rediscovered that a ley line marked the route of this 'magnetic' energy, giving the concept a wider audience who have responded with increasing fascination. Dowsing the actual energy involved brings a new dimension into play where the abstract concept assumes a reality that can be measured, or at least felt, by most people. This in turn creates a fresh scenario where those who feel drawn into the mystery can personally interact with the elemental forces involved. What may appear at first to be an unsubstantiated theory crystallizes into a vivid experience that communicates itself to others. This in turn may have consequences that we can only guess at from our current level of understanding.

Much mystery hovers about the idea of a latent sixth sense which can, with the aid of rods or pendulum, detect and measure the energies emanating from the earth, yet it is clear that when refined, dowsing can be an extremely accurate method of sensing the unseen. Like any other talent, it can be developed to a fine degree of sensitivity, and the fact that so many people can dowse to some extent may indicate that what we are really dealing with is a sense that has atrophied through disuse, a side of the human mind that has been locked away for a very long time.

In the past, the technique of dowsing has had many useful applications, and a large proportion of those who find that they can trigger the residual memory in a basic manner can go on to more sophisticated interpretations. These can include the detection of underground water and minerals, lost objects and the measuring of subtle energies. This latter category is one of great potential for the future, as many people find that it is possible to dowse the bio-magnetic fields around those who may be suffering from illness or disease so that imbalances can be detected and rectified.

The present book is concerned with the detection of these invisible energies that surround living bodies. Humans, animals and plants possess their own individual energy fields whose harmonious state is essential to good health. Rocks, water and other 'inorganic' material also have their own associated fields, each unique in its own right. The planet itself has an enormous field that exists far out into space and interacts with those of other heavenly bodies. It also possesses other energies which, as in all living beings, operate in channels and flowing currents, the meridians of Oriental acupuncture. Dowsing these unseen energies leads into the world of multi-dimensional forces that lie behind the physical reality we observe with our ordinary senses.

For many years now, dowsers investigating earth energies have discovered that old sacred sites emanate powerful forces that interconnect with others within the landscape. These flows of energy affect the sensitivities of living creatures, and can trigger the dowsing response in many people. It is fascinating to watch the faces of people who have never dowsed before experiencing their first positive reaction. There is an unforgettable sensation of awe in that magical moment. After the first joyful reaction the real work begins—in refining and understanding precisely what is being indicated by the dowsing rods or pendulum. The questions asked and the concepts sought must be defined and held in the mind with rigid precision. The description of the right mental approach is at first perplexing and contradictory—relaxed concentration. If you concentrate too much you get nothing, and if you relax too much you get spurious results. In essence it is a matter of reaching an almost meditative state with one razor-sharp part of the mind inflexibly focussed on the precise thing that is being sought. Like many other arts, there is a knack to it.

This precision is eloquently illustrated by dowsers employed by electricity and telephone companies, who are able to differentiate between the two types of cable. These are both made intrinsically from the same materials, yet the refined sensibilities of the dowser can clearly detect the difference. In other words, provided your concept or visualization is finely tuned, the degree of accuracy in dowsing is limitless.

Sig Lonegren's book *Spiritual Dowsing* and Tom Graves' *Dowsing, Techniques and Applications* provide detailed instructions on the basic art and the beginner can have no better initiation into this fascinating subject. For those who wish to bring their own hidden talents to bear on the material in the current book, and explore these mysteries in the field, it would be wise to study the disciplines involved before attempting to make sense of the intricate web of subtle forces that lies behind physical reality. A learner driver could never cope with the potential of a Formula One racing car, and it would be just as difficult for a neophyte dowser to make sense of the subtleties of the dowsing reaction without considerable application.

Having said that, the energies associated with the St Michael Line are particularly powerful, and it is certainly possible for those who can dowse to detect them with the minimum of effort by visualizing a current connecting, for instance, St Michael's Mount to Glastonbury Tor. This is especially so if the precise location of the energy flow is known, and throughout the book specific indications are given whenever possible. However, there are many other forces interacting, and a clear, unambiguous mental approach is essential if confusion is to be avoided.

The explorer who enters into the search to define the path of these invisible energies soon becomes aware that the people of previous times knew of these things quite naturally without having to resort to using pendulums, rods or bits of twig to understand what was happening to the Earth's elemental forces. Initially, such a realization is difficult to grasp, but there are many examples of experiments with birds and animals which use a recognition of electro-magnetic or bio-magnetic lines of force for guidance in flight and movement, and there would appear to be no reason why Homo Sapiens cannot rediscover this lost sensitivity that was once thought to be so essential to a harmonious relationship with Nature. It is an inescapable conclusion that the need to become aware of the terrestrial and cosmic forces which deeply affect our behaviour patterns is of fundamental importance to the evolution of the species.

Before the hunt for the St Michael Line started there were a number of experimental attempts to locate it, and compass bearings of its direction indicated initially confusing results. This was very disconcerting to begin with, and it looked as though other energy flows were interfering with the reactions. It seemed that it was impossible to differentiate between this particular current and the many others that exist, yet the British Society of Dowsers have used the location of the St Michael Line as a test to check the accuracy of their members, showing that such detection is a practical possibility and by no means a subjective phenomenon. It was only after some time that the reason for the error was somewhat painfully discovered, and this clearly demonstrated the essential lesson that all dowsing interpretations have to be assessed with care and honesty. The absolute necessity for precision cannot be over-stressed.

It was found that using fairly hefty forged dowsing rods had a number of advantages in a project such as this. The most important was that they are unaffected by varying weather conditions and allow for accurate tracking in high winds at exposed locations. They also, by sighting down them like a rifle barrel, give clear and positive direction and quick results in determining frequency, pulse, width of line and other minutia, always of course providing the right questions are asked. The flattened handles give a sensitive indication of the strength of the field and seem to help eliminate spurious readings when concentration begins to flag at the end of a long day's dowsing. Many other splendid uses of these rods were discovered during the course of the project; they are an excellent defence against belligerent animals, they can be used as climbing aids while negotiating muddy tors, they do an excellent shish-kebab and make very satisfying back-scratchers!

The technique of driving whilst dowsing, (using only one rod, of course) became quite polished after some practice and had the added advantage that the driver/dowser became disoriented and was for the most part dowsing blind, ensuring that preconceptions were overruled. The navigator similarly developed a curious relationship with tenuous markings on maps, forgotten trackways and indescribably muddy lanes, which occasionally led to hair-raising situations that are the stuff of quests and adventures. One of the delights about dowsing in the field is that it can be great fun . . .

The romantic element of such an exploration is also powerful. To be drawn to ancient temples and forgotten shrines sensing a profound purpose is to step through the barrier of time. Weather-worn relics come alive and cold stones glow with a power that has been imprisoned by neglect and misunderstanding. There is an unmistakeable impression that the old sites respond to an approach that does not impose on them images formulated in the minds of historians and archaeologists, images of death and terror that only create fear in the observer. Fear is the one emotion that is guaranteed to block out the finer sensitivities, erecting an impenetrable wall between the rational and the magical, intuitive part of the mind that works with more refined energies of perception. Perhaps that is why it has been so heavily used in the past.

To begin to communicate with the Earth at these special places an almost childlike reverence is necessary. Preconceptions must be held in check and the mind emptied of trivial everyday clutter. Then one enters a different world. Old stones appear as friends, relishing the contact of a willing mind and triggering revealing insights into their past. Protective spirits seem to hover around them as the veils of vanished aeons evaporate and the past merges with the present. There is a sense of continuity that is inspiring. Standing in the twilight at a place where the spirit is strong there is a recognition that in the end, time is like a spiral where places once central to more perceptive minds are revisited, drawing us to them by a power we hardly understand. Yet there is an impression that the secrets contained within them are ready to be revealed, as if the memories of a world that is barely imagineable today are slowly being restored.

This ancient rapport with the hidden energies that surround us opens up limitless possibilities only bounded by the imagination. To focus the attention on the invisible side of Nature is to create a bridge between the intellect and the intuition, striking a balance that is desperately needed in a world where rampant rationality has brought us to the edge of cataclysm. Experienced dowsers often find that after some years, they can throw the rods or pendulum over the nearest hedge, for they learn to sense the object of their quest without tools, seeing it with their inner eye. Dowsing, it seems, is the first stage of developing a form of clairvoyance, and perhaps an important part in the next stage of human evolution.

There can be little doubt that ancient peoples exercised the dowsing faculty in a totally natural manner. They were intuitively aware of special places where the Spirit of the Earth was strong, certain spots where the forces of Nature were concentrated and could affect human consciousness. When prehistoric people approached such a shrine, it may well appear to us that they were worshipping strange gods, yet their true purpose, divested of our own cultural projections, was to communicate with the forces and intelligences of Nature, so that their conduct would be harmonious with the influences from the Earth and cosmos. Their preoccupation was with the health and fertility of the Great Mother, and the eclipses, planetary, stellar and solar events that affected her. Thus stone circles are instruments where the planetary body interacts with the endless round of celestial events, creating a harmonic fusion between them. At the heart of the entire enigma is a view of the universe as a single, self-regulating system, an organism that must be constantly communicated with in all its myriad diversity of moods. The siting of such sacred places was determined by the Earth itself, the currents and channels of her life-giving energy flowing through places recognized as centres of illumination. These centres are today rarely found in a state that reflects their original function. The ruined remnants of a vanished cosmology tantalize the imaginations of hordes of modern pilgrims, whilst many of the ancient shrines are now the sites of churches, chapels and cathedrals, some still vibrant with spirit, yet many ignored and neglected except by the occasional itinerant explorer.

The major meridians of the Earth's subtle energy animate correspondingly important sites within the system. It is no accident, therefore, that places such as St Michael's Mount, Glastonbury, Avebury and Bury St Edmunds occur on a terrestrial current whose significance has spanned all ages. The knowledge of such arcane matters has often been deliberately obscured in the past, for knowledge is power. Esoteric brotherhoods and orthodox religion alike have maintained a secret hold over the hearts and minds of ordinary people throughout the world during centuries when domination and exploitation have been the rule. Yet evolution moves on, and it now seems likely that the true and original use of the old centres of the Earth Spirit, as places of communication and transcendent perception for all who recognize them, irrespective of cultural conditioning, may be reinstated. A common purpose that overrides all artificial barriers is perhaps the only avenue open to us at this late stage. We must listen to the Earth as we have not done for a long time. The whisper of her breath awakens old memories which are of immense power. Let us listen.

THE ANGEL AND THE DRAGON

The image of St Michael that comes down to the modern world is of immense antiquity. The Christian archangel, often depicted thrusting his sword down the throat of a fearsome dragon, supplanted older gods such as Apollo or the Celtic Sun-god Bel and took over their sanctuaries, the sacred hills and high places which appear to guard the landscape. In the Book of Revelation, he is the one who clears the way for the second coming, a destroyer of demons and great Angel of Light. He also seems to have absorbed the spirit and attributes of other gods associated with light, such as the Roman Mercury or Greek Hermes, who traditionally have special charge over the mercurial currents of the Earth and the hermits who live on them, guiding pilgrims and kindling beacon fires for travellers. The earth currents were understood in the ancient world to be the raw dragon force of Nature, subdued in Christian mythology but previously venerated for their beneficent powers.

The graphic image of St Michael's sword piercing the dragon is an adaptation of the hermetic wand or Caduceus, where a central staff has serpents entwined around it in a double spiral, a timeless symbol of natural energies operating in harmony, and, as modern science has discovered, also a striking glyph of life itself as represented by the DNA molecule. St Michael is also often depicted holding the scales of justice, with which to weigh human souls after each incarnation before guiding them into the afterworld. This was one of the functions of the Egyptian deity Thoth, God of Wisdom and scribe of the gods, as painted on a thousand tomb walls, and shows the great antiquity of this archetypal image. The ibis-headed Thoth was the original owner of the serpent staff, the Caduceus. There also exists a curious sympathy between the god of the Egyptians and the British landscape, for across the country many natural and artificial mounds known as Toot hills are found, once thought to be ancient watch-towers and referred to by some authorities as having a special association with Thoth, or Tahuti, whose archaic name is echoed in folk memory.

In later times, Thoth was overshadowed by his Greek equivalent Hermes, father of the Hermetic arts and originator of magic and religion, who was born in a mountain-top cave and became the spiritual guardian of high places. As well as an affinity with caverns and mountains, both traditional places of mystical initiation, he had a special association with roads and standing stones, examples of which, called Herms, were to be found at the centre of Greek market places. The Roman god Mercury, messenger of the gods, continued the tradition and Mercury stones marked the Roman roads. Other cultures had their equivalent counterparts; in the Aztec pantheon he was the feathered serpent Quetzalcoatl; to the Gauls, Teutatis; in Islam, Idris.

The Christian archangel who succeeded the old gods adopted their magical and mystical attributes, and so he is also the spirit of revelation, giving inspiration and visionary glimpses of divinity, the great initiator into the hidden mysteries. In the esoteric tradition, he is the one who transmutes lower, base energies into those of a more refined, spiritual type, thus allowing him to vanquish demons. This would seem to be the real meaning behind the glyph of the slain dragon—the archangel transfixes the raw, dragon energy of the Earth with the Will (of which the sword is a traditional symbol), and transmutes it to a higher rate of vibration.

In the Middle Ages, the cult of St Michael reached its peak. Pilgrims from all over Europe would embark on journeys to the major shrines such as St Michael's Mount, Cornwall, or Mont St Michel in Normandy, both places where shining visions of the saint were reported to have appeared in the early centuries of Christianity. Places once used by Druids to invoke their own mercurial god of light became the focus for great pilgrimages, continuing a tradition that stretches back into prehistory. Chapels to St Michael crowned sites of ancient sanctity; at Glastonbury, one of the greatest of the English centres, a church dedicated to the saint stood on the Tor until demol-

St Michael slaying the dragon, from an original drawing on a copy of the Royal Charter for St Michael's Mount, 1465.

ished by an earthquake in the 13th century. This was later replaced and its remaining St Michael's Tower is still today a potent symbol all over the world.

One of the main routes for those visiting the sanctuaries of St Michael in Britain was along a way that ran south west/north east across country. This led the traveller to a number of churches dedicated to the saint and his more earthly counterpart St George, also famous for subduing dragons. Along the way were dramatically situated hilltop shrines such as St Michael's church on Brentor and St Michael's chapel and hermitage on Roche Rock, Cornwall. Those that followed the old path were led past the remains of stone temples and great earthworks, imposing monuments to another age when the same spiritual presence was

St Michael, holding his sword in the right hand and the balance in his left, shines in stained glass in England's most innaccessible church, Brentor on Dartmoor. At 1100 feet above sea level, it is a dramatic example of a site dedicated to the angel of high places.

honoured under a different name. Finishing at the rock-cut chapel on the legendary St Michael's Mount, the pilgrim would pray for inspiration and healing, and fragmentary records of the many miracles that took place in those days of pious innocence can still be seen in the remaining archives from Mont St Michel, that other rocky citadel dedicated to the archangel similarly situated off the French coast. The continuity of this route from great antiquity into historical times demonstrates something of its true significance, for hidden beneath the St Michael associations appears to be a race memory from a very remote time when humanity wandered the land in sympathy with the cyclic rhythms of the universe. The impulse to follow in the footsteps of ancestral tradition was so strong in a non-materialistic culture that people felt called by the land and an ancient God, later clothed in the stained-glass colours of a Christian saint. The further back in time one probes, the more magnificent are the achievements of those who marked the route. Medieval churches and chapels perch on prehistoric mounds which often appear to have been artificially shaped to coincide with the direction of the pilgrim route, whilst at Avebury, the scale of the vision, sculpted in earth and stone, is breathtaking. These works were nothing less, it seems, than the instruments of a science and philosophy that was so vast in its scope that a memory of it has spanned all ages, until it appeared to be lost forever. But forgotten memories flood back to the old man in his dotage, and this may also be true of a time when humanity itself is about to move forward into another evolutionary phase, one which, if we are to believe a persistant mystical tradition, will be presided over by St Michael.

In a booklet dedicated to the archangel, a foreword written by the Bishop of Coventry on St Michael's Day, 1951, urges us to continue the ancient practise of visiting the old shrines; 'Behind the faith in St Michael there is an age long experience of the Christian Church and even of the human race ... Our Faith looks to revelation from above. In our time we are to look for this revelation on the sacred sites belonging to our Faith. It is the privilege of pilgrims to re-sanctify these sites as holy places ... '

The series of articles that follow in *Michael: Prince of Heaven*, compiled by the remarkable mystic Wellesley Tudor Pole, invokes the spirit of St Michael in often ecstatic, inspirational prose. Historical and legendary accounts of the archangel and his shrines across the world are given colour by poetic images of the landscape encountered by the pilgrim. The various writers foresee the dawning of a New Age, brought about by revelation, and prophesy that Cornwall, with its network of St Michael sanctuaries, has a special role to play. For the county has an intimate relationship with St Michael, who is its original patron saint and who, like the legendary Merlin and King Arthur who slumber in the landscape, is awakening from his long sleep. An image of Cornwall is evoked which echoes its role in past ages, as a centre for Celtic saints and visionaries who dwelt in its secluded sanctuaries; 'Why should not St Michael's Mount become a Mount of Vision once again and the sacred places and pilgrim centres throughout Cornwall glow once more with radiant Light that would be visible to all who know how to perceive and understand its message? . . . Let Cornwall light the

Lamp that is to cast its radiance across the whole of England and beyond . . .'

However, while St Michael may have a special affinity with the romantic land of the far west, as the spirit of revelation he has the power to affect the whole of humanity. As guardian of the Mysteries, earthly harmony is his special responsibility, symbolized by the balance he often holds in his hand. His feast day falls on September 29th when the Sun is in Libra, the sign of Justice, when the hours of darkness and light are evenly balanced, a day when pilgrims of previous times would gather at his shrines and fairs were held in his honour. The rediscovery that these places possess natural qualities which have the potential to change human perceptions, as acknowledged in past ages, may perhaps encourage modern pilgrims to seek them out and, as suggested by Wellesley Tudor Pole, rededicate them to the ancient Spirit of the Earth, and the archangel who presides over it.

The legendary holy island of St Michael's Mount.

NATURAL GNOSIS

The record of the quest that follows is written in the form of a journal. This approach is chosen for many reasons. Firstly, the gradual unfoldment of the principles involved can be recounted in the sequence in which they occurred; the inherent complexity of some of the concepts involved may otherwise be difficult to grasp. Secondly, the nature of the adventure means that there may be, concealed within the chain of events, some significance of which we are unaware, yet which may strike a chord in the detached observer. Also, it is a record of subjective impressions and changing perceptions triggered by a pilgrimage into the unknown, and as such is offered in the spirit in which these discoveries and conclusions were revealed.

It is presented as an honest account of an investigation into matters that are largely intangible. Despite this, the results can be demonstrated by reference to the landscape and the great diversity of places of ancient sanctity that are implicated. The exquisite beauty of the way the terrestrial current interacts with the countryside through which it passes may have a poetic appeal, but the energy itself is specific, measurable and alive. No doubt many mistakes and misconceptions can arise in the course of such an investigation, and these will be brought to our attention by those who possess an eagle eye for such matters. It is also inevitable that there will be criticisms and disagreement about some of the conclusions in such a work; to all such criticism we are content to allow the record to speak for itself, and the future to judge our efforts in trying to make sense out of matters that have rarely been exposed to the clear light of common-sense scrutiny. It may well be that as understanding grows, and the veils of Nature are penetrated, such ideas will once more become as commonplace as they were in the past.

It is the intention of the current book to place the data before the discriminating eye of the reader, and to invite the participation of other dowsers, sensitives, researchers and anyone else who feels drawn into these matters to confirm or elaborate the conclusions within these pages. A series of maps is available (see page 211), showing the routes taken by the energies associated with the St Michael Line. From experience, we are aware that each particular area through which it runs is connected into the network, and that churches and prehistoric sites in the vicinity are joined to it as if we are looking at a river system of streams and tributaries, or a nervous system of ganglia and communication channels. By allowing those who are attuned to their own local landscape to explore where these currents run, it is hoped to initiate a rediscovery of the unseen spiritual energies of the Earth and the laws that govern them, a renaissance of the principles of Natural Science, a gnosis of Natural Religion.

Chapter Two

CHASING THE DRAGON

Heaven Above, Heaven Beneath,
Starres Above, Starres Beneath,
All that is Above, is also Beneath.

William Blake

ST MICHAEL'S MOUNT, CORNWALL. According to legend, the first association of St Michael with the romantic island situated in Mount's Bay was in the year 495 AD. On a rocky ledge near the summit a group of local fishermen experienced an incandescent vision in which the archangel appeared, starting a tradition of Christian pilgrimage that led to the Mount becoming one of the most important St Michael shrines in Britain. In its heyday, when it was the terminal point for those journeying from all over the West of England and beyond, miraculous healings and revelations appeared to have been almost commonplace.

In the earlier years of this century, a local clergyman, Canon G.H. Doble, came across the most valuable book to be lodged in the public library at Avranches in France, a remaining fragment of the archives of the Abbey of Mont St Michel. Within its faded pages, he found the story of a certain blind woman, named Christina, from the neighbourhood of Glastonbury, who arrived at St Michael's Mount on 14th May, 1262. Just before High Mass, surrounded by a crowd of monks and pilgrims, she 'by the intercession of the Blessed Archangel Michael, recovered miraculously the sight of her closed eyes'. In the same year, on the 11th June, another woman from the nearby village of Gulval was taken in a state of catalepsy to the church, where she was immediately healed. A girl called Alice from Hereford was cured of her blindness 'on 29th January, before the rising of the sun'. A fourth miracle, when a dumb man regained his speech, is also mentioned. The book, it appears, contains remnants of a register of cures, recorded in the matter-of-fact manner of a journal of commonly accepted events.

Previous ages had also looked upon the Mount as a place of special power. Medieval pilgrims would pass the 'Giant's Well' on their way to the summit, a reminder that Cornish legend refers to the rock as the abode of a Giant called Cormoran in the days when giants were as common as juggernauts. Yet as with many old legends, there may be some hidden truth concealed in this story. For in the fourteenth century, during the rebuilding of the church which had been destroyed by the same earthquake of 1275 that had demolished St Michael's church on Glastonbury Tor, astonished monks came across the skeleton of a huge man. Estimated at about eight feet tall, his bones were removed and buried nearby, only to be disturbed again in 1864 when they were finally laid to rest in the cemetery at the foot of the hill. His rock-cut tomb, roughly nine feet square, still exists near the altar of the chapel, and is entered by means of a small stone stairway behind the wooden pews.

In the old Cornish language, the Mount was called Carreg Luz en Kuz, a term translated by the chronicler William of Worcester as the 'Hoar rock in the wood'. The word 'hoar' in Celtic, Europe's most ancient language, often refers to menhirs or standing stones, a memory of prehistory when megaliths may have preceded the later stone buildings. The idea that the Mount once stood in the middle of a wood, before an inundation of the sea changed the landscape, was once thought of as fanciful romanticism associated with the idle ramblings of those who whispered of sunken lands and Lyonesse. However, within recent times petrified stumps of various varieties of trees, examples of which can be seen in the local museum, have been revealed by the shifting sands, and in Victorian times boatmen used to take visitors out into the bay at low tide to peer into the waters to see them.

The great antiquity and mystical associations of the sacred Mount certainly lead back to a remote era. One authority states that 'It was famous as a centre of Druid worship from early times', and that it was first known as Dinsul, or Citadel of the Sun. The imagery of St Michael who replaced earlier gods of Light and Creation points to a clear tradition of ancient sun worship and a divinity connected with solar energies.

FEBRUARY 1st, 1987. The beginning of our quest to track the energies of the St Michael Line began, appropriately, at the old sanctuary, with the grey castle perched on top of its rocky eyrie partly veiled by a haze of damp mist known in Cornwall as 'mizzle'. The tide was out and the island could be approached across the causeway that links it to the mainland, a route trodden by thousands of pilgrims, their gaze fixed on the object of their pious labours after many a long month on the open road. Setting foot on the Mount, an exploration of the deserted lower reaches revealed something that was to affect the whole thinking behind the project. Any preconceptions about how the dowseable energy flow operated had to be dismissed. Its course across the island did not, as we had fondly imagined, pass through the summit with its church and castle, but through a gap in a prominent rock outcrop on the western side, continuing through a row of old buildings on the left of the causeway and finally disappearing off across the bay in the direction of a small cove to the south of Marazion.

On that grey February day the castle was closed, and as we headed damply back to the mainland, there was an understanding that whatever the expectations might be, the energy that we had located would not obey the preconceived notions of human minds. This was, we were later to realize, a clue to its quicksilver character, and, in its own modest way, an important foundation for the enterprise. At least we could be sure that we were not following a mirage.

Some hours later, the first half-dozen dowsed points had been transferred to the Ordnance Survey map of the surrounding area. They all seemed to coincide fairly accurately with a straight line drawn through the Mount at the generally accepted angle of the St Michael Line of 27 degrees north of east. As dusk fell, we found ourselves at a tiny Victorian chapel at Leedstown, a small village a few miles inland from the Mount, with no inkling that this place was to provide an initiation into the considerable importance of the current we were tracking, and its acknowledgement by both past and present Church authorities. The spirit of the enterprise was immediately transformed, for here was a chapel that had been built directly on the line we had followed from St Michael's Mount.

As we entered through its creaking doors, ivy leaves fluttered against the windows. The place seemed to be buzzing with an almost audible static, producing a curious feeling of light-headedness as we stood there in the half-light soaking up the atmosphere. By now, we had discovered that what we had been referring to as the 'line' was a broad band of energy approximately twenty paces wide. It took in the whole building, with the centre, the most powerful and easily detected part, running along the precise axis of the chapel, passing through a bell hung high on the west wall, down the central aisle and right through the crucifix on the altar.

On the Sunday morning a week later, bells were ringing out across the Cornish countryside, the service at Leedstown chapel was just finishing and the vicar was getting ready to leave. We approached him with a sort of naive bravado and asked if the chapel had been built on an ancient site, as it appeared to be in a significant location. He told us that it had been built in the last century on virgin ground. Yet another preconception evaporated. It seemed that someone in Victorian times had acknowledged the existence of the energy flow, and deliberately erected the tiny building in its path. This had very interesting implications, as we were more accustomed to thinking about such matters in terms of remote history than the staid world of nineteenth-century clerics. The chapel had been built by Edward White Benson, Bishop of Truro, and no previous structure could be recalled. We speculated on whether the choice of site and specific orientation of the building was determined by direct knowledge of the St Michael Line or by some form of intuitive inspiration. Whatever the reason, it was intriguing to learn that this particular gentleman later rose in ecclesiastical office to become Archbishop of Canterbury . . .

There was more to come. A short conversation with the vicar proved that he was immensely knowledgeable about these matters. The Revd Robert Law is in fact the exorcist for the diocese, and has spent much of his life dealing with the unbalanced energies created by our modern ignorance of how they function. He had known the celebrated earth energies ecclesiastic Dom Petipierre, well-known for his understanding in this field, and knew about the St Michael Line, and the fact that his chapel was built in its path. The energy, he said with a refreshing openness, was neutral until used, and it was the practice in the past to site religious establishments on the flow to keep it pure. The chapel, crucially situated near the Mount, had, since being built, been allowed to deteriorate spiritually, and he had been charged with the reversal of this downward trend. It certainly seemed he had done an excellent job, for it is now a place that uplifts the spirits.

Leaving the chapel with its invigorating atmosphere and surprisingly knowledgeable and frank vicar, we felt inspired and encouraged, but with a sense of considerable humility. It appeared that the phenomenon we were investigating was no forgotten facet of some archaic philosophy, but an aspect of something very much alive and well understood by those within the established Church. Setting off on another afternoon's dowsing, we were convinced we were on the right track. This impression, however, was not to last for long.

CATHEDRALS AND QUOITS

The next few results were perplexing. Heading away from the Land's End towards the population centres of Camborne and Redruth (the closest thing you can get in Cornwall to industrial conurbations), there was an increasing tendency for the St Michael energy current to lead away from the beautiful straight line we had drawn on the map indicating the countrywide alignment. With much scratching of heads the dowsing reactions were checked and re-checked only to affirm that the energy did indeed appear to be curving gently away from its expected route. According to the map, it appeared to be heading towards a prehistoric monument known as the Giant's Quoit near Carwynnon. On closer investigation, the quoit, which at one time, judging by the immense size of its capstone, must have been a formidable structure, was found to be a sad pile of old stones heaped unceremoniously in the middle of a ploughed field. It had evidently been destroyed during a violent storm in the last century. The line did not pass through it, but swept through the adjacent countryside. Sitting on the enormous capstone, we pondered on the meaning of this new mystery.

Was it true that the line was bending? The dowsing results certainly indicated that this was the case. Baffled by the last few miles, we were to be utterly bewildered by what was to follow. The line seemed to be giving the Camborne/Redruth area as wide a berth as possible, deliberately steering clear of this concentration of sprawling industrialism. With the great granite mass of the prehistoric centre of Carn Brea looming from its lofty pinnacle, confusion ruled. By definition, a ley line was straight. Yet this most remarkable example that ran right across southern Britain was, according to our dowsing, becoming distinctly curvaceous. If it had zig-zagged from one ancient site to the next, then it would perhaps have been easier to understand. But it was meandering through the countryside like a great snake. The gaunt, eyeless chimney stacks of the surrounding mine-workings gazed on our incomprehension, and it was to be some time until we discovered the meaning behind this tantalizing enigma.

The city of Truro is famous for its cathedral, with its three spires dreaming over the old town like something out of the Renaissance, a magnificent example of Victorian Gothic flamboyance. It is built on the site of the old parish church of St Mary's, part of which remains incorporated into the eastern section of the more modern building. The 'line', a term which had now become somewhat inaccurate, had swept off to the north of the city to skirt around an ancient settlement at the head of the beautiful verdant valley of the River Kenwyn. It had led past the railway station to the cathedral. Dowsing around the building on a quiet sunny Sunday afternoon, we discovered that it ran right alongside it, through what is now a modern chapter house built on pillars, echoing many of the above-ground altars traditionally dedicated to St Michael, the angel of high places. Beneath it is to be found a great equal-armed cross inlaid into the paving.

Even more intriguing, another building was originally destined to occupy this particular site earlier in the century. Partly-constructed arches which would have completely enclosed the path of the energy protrude enigmatically from the cathedral and the school opposite, although for some reason the plans were never carried out. It seemed we were again coming face to face with a Victorian revival that apparently indicated a recognition of the Earth's subtle energies. In this case it had involved a massive expenditure of finance and considerable expertise to construct Cornwall's only cathedral on the site of the old parish church. This church had traditionally been dedicated to St Mary, commonly held to be a Christianized version of the Earth Goddess of the great Nature Religions.

It was also heartening to discover, a short distance away, that old St Paul's Church, an ancient-looking, mellow building, was precisely aligned on the energy flow. This confirmation of the accuracy of the dowsing reinforced our enthusiasm again, after a time of considerable confusion. Inside the church, the air was heavy with incense after the Sunday service, and the atmosphere was strangely exhilarating. Standing there in the centre of the building with the energy current running directly down the aisle and across the altar, we had further evidence that religious authorities knew all about the existence of this natural energy, and had constructed their buildings in its path, presumably to utilize it for spiritual purposes.

A long evening's discussion followed. It was difficult to come to terms with the latest developments, and we recoiled from the necessity to rearrange all our carefully nurtured conceptions in order to accommodate the new findings. Despite this, there was the irrefutable evidence of a church, a chapel and even a cathedral, aligned on the meandering St Michael Line, so it seemed reasonable to assume that at the very least we had stumbled across some generally unacknowledged facet of the ley system. Our previous simplistic notions of a neat, orderly pattern was far too naive. The energies involved were of a more flowing, organic nature.

Searching for references which could throw light on the dilemma, we turned to the writings of John Michell, who had been responsible for our current involvement in this most confusing world of earth energies. Immediately, we came across passages which had somehow been overlooked before, as if the inner eye had not been ready to see and understand. In his lyrical and moving essay in *The Earth Spirit: Its Ways, Shrines and Mysteries*, he writes that sacred rocks and other natural shrines and the paths that connect them were once inhabited by an ancient spirit, revered for its divine attributes:

> '. . . for they are ways of the earth spirit, not merely secular routes but natural channels of energy, first traced out by the creative gods, followed by the primeval wandering tribes and still in settled times used by religious processions or pilgrims to a shrine. Traditionally they are also paths of psychic activity, of apparitions, spirits of the dead or fairies, particularly on one day of the year.'

> 'All these various traditions, which occur universally and evidently derive from some once unified system of knowledge about the ways of the earth spirit, refer to, as it were, a stream of magnetic current, fertilizing, and accompanied by manifestations of spirit, that passes through the country on certain routes and on certain days, its seasons determined by the positions of the heavenly bodies.'

The true nature of the terrestrial currents, it seems, is serpentine;

> '. . . the serpent represents the mercurial currents of the earth spirit gliding in serpentine channels through the earth's crust—the yin force of nature . . . When the serpent current of the earth spirit is transfixed by the lance of the dragon killer, it can no longer move freely about the earth, for its energies are now fixed and concentrated on one spot . . . For many years now, experienced dowsers, including Merle and Diot in France and Guy Underwood, Reginald Smith and many others in Britain, have observed the fact that every megalithic site is over a centre or channel of the terrestrial current whose emanations are detected by the dowser's rod. All ancient tombs and stones were placed so as to coincide with and accumulate the flow of the earth's vital energy, its 'spirit'. . .'

Here, then, was the explanation of the current of energy we were tracking by dowsing. The natural planetary energies flowed along channels or meridians that were curvilinear, animating the Earth with vitality. They linked prehistoric sites which had always been understood to be crucial to life, places where in some way this divine force was concentrated. As religions had changed, so had the mythological symbolism, and the Solar deities of ancient times had been overlaid by Christian images which continued the old ways under a new ethos. St Michael had vanquished and transfixed the serpent of old, the spirit of Nature that flows through the land, but it was not killed, merely subdued. The system was not static, an outmoded concept frozen in time, but still evolving. Its recognition in even relatively recent times showed that the Earth Spirit was continuous and dynamic, despite its apparent neglect. In the minds of humanity, it had been slumbering. For us, however, the Spirit was again beginning to stir.

A VAST INTELLIGENCE...

The conversation grew animated as things began to fall into place. We recalled the ideas of the eighteenth-century antiquarian William Stukeley, who, as well as being a man of the cloth, espoused the antique religion of the Druids, the old serpent worship. Images of engravings of Stonehenge came to mind, of white-robed Druids displaying vast banners decorated with serpent motifs. Then, the serpent was regarded as a symbol of wisdom, as it was in Ancient Egypt where the Pharaohs always wore the Ureaus snake entwined about their heads, a perennial glyph of godlike qualities. Perhaps the Christian identification of the serpent with the Devil was no more than an attempt to divest the Old Religion of its power over the land, while the new faith, a reformation of a religious ethos that had become corrupt, built its churches on the old places of serpent worship? By the time the first rays of dawn penetrated the heady atmosphere of esoteric speculation, we were quite convinced after the confusion of the previous long day that the results were beginning to make sense. Before we retired to grab a few hours' sleep, another interesting fact emerged. We had started the project on February 1st, a date that was one of the most important of the old Celtic calendar. It was the time of Imbolc, one of the great fire festivals of the ancient world, a curious coincidence as the countrywide lighting of beacons obviously had an affinity with St Michael, the light-bringer and patron saint of hills and high places. As the clear light of dawn dissolved the strange shadows of our nocturnal ramblings, there was a sense of discovery in the air.

Sleep has the peculiar effect of drawing rational problems from the conscious mind down into the subconscious, and allowing them to emerge purged of the accretions of everyday confusion. Doubts and difficulties often disappear when the thinking mind actually stops dwelling on them, and a new day brought a clearer understanding. Filled with an almost childish enthusiasm, we grabbed dowsing rods and maps, and headed off to explore the Land's End area.

Fogous, standing stones, holy wells and stone circles all abound in this strangely remote part of the country, called by the ancients Belerion. There is a certain atmosphere about the place, an echo of a life that is hidden deep in the recesses of the mind. Poetic and imaginative, it is a magic that almost everyone feels as they pass the Mount into what may well be part of the drowned land known in legend by the name of Lyonesse. But any romanticism was severely dented on driving past Newlyn Fish Market towards Mousehole, for the St Michael current was rapidly located running right through the Penlee quarry complex on the edge of Mount's Bay, a place of shabby concrete buildings and rusty corrugated iron. Mystical sensibilities took another battering as it was tracked across the peninsula to reveal that it gently curved around as if trying deliberately to avoid all the famous landmarks associated with prehistory.

After passing the Merry Maidens stone circle, it occurred to us that there could possibly be a connection even though it was not situated directly on the flow. This proved to be an idea which led to a greater understanding of how the energies operated, for we found that it is joined to the main channel by a minor artery. A picture of a living system was emerging, exactly like a great river of energy that had streams and tributaries flowing into it. Whilst bringing an entirely new perspective, however, it also introduced a potential complexity, and it was necessary to decide not to be side-tracked into investigating all the possible connections with the main line, otherwise there seemed little doubt we would never get further than the area around Land's End.

It was late afternoon. The February sun was sinking in a haze of orange and the sea breeze was as gentle as a spring day as we followed the dragon line to the coast. As we trod the springy tufts of sea-pink it suddenly started to make a tight curve to the right. We tracked it towards the cliffs, following the rods as they led away to the sound of the sea. Dowsing it in such an intimate manner was a humbling experience. There was a feeling of spontaneous rapport, an awareness of some vast intelligence at work as the dowsing rods twisted and led away to a rocky promontory. It looked ordinary enough, except that a large erect granite rock guarded the entrance to a rugged crag, perfectly vertical like some sentinel posted there millennia ago, overlooking the Atlantic. On the map, it was marked as a hill-fort with the name of Carn Lês Boel. Just along the coast, the tip of Land's End jutted out into the ocean.

What we found at this spot was inexplicable. The broad band of energy converged to a point at a great slab of horizontal granite and apparently disappeared into the ground. Then, slightly further on, it re-appeared in precisely the same manner, heading off into the reddening glow of a late winter sunset. On further investigation, and with a strange sense of unreality, we found that a five-pointed star was clearly dowseable in the earth's field around the point where the line converged and disappeared. However, it was not the traditional pentagram, the universal sacred symbol that appears in all religions, but a distorted version, with strangely elongated and foreshortened arms. What all this could possibly indicate was beyond our understanding, yet there was a most moving inner conviction of contact with an intelligence that was far greater than either of us had ever known. In a peculiar mood of mystical reverie, we sat on the crag gazing out to where the line flowed in from the gently-lapping waves, dreaming of lost lands and vainly trying to gain some insight into what on earth it could all mean. One thing, though, was certain. Carn Lês Boel was a very special place.

ECHOES OF OLD CORNWALL

'Passing onward, the traveller will pause amid a winding outline of unhewn granite pillars, and he will gradually discover that these are set up to represent the coils of a gigantic serpent, traced, as it were, in stone.'

R.S. Hawker
*'Footprints of Former Men
in far Cornwall' (1803)*

A few weeks later, we were back 'chasing the serpent' on its sinuous path up through Cornwall. Since the last expedition a lot of thought had been devoted to the concept of serpent energy, which had well and truly ensnared us in its coils. To begin with, it had become apparent that 'serpent' and 'dragon' were interchangeable terms. The dragon energy of St Michael was exactly the same as the serpent energy of the Druids, both symbolic images of the vital principle of nature, the Earth Spirit. The two words were even drawn from the same source, the Greek Draconis, meaning serpent.

Research was revealing a surprising wealth of references to this energy: Druidic sources spoke of the *Wouivres*, meandering channels of invisible force that flowed through the surface of the Earth and crossed at special places; a living tradition still existed in Australia, where the Aborigines used their wandering dream paths to honour the spirit of the land, as their nomadic ancestors had done by their annual migrations across country; an exact science of these currents had existed since early times in the Chinese discipline of *Feng-shui*, and was still in operation; and there were many references to them in accounts of European folklore such as W. Evans Wentz' *The Fairy Faith in Celtic Countries*, published in 1911;

> *'An Irish mystic, and seer of great power, with whom I have often discussed the Fairy-Faith in its details, regards 'fairy paths' or 'fairy passes' as actual magnetic arteries, so to speak, through which circulates the earth's magnetism . . . when the house happens to have been built in a fairy track, the doors on the front and back, or the windows, if they are in the line of the track, cannot be kept closed at night, for the fairies must march through.'*

There is in fact a universal tradition of the subtle energies of the planet which has been submerged beneath the mechanistic philosophy of recent centuries, ignored by a world more interested in extracting and converting the natural resources of the Earth than of utilizing its beneficent natural forces. These were, as we were in the process of discovering, central to the people of previous times, and held by them to be sacred.

Passing by the distant spires of Truro cathedral, we picked up the serpentine current that had run alongside it and followed it as it swept along the valley of the Tresillian river and out towards Ladock. It passed through the private estate of Trenowth House, disappearing into the seemingly impenetrable woodland. Peering over the fence into the half-light of ancient trees, we knew that somewhere in the tangle of undergrowth were the ruins of a Celtic chapel, marked on the map but, according to a helpful local, now little more than a few old moss-covered stones. A short walk later and we stood at the little-visited earthwork known as Resugga Castle on the opposite side of the River Fal. The line ran right through the centre of this beautiful and strangely moving place, and as we gazed across verdant countryside to the unnatural lunar landscape of the Cornish clay country, where the countryside has been raped unceremoniously of its mineral content, the mood was poignant as the stark contrast presented itself. The 'Castle' with its earthen embankments may well have been used as a fortification in times of threat, but there seemed little doubt that it had originally been a sacred site or ritual centre. It would have been natural to protect such a place from invaders. In the distance, the drab greyness of a totally man-made landscape loomed, with little redeeming greenery. It was impossible not to wonder how such devastation might affect the secret forces of Nature.

A gentle curve inland towards the village of Foxhole, and we were in the midst of the weird science-fiction dreamscape of glistening white pyramids and gaping chasms filled with arctic green water. As we stood on top of St Mewan Beacon, positioned in the path of the sinuous flow, the entire surrounding landscape and the whole of St Austell Bay was spread below; we wondered about the significance in pre-Christian times of lighting great fires at these beacon points, and concluded that such acts were no empty rituals but something far more potent. A ghostly white pallour of fine dust hung over everything and huge machines were grinding away in the distance. It was difficult to imagine how beautiful the place must once have been.

Along the Gover Valley, we were led to the outskirts of St Austell, under a railway bridge, and then, quite suddenly, we found ourselves in the cloistered calm of old trees and towering rhododendrons, a magical place where a milky-white stream flowed down from the hills above. A beautiful Gothic-style holy well was built into the side of a rock face and heavy traffic thundered along the main road twenty feet above. This was Menacuddle Holy Well, a place long revered for its mystical virtues, and the only physical remains of an important Medieval religious foundation. It is one of those special, inspirational places where mysterious ideas which seem to have been created in another dimension creep into the mind. No one would be in the least surprised to catch a glimpse of hooded monks or even one of the faery folk whilst brooding in the sculpted stone known as the Druid's chair. Whether this special atmosphere is due to the ghosts of those who once inhabited the place or to the presence of the Earth Spirit is difficult to know; perhaps it is a combination of both. But once again, we had found the serpent energy passing through a powerful site, used for religious purposes until relatively recent times. It seems that far from banishing the serpent and equating it with the Devil, the monks of old were actively engaged in using its refined energies for their own mystical purposes.

THE GARGOYLE

Continuing through the disturbed landscape of China Clay works and skirting the slopes of Knightor, the course of the current took little account of the damage caused by man in search of mineral wealth. The impression was of a vast and powerful body whose skin had been torn and wounded, leaving ugly scars that were superficially devastating, but which left the basic life force unaffected. Nevertheless, it was a relief to leave behind the scenes of despoilation and travel once more through the seductive Cornish countryside. The Luxulyan valley is justly famous as one of the most beautiful in the county, and driving down the steep lanes with the sunlight filtering through a dark canopy of ancient trees was invigorating. The serpent wound through the landscape to the town of Lostwithiel on the banks of the River Fowey, once a thriving port and for centuries the capital of Cornwall, where part of the royal palace still remains. Dowsing in the narrow streets we were not greatly surprised to find the line heading straight through the centre of the town, towards the imposing spire of Lostwithiel Church.

The line entered at an angle from the south-west, passing through an unusual ancient stone in the churchyard. Inside, everything was relatively modern, with little sign of the artefacts of great antiquity that usually abound in old churches. The most ancient and intriguing object was to be found just by the south door. A unique font, far more pagan than Christian, and heavily carved with lively hunting scenes, stands out as the only archaic remnant. It possesses many curious features. Strange lions are carved on one side of its octagonal granite bowl, with other figures that have been defaced down the centuries. A 'Green Man' in Celtic Bishop-style hat has florid foliage spilling out of his mouth, a commonly-accepted memory of the pagan Nature gods of fertility. But the weirdest, most startling feature of all is the grotesque gargoyle that juts out irreligiously from the other, more mundane, decorations. Why this striking face should have been spared destruction when the heads of the other carvings have been deliberately chiselled away is intriguing. The head itself is like no other ecclesiastical gargoyle in the country. Two serpents writhe across its head and ears, and a curious projecting forehead has a spiral encompassing it, worn and discoloured by thousands of hands that must have rubbed it as a good-luck fetish. In fact it is impossible to look at this peculiar image without finding yourself naturally fondling it, such is its power. It seems to leer out from another time, a time so strange that it beckons to some atavistic urge within, with its swirling vortex of energy carved exactly where the third eye is located. The existence of such a curious object in a Christian church is remarkable. But its effect upon the energy flow was even more so.

The remarkable gargoyle on Lostwithiel font, with a spiral carved on its projecting 'third eye', and serpents entwined about its head.

At the exact location of the font, the energy focussed to a point in the same way that had been observed at Carn Lês Boel, and yet again a distorted pentagram was dowseable. Equally interesting, the serpentine nature of the flow suddenly changed, coming in from the south-west and immediately realigning to a direction that was practically due east, leading across the altar. Why something that seemed essentially flowing should quite suddenly change its direction in such an abrupt fashion was beyond comprehension. In some inexplicable way, the ancient font with its grotesque head and strange serpents radically affected the usual pattern of flow.

ROCK-IDOLS AND THE NATURE MYSTIC

Tracking it east, the line crossed the River Fowey just by the old 13th century bridge and hugged the lower slopes of Beacon Hill. It led to a secret, magical place on Druid's Hill, a wooded area in the private Boconnoc Estate. In the midst of thick rhododendrons and ancient trees was an enchanted glade, where there stood a twenty-foot high granite cross on its huge plinth. Eight tracks radiated out into the surrounding woodland in what could only be a ceremonial arrangement. This particular spot had been remembered since remote times as a Druidic ritual centre, and later as the site of confrontation in the Civil War. The Michael serpent ran through the great cross, now forgotten and neglected, on which were inscribed the words: *'On this hill, once the site of Druid idolatry and in later times the scene of civil bloodshed, This ancient symbol of the holy religion of the redeemer is erected in greater acknowledgement of the blessings of a pure faith and of a peaceful country'*.

The route took us to Fairy Cross, following the course of the main A390 road and weaving through an impressive collection of scattered tumuli grouped in varying numbers and visible from the road. Then it left the traffic of the twentieth century and veered past ancient earthworks and a hill-fort into the beautiful Glynn Valley, crossing the Fowey once more. Our minds were not a little confused at this stage, weighted down as they were with the concentration on dowsing, navigating and attempts to grapple with new concepts. As if the gods were tuned in to our mood and anxious to encourage us through our period of doubt, the next turning brought us to a tiny hamlet on the edge of Bodmin Moor where we found the serpent running

Druid's Cross in the last century.

through a crossroads. To our initial disbelief, and then our great amusement, the village was called Ley!

We headed out across the moor, past a tumulus on Goonzion Downs, and found ourselves in the village of St Neot. This place has been renowned for many centuries as a religious centre, as its magnificent church with its famous stained-glass and collection of ancient stones testify. It had always seemed strange that such a cathedral-like church should stand in the middle of the hostile moor. Even its holy well, in a meadow below the church and now a travesty of its former glory, was one of the most famous in Cornwall. The line passes right through the church, entering at the south-western end and emerging at the north-east to head for Berry Down, through an earthwork marked on the map as a 'fort', on through the hamlet of Draynes and past the reservoir at Siblyback. We were suddenly into prehistoric Cornwall. Within a few miles were the Hurlers, three Bronze-age stone circles which stood in the shadow of the Cheesewring with its remarkable 'fort' known as 'Stowe's Pound', and a whole array of ancient relics including carved stones, Celtic crosses, St Cleer Holy Well and the most impressive megalithic structure in the county, Trethevy Quoit.

Driving along the open moorland past the crooked shape of the stone cross known as Long Tom, we recalled R. S. Hawker's description of the old tracks across the moors. The visionary poet, mystic and Vicar of Morwenstow had written 'Wheel-tracks in Old Cornwall there were none, but there were strange and narrow paths across the moorlands, which the forefathers said in their simplicity, were first traced by Angel's feet.' As we pulled up near the frozen shapes of the Hurlers and stood in the dusky glow of a fading sun, cattle grazed contentedly amongst the old stones. Other than the distant singing of a skylark, the entire scene was hushed and deserted. The energy passed through the first (now almost unrecognizeable) circle, followed the path and went straight for the middle of the three circles. As on the cliffs at Land's End, it tapered to a point, disappeared into the ground where an oddly-shaped five pointed star was dowseable, and re-emerged to head towards the third circle. This last ring of stones is most mysterious. Inside, a seemingly infinite succession of shapes are dowseable, from geometrical designs to inexplicable organic patterns. It gives the impression of some sort of 'Rosetta Stone' of subtle energies, impregnated into the Earth's field at this spot.

After some time exploring the apparently endless display of energy forms, we found that the current did not enter the last circle, but suddenly changed direction and followed its outline in the most uncanny manner, curving tightly around its perimeter. We felt that the serpent was studiously avoiding the third stone circle in order not to disturb the energy forms, weaving around it and pointing straight towards the Cheesewring.

We walked over to the great rock-pile with its weird top-heavy formation that towers over the countryside, past the remains of excavations of long-lost tin miners, as if in a dream. We talked of the strange tale of Daniel Gumb, an eccentric figure from the eighteenth century whose spirit hovers over the place. As a boy he was highly intelligent, strange and unsocial, having nothing to do with

Sacred geometry at the Cheesewring . . . a geometrical carving on the roof of 'Daniel Gumb's House', within a short distance of the former Druid idol.

the ordinary pastimes of his peers. He preferred to wander alone on the moors with a book, spending nights at places such as Roche hermitage where he would lose himself in the wonders of the night sky. The Revd R.S. Hawker wrote that even in the last century, local legends still identified the tall and craggy places with the youthful scholar who spent his nights 'learning the customs of the stars' and 'finding out by the planets things to come.'

In later life he was a stone-cutter who became obsessed with Euclidean geometry, and, having married a local girl took up residence in a stone-built cavern directly below the Cheesewring. The mundane life of a cottager did not appeal to the visionary mind of Daniel, who was happier to follow the ways of a more ancient persuasion. The remains of 'Daniel Gumb's House' are still there to this day, with the roof fallen in and a stone beside the doorway carved with his initials and the date (1735) when he forsook the ways of the world. It was here that he lived, winter and summer, on the bleak moors, gazing out in mystic reverie and pondering the mysteries of sacred geometry. His wife and children were equally happy, it seems, to live amidst raw Nature, and he had no time for the parsons whose parishes bordered the moor, who he thought utterly ignorant of Nature's principles. The roof of his house and many other stones around the edge of the desolate moor are carved with geometrical theorems as testimony to the existence of this curious mystic.

Nevertheless, even though it seemed he had been totally involved with the landscape and the ways of Nature, it still came as something of a surprise to discover that old Daniel's stone-age dwelling was directly in the path of the serpent. It took in the whole of his 'house' before heading right to the startling formation of the Cheesewring. It was beginning to appear increasingly likely that the association of this place with the Druids might well have been more than imaginative fancy. Antiquarians such as William Stukeley had always claimed that these rock-piles were connected with serpent worship, and even until fairly recent times had been revered by the local people. Writing of them in the eighteenth century, the Cornish 'Father of Archaeology' Dr Borlase had recorded that 'the vulgar used to resort to this place at particular times of the year, and payed to this stone more respect than was thought becoming for good Christians'. Perhaps old Daniel was nothing less than a latter-day Druid, hopelessly out of time, but with a mind attuned to the landscape and engaged in the mysteries of something that was truly timeless.

The serpent did indeed travel right through the rock-pile, on through the impressive hill-top enclosure of Stowe's Pound where there is a collection of similarly enigmatic formations, and headed off in the direction of the dramatically-shaped Sharptor. As the sun lost itself in a blood-red haze, the old stones were lit up by the colour of living fire. We stood there, two tiny figures dwarfed by the massive shape of the rocks worn smooth by millennia, peering out over the ethereal moorland landscape with its stone circles, and felt very small indeed.

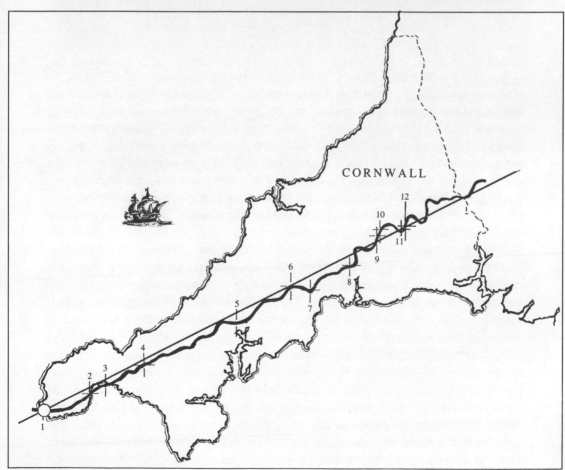

The St Michael current in Cornwall: 1. Carn Lês Boel; 2. Penlee; 3. St Michael's Mount; 4. Leedstown; 5. Truro; 6. Resugga Castle; 7. St Austell; 8. Lostwithiel; 9. Ley; 10. St Neot; 11. Hurlers; 12. Cheesewring.

Chapter Three

THE SERPENT POWER

*'On attempting to investigate the conditions at the centre of the earth
we find there a vast globe of such tremendous force that we cannot
approach it. We can only touch its outer layers; but in doing even that
it becomes evident that they are in sympathetic relation with the
layers of kundalini in the human body . . .'*

C.W. Leadbeater
THE CHAKRAS (1927)

B EFORE THE NEXT STAGE in the quest a natural hiatus occurred, giving us
the opportunity to research a little more deeply into the complex associations
that surround the idea of serpents, their mythology and the natural energies they
symbolize. What was revealed was an intriguing insight into how a once-universal
image of divinity had been debased into one of fear and contempt. A
misunderstanding of the Biblical Garden of Eden story appeared to be at the root
of this, where the symbolic serpent has become the focus for the projections of
centuries of hatred and bitterness. This was a complete reversal of the veneration
of an archetypal image that had been considered sacred in all previous cultures.

Looking back over the last fifteen hundred years or so, there can be little doubt
that serpents have suffered from more than their fair share of bad publicity.
Vilified and scorned by orthodox religion and cultural conditioning, both the
creatures themselves and their symbolism have been subject to irrational loathing
and contempt to a degree that seems quite remarkable. In the ancient world,
exactly the opposite was the case. They were regarded as especially holy, in fact
one of the most divine of animals; wondrous creatures who represented the
quicksilver motion of the forces of Nature and the secret side of existence. Powers
of prophecy and divination were ascribed to them, and at the famous Greek
Oracle at Delphi, the resident priestess held the title of Pythoness, and would
enter into a trance state under the influence of the spirit that flowed from the
Earth, enabling her to penetrate the veils of the material.

As soon as one begins to delve into ancient history or esoteric science, it quickly
becomes apparent that the serpent power occupies a unique position in all the
religious and philosophical traditions of the world. Throughout history, and in all
corners of the globe, that energy known as the fire-serpent has been held to be the
motive force behind evolution and spiritual development. In traditional Western

mysticism, it is symbolized as the Caduceus of Hermes or the Greek god of healing, Aesculapius, whose serpent staff is still in the modern world associated with the power of healing and mystic unfoldment. In Oriental tradition it is famous as Kundalini, a serpent coiled at the base of the spine, which can be awakened by certain techniques to emerge at the pineal gland or 'third eye' to bring enlightenment, like the image of the Egyptian Ureaus, a cobra-like serpent coiled around the heads of gods and pharaohs.

'As above, so below' is the enduring tenet of esoteric philosophy. The idea that the forces behind the microcosm are the same that underlie the macrocosm is universal, referring to the manner in which the universe functions, irrespective of scale. The laws of attraction and repulsion, and the basic forms of energy all obey the same rules whether the object of scrutiny is an atom or a stellar system, a DNA molecule or a spiral nebula. Such an understanding of the creative forces of existence seems to have been mythologised in all cultures, usually by symbols drawn from the natural world. Prominent amongst them is the snake.

Wherever one looks, from the most remote civilizations to modern occultism, the ever-present image of the serpent can be traced through endless patterns of sculpture, painting, poetry and the myths of divine beings. Early female deities were often represented as snake-goddessess, like the famous image of the Minoan statuette who brandishes twin serpents aloft in triumph. The Aztecs worshipped Coatlicue, snake-goddess and earth mother, whose head was formed by those of two opposing serpents. In ancient Greece, the dragon or serpent was the animating spirit in every place, the *genius loci* of rocks, pools, rivers, mountains and oceans. In Europe, hills, mounds, sacred pools and holy wells are still referred to as abodes of the dragon, a vestigial memory of the ancient wisdom of natural energies. Gods as well as goddesses have a special relationship with serpents also, for they too wield the powers of creation. Thus, the great teacher of the Aztecs was Quetzalcoatl, the feathered serpent, and on the arrival of Cortez on the shores of Mexico, the emperor Montezuma presented him with a turquoise mosaic mask, believing him to be the great God himself. It was in the form of two snakes, one green and one blue, symbolizing the energies of earth and sky. Aztec tradition says that he will one day be reborn on Earth. Conchobar of Ireland was born at the winter solstice with a baby dragon clutched in each fist, over which he presumably had divine power, and Hercules, also born at the solstice, strangled

Minoan snake goddess from Knossos, Crete, c.1600 BC. Full-breasted, the essence of fertility, she holds aloft twin serpents representing the elemental forces of Nature.

two serpents on the anniversary of his birth. The Celtic ram-snake, with its spiral horns, is one form of Cernunnos, potent God of Nature and a symbol transferred to the astrological sign for Capricorn, which rules the energies of the Earth.

In China, dragons have never been vilified as they have in the West. In the ancient science of natural energies known as *Feng-shui*, the Dragon Man is still called upon to determine the most suitable site for homes, temples, tombs, offices and factories so that they may exist in harmony with the surrounding environment. *Feng-shui* can be translated as 'Wind and Water', perhaps the nearest we can get to describing the intangible qualities of unseen energies that course like streams of water or travel between one high point to the other like the wind. Through this science, the terrestrial currents determine the position of buildings which must not block the free flow of energy, for to interfere with the flow of spirit is to work against Nature, to create imbalance and invite misfortune and disharmony. In this way, dragons are courted for their beneficent power over the affairs of humanity, animals and the environment, and traditionally inhabit the three worlds, the firmament above, the firmament below, and the Earth between. They are the ultimate royal symbols, and a true king is one who has both the dragons of the Earth and the heavens at his command.

Dragon or serpent symbolism has many branches, but the most powerful of its guises is always as a recurrent image of the natural elemental energies of the Earth. The health and fertility of the landscape is guarded by dragons, often slumbering in a well or pool, or guarding buried treasure in some legendary hill. Other dragons exist in the heavens, and breathe fire, illuminating the countryside with displays of pure, raw energy manifesting as electrical discharges. Nature itself is a dragon, sometimes gentle and fertile, sometimes inspirational and transcendent. When mistreated or abused, however, she can bring catastrophe and utter ruin to those who, through ignorance or antagonism, deliberately flout her Laws. In one of her more mischievous aspects, she is Typhon, who creates devastation by Typhoons and other destructive manifestations which often operate in a spiral.

The knowledge of the harmonious use of the Earth forces that are represented in *Feng-shui* was apparently once universal, with every structure built according to principles that seem obscure to the modern world. All temples and prehistoric sites were positioned on centres of energy that had the power to transform perceptions and give glimpses into the true reality behind physical appearances. Energized by the science of ritual, the elemental serpentine forces of the Earth were focussed for inspiration and rapport with the evolutionary momentum that is the motivating force behind life.

So another essential aspect of the serpent is as a universal symbol of rebirth and rejuvenation, an image of transcendent change. This is no doubt partly because snakes often shed their skins to appear miraculously renewed, and so they have become potent images both of reincarnation and metaphysical rebirth. This principle is also represented in the glyph of the serpent's egg, a device employed by Druids, alchemists and others to invoke the potential of the human spirit for total transformation. The remarkable seven-hundred foot long Serpent Mound in

Ohio has an egg in its opened mouth, while the Ouroborous symbol of the serpent swallowing its own tail also echoes the endless continuity of the energies of creation. Greek gods and goddesses are often depicted in the presence of serpents representing the forces behind harmonious Nature, and statues of Aesculapius' daughter Hygeia who looks after the health of humanity show her offering the sacred serpent a bowl of milk. So widespread was the reverence for snakes in ancient Greece that the private temples in every house had representations of them painted over the altar, and each house had its pet snake which was fed milk and honey and treated as an honoured and welcome guest.

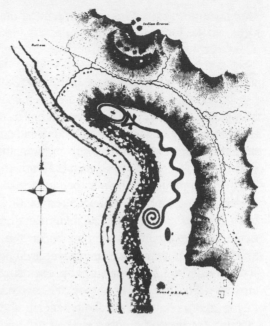

The Ohio Serpent Mound.

Such was the traditional image of the serpent or dragon when the Earth was always thought of as an entity that was alive, its inward and outward breath marked by night and day whilst its body reacted to the rhythms and resonances of the surrounding cosmos. As a planetary entity, it has its energy meridians and node points which function in a similar way to their counterparts in the human body, and which are increasingly used today in the techniques of acupuncture and spiritual healing. In human medicine, the subtle energy channels are stimulated in various ways which cleanse them, allowing a natural harmony to re-establish itself by the marvellous self-repairing mechanisms that exist in living organisms. These are often stimulated by the insertion of needles which excite the currents of the subtle body, and it is beginning to look as though the ancient people who erected standing stones at special places on the surface of the Earth were employing the same principles on an accordingly vaster scale. Perhaps the most powerful method of stimulating sluggish energy flows in the human body is called moxibustion, where a ball of wax is placed on a needle and ignited. When one considers the great importance of lighting beacon fires across the countryside at crucial times of the year, which was widespread in the ancient world, there could well have been a definite scientific principle involved. The node points of the countryside would have been purified and the channels that connect them cleansed, maintaining the maximum health and fertility of the body of the Earth. The unseen energies would course freely across the land, interacting at certain places where the spirit was concentrated, creating a powerful fusion between the mercurial energies of the planet and those from the heavens. Unknown or unidentified by modern science, these principles of Nature appear to be fundamental to existence, as powerful in their effect upon life as the inexplicable forces of gravity and magnetism.

THE CHURCH ON THE ROCK

MAY 30th, 1987. The Hurlers and the Cheesewring had made a great impression on both of us at the climax of our last expedition. It was beginning to seem likely that the three stone circles were in the nature of scientific instruments, each one with a specific function associated with the serpent current. The Cheesewring itself, often thought to be a stupendous work of art created by natural forces, now appeared to us as the weathered remnant of an enormous structure that may have been erected as a marker or focus for the energy. The fact that such a natural stone edifice should happen to lie on the exact centre of the flow as well as marking the countrywide alignment seemed to be more than coincidence.

Leaving the prehistoric hilltop enclosure of Stowe's Pound, we tracked the current across the lower slopes of Sharptor, where it ran through a collection of farms and cottages crouched beneath the distinctively-shaped tor. It led on through Henwood, across Darley Ford and into Upton Cross, a village that has grown up around an old crossroads a mile or so away from the Cheesewring. The line seemed to be developing so many tight curves that signs of stress from the navigator and vague feelings of discomfort from the dowser began to appear. We were only prevented from erupting into exasperation when, just before a particularly fiercely-braked stop, the rods crossed at a farm where it passed right through a farm building, the exact centre of the flow running through the nameplate. Just one word was painted on the sign. LEY. This was the second time the current had led through a place with this singular name. Perhaps, we thought, someone was trying to tell us something.

The line continued its meandering route through the early summer countryside, crossing the beautiful River Lynher at Plushabridge and weaving about through Bray Shop and Sydenham Damerel. It passed diagonally through the porch and tower of Stoke Climsland church, and at Horsebridge we noticed an oddly-placed tumulus at the bottom of the river valley. These mysterious earthen mounds that occur in such numbers and diversity throughout the country are invariably found on high ground, where they can usually be seen from a great distance. Such a lowly position seemed curious. In the shadows of old trees, we noted that it had been put there for what must have been a very good reason. The Michael current flowed right through it.

Suddenly, we were in Devon. Our early adventures lay behind us on the other side of the River Tamar, and there was a certain sadness in leaving the land of the far west, even though we both lived there and would be returning very soon. It was as if a distinct phase had ended, like saying farewell to a lover for the first time. Of course, the love may grow deeper, but it will never have that quality of naïveté that characterizes the first flowering. For us it had been a time of initiation, and we wondered whether it was this essential facet of its nature that had led to the county's ancient tradition as a land of Druids, Celtic saints, holy men and hermits.

Through a soft but steady drizzle, a tantalizing shape could be glimpsed ahead. As we travelled along the dead-straight road over two miles long that led directly to it, the dark shape grew in clarity and power the closer we approached. Its presence seemed to dominate the wet, grey landscape in the descending dusk. The tiny, isolated church dedicated to St Michael that stands on the pinnacle of the rocky crag of Brentor looked full of mystery as we drew into the deserted car park at its foot. Trudging through the dampness with drizzle collecting in silver droplets on the dowser's beard, we found the current sweeping across the road towards an area marked by old trees. Clambering over a fence, we found ourselves at the base of the hill, in the midst of an interesting collection of old earthworks despoiled by the opportunism of open-cast mineworkers. Mounds and hummocks, pathways and small valleys are worn and sculpted into the earth, creating a miniature landscape that looks as if it must surely be inhabited by the Piskies.

The mist grew thick; a strange sense of peace descended. There was an indefinable feeling that we were being observed. On a flattened mound, with the church above obscured by cloud, we found what we had come to think of as a node point, where the current focussed and entered the ground, accompanied by a strangely-shaped pentagram. There was a long period of silence.

For a second or so, the mist momentarily lifted and we caught sight of the church, looming above our heads at 1,100 feet above sea level. At the same moment the bell rang seven times, echoing over the damp Dartmoor countryside. It was an eerie experience, yet not in any way forboding. We scrambled up the hill in the twilight, boots wet and muddy from the soft, drenched ground, and the door to the church opened to our touch as we sought sanctuary. Inside, there were no footprints. The church was empty. The only sign of life within the tiny rock-fast building was a glorious stained-glass window of St Michael, sword in one hand and scales in the other, positioned in the east behind the altar. Coloured light filtered into the gathering darkness, making the polished brass glow with rainbow fire. Silently, we paid our respects, and then slipped and slid down the hillside, past the encircling earthworks, to home and a hearty blazing fire.

The following morning was bright, and so was the mood. Gone was the greyness and air of isolation that had led Tristram Risdon in 1625 to describe Brentor as 'a church, full bleak, and weather beaten, all alone, as it were forsaken'. Today it sang out over the Dartmoor hills, cocks crowed at a nearby farm and the atmosphere glowed with the promise of summer.

The name itself seems to have ancient significance, and occurs in other important places such as the legendary Brent Knoll in Somerset. Archaeologists date the earthworks around the volcanic hill to the Iron Age, yet as always, these may be of far older origin, the Celtic remains merely built on a previous site. According to local legend, when the original church was being built the foundations were set at the foot of the hill, but the Devil, evidently in an effort to deter worshippers, carried them to the summit during the night. This apparently explains the exposed and inaccessible position of the present church. However, it occurred to us that this legend could well be a folk memory that the original sacred site, located below the church, was transferred to the top, perhaps during Medieval times when the existing building was erected, and indicates that the discovery of the energy node in the earthworks below may pinpoint a former site of prehistoric antiquity. Why the Devil should have been held responsible for the siting of the church is perplexing, unless it is a memory of the old religion of natural forces, considered to be 'the work of the Devil' as Medieval Christianity became more institutionalised.

The first church was built about 1130 by Robert Giffard, whose father came to England with William the Conqueror. A charter to Richard, Earl of Devon reads 'My father, Robert Giffard, gave the Rock of Brentor to God, St Mary and the church of Tavistock as a perpetual gift . . . and the church of St Michael which he built on that same Rock at his own expense'. This gift has been both cursed and blessed down the centuries, for the chronicler Richard Polwhele wrote in 1806 *'it has been shrewdly said of the inhabitants of this parish, that they make weekly atonement for their sins: For they can never go to church without the previous penance of climbing up this steep, which they are so often obliged to attempt with the weariest industry, and in the lowliest attitude. In windy or rainy weather, the worthy pastor himself is frequently obliged to humble himself upon all fours, preparatory to his being exalted in the pulpit'.*

A fair, mentioned in a twelfth-century charter, used to be held at the Tor at Michaelmas in previous times, no doubt an echo of an even more ancient custom. There is also reference to an unusual stone at the foot of the Tor, on which a pole, festooned with flowers and ribbons, was erected as the centre of the festivities, but which has long since disappeared.

The question of what exactly was happening at the node points we had so far discovered was greatly exercising our imaginations. No easy explanations were forthcoming, and the more we thought about it the deeper appeared to be the mystery. There was a distinct impression that the energy was somehow entering deep into the Earth, perhaps creating the curiously-shaped stars that were dowseable in the field at these spots. They always occurred at special places and must have had considerable importance in the past. We resolved to mark out meticulously on the ground the precise shape of the one at the earthworks.

An hour or so spent dowsing it accurately and marking it out with a ball of white wool and wooden pegs revealed a peculiarly distorted pentagram, with no two 'legs' the same. Later, we were to return to The Hurlers to do the same, and record the exact dimensions of that particular star. Each seemed to possess its own unique characteristics. After marking out the pentagram at Brentor, though, we were none the wiser, and were only left with the fervent hope that we would discover more about this perplexing phenomenon in the future. We followed the Michael current up the hill, where it passed through the rock on which the church tower is built. It was on this tower, according to writer James Hine in the last century, that flaming beacons were formerly set at the old fire festivals or during threat of invasion.

Hamish Miller and the pentagram at the prehistoric earthworks below Brentor.

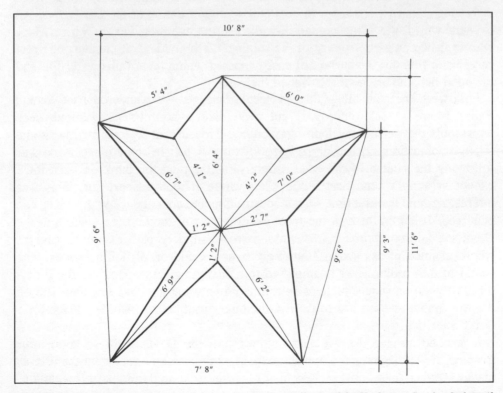

The dimensions of the pentagram found in the central stone circle of the Hurlers on Sunday 3rd April 1988.

A HAUNTED PLACE

A mile to the north east of Brentor is the hamlet of North Brentor, where its church, closely linked to its neighbouring St Michael de Rupe (of the Rock),is aligned on the direction of flow. Strangely, it seems that the building was quite recently erected (1856), and there is no mention of a previous structure. Perhaps it was part of the revival in Victorian times, built, like Leedstown chapel, close to its respective mount dedicated to St Michael.

To the east, the dappled hills of one of the Westcountry's last wildernesses shifted and changed as clouds moved across the sun. The serpent was winding its way around the north-western extremity of Dartmoor. It looked as though it was heading for the ancient village of Lydford. It crossed the bridge near the entrance to Lydford Gorge, one of Devon's most beautiful wooded valleys, a place with exhilarating atmosphere and more than its fair share of legends.

Few people were about as we walked the path through the steep tree-lined slope to the River Lyd below. The hissing, tumbling sound of a waterfall drifted through the branches, and then we were standing at the foot of the White Lady waterfall, in clouds of spray whipped up by the breeze. As the name suggests, this is a spot where apparitions of a white lady are said to have appeared, and a handy tip for travellers, preserved in local folklore, recalls that anyone who falls into the river here and sees the figure of a woman dressed in white will be saved from drowning. Such visions seem to be a classic manifestation of the Earth Spirit all over the world, where the woman-in-white is often interpreted as the Virgin Mary who replaced an earlier image of the shining Earth goddess. It came as no great surprise to find that the current of energy passed within feet of this waterfall, and included half the bridge that spanned the river.

Following the path along the spectacular Gorge, we wandered past Tunnel Falls, where a rock outcrop is cut away like a hermit's cave above deep whirlpools that seethe and foam way below. The serpent was performing some strange contortions. It had narrowed to about six feet in some places, and was following the course of the river, slightly overlapping the bank on occasions, except at a tight bend near Pixie Glen where it took a short cut. This was interesting, and the first time such a constriction and coincidence with a river had occurred. It led on through the most exciting part of the Gorge. Visitors to the Devil's Cauldron approach it down a narrow, slippery path to a dark cavern, where chained planks swing alarmingly over a cauldron of boiling water. The sound of the rushing river is amplified to a deafening crescendo, and those of a timid disposition should perhaps refrain from entering the cave lest they slip on the wet timber and are lost forever in the maelstrom below. An ideal place for a Druid sacrifice.

It seemed strange that we had bumped into the Devil again so soon after Brentor. It was beginning to appear as though this may be a recurrent feature, as places ascribed to 'that old serpent' as he is referred to in the Book of Revelation, apparently harboured a memory of archaic rites.

The village of Lydford on a pleasant June day seems ordinary enough. Only the sight of the grey, forboding castle on its mound reminds the visitor that it was once a place of power, the capital of Dartmoor. In the Domesday Book it is taxed equally with London, and the time of Ethelred the Unready saw it as a Royal Mint, examples of the coinage today being extremely rare. The square castle was built by the Normans on a Saxon mound, and is a sight that could not be described as picturesque, even by the most enthusiastic artist exercising his creative imagination. We tracked the Michael current across Lydford Bridge;

> *Where, 'mid the shrieking night, the maniac rush'd*
> *Despairing to the black abyss below.'*

As the poet Browne, from nearby Tavistock, wrote in grim mood.

It led straight past Lydford Church and the prehistoric earthworks behind to the knoll on which the castle is built. In the castle an intense black atmosphere pervaded the gloomy building, and an almost physical nausea affected us both. It was emanating from a dungeon on the side next to the road, a stark stone pit that one can peer into from above. We had occasionally come across 'black lines' or 'black streams' before, which dowsers had recognized for years as flows of energy that were in some way harmful. They can affect mental and physical health and cause much misery, and this one was the strongest we had come across, sweeping out into the surrounding country. Various techniques have been employed to bring these disturbing forces back into a more harmonious state, and sometimes metal rods are hammered into the ground to neutralize or divert them. However, we had for some time practised a simpler, and just as potent, method which had been used successfully on a number of occasions, and which we found effective in clearing energies that were adversely affecting the environment. Mentally we attuned to the site, and asked with great humility that if the place needed to be re-harmonized, then we should be used to help. An impression of anguish, a cry for release, was almost audible. In quiet meditation, we visualized a clear white light descend on the castle where we stood, healing and purifying everything it touched. The place was so depressingly black that some time passed before, finally, a lightness became discernable. The depression lifted. A great sigh seemed to seep out of the old stone walls. The fierce black stream had been transmuted to one of a different frequency, a clear, balanced, healing energy. It was still dowseable and just as powerful as it passed through the dungeon into the enclosure behind, but was of a radically different nature. The whole site seemed lighter than before, as if it had been cleaned and polished. We thanked our God, and, a little drained by the concentration required in this strange encounter, we repaired to the Inn next to the castle to recover.

The Castle Inn is a mystical sort of pub. On entering, a superb stained-glass window of a Green Man, the old fertility god of Nature, extends a warm and timeless welcome to the weary pilgrim. In one bar, genuine witch-balls for averting the Evil Eye hang from the ceiling, whilst a faded photograph of the famous spiritualist Sir Arthur Conan Doyle peers down on those that still inhabit a mortal coil and can enjoy the physical pleasures of a pint of good ale. In the other, an ancient fireplace is hung with many curious artefacts, among which is a three-dimensional fourteen-pointed star made of stained glass. Just what every old pub should have, we mused. Especially if it was next to Lydford Castle. The conviviality of the hostelry soon revived us and admirably made up for the experience of the last hour.

Lydford Castle, we discovered later, was infamous for its depressing effect upon everybody who passed that way. It had always been passed on with the manor and forest in Royal Grants, which even in the nineteenth century extended to 53,900 acres. In the time of Edward I, it became a prison with an evil reputation above all others, a vile and loathsome place where people were incarcerated in chains. In the reign of James I, the poet Browne wrote;

> 'They have a castle on a hill;
> I took it for an old windmill,
> The vanes blown off by the weather;
> To lie therein one night, 'tis guessed
> 'Twere better to be stoned or pressed
> Or hanged ere you come hither.'

If further proof were needed of its fearsome repute, an order of Parliament at the time of Henry VIII refers to it as 'one of the most heinous, contagious, and detestable places in the realm.' Apparently built on a prehistoric mound, the effect of such a place on the quality of the energies that make up the St Michael current can be vividly imagined.

THE FIRES OF BEL

After following the line through a tumulus in the middle of a field outside Lydford, we were heading away from civilization. It ran through a crossroads near the Dartmoor Inn and off into the wild blue sweep of Dartmoor, with its great tors breaking through the otherwise curvaceous landscape. As we strode off across the moorland turf, the wildness of Earth and sky ran through the mind like a crystal stream, sharpening the senses. A buzzard hovered overhead.

We were led down towards a tributary of the River Lyd. On the opposite bank, the remains of a curious building attracted our attention. In the middle of nowhere, a large structure of unusual dimensions and shape for a dwelling or farmhouse had once been sited on this spot by a trickling stream. It will remain an enigma for the time being, for research so far has revealed no knowledge of its purpose. Yet it is built exactly on the serpent current, and across its entire width.

Right in front of us the rocky mass of Widgery Tor beckoned. On its summit, an enormous granite cross guarded the Moor. Erected by an Exeter artist named Widgery in the last century, it marked the centre of the line which flowed through it and on into the dangerous bogs and uplands of the north.

The current flowed around the southern slopes of Great Links Tor, crossed the

West Okement River and ran across Yes Tor. The gaunt granite crag of another Tor, West Mill, looked down on us with stony indifference as we tracked it through the exposed high ground. It led to Lower Halstock Farm, set in a valley on the edge of the moor. The farmer told us there had once been a large chapel on his land down by the river. Later, in *An Exploration of Dartmoor and its Antiquities* by John Page (1892), we found a reference to this chapel. It had been dedicated to St Michael.

The itinerant wanderer who comes across the Ninestones circle below Belstone Tor could be forgiven for scratching his head and wondering whether he has been pixilated. He may count the stones once or twice, but will scratch his head again on the discovery that there are considerably more than nine stones. Why this should be is open to question. As the serpent runs right throught the centre, it must once have been a sacred site. Perhaps, in more secular times, it was converted to a shepherd's shelter or hermitage, and the original stones filled in with others to create a 'hut circle' dwelling. Whatever the reason, this twenty-seven feet diameter circle shares the common name of Ninestones or Nine Maidens with many other stone monuments throughout the country, and it was interesting that when dowsed, only nine of the stones had energy lines connecting them to the centre within the circle.

It also shares a common legend. As with the Hurlers on Bodmin Moor the stones are supposed to represent Sabbath-breakers, who were turned to stone for enjoying themselves on a Sunday. The clergy of a previous era were particularly fond of this tale, it seems, judging by the enormous numbers of petrified people who inhabit the ancient landscape. And such a terrible fate for those who enjoyed innocent revelry at noon, so the legend says, on the day of the Sun . . .

Breathless, we arrived at the crown of Belstone Tor. Sitting on top of the world, we scanned the horizon. Green fertile country to the north, open wilderness to the south. The energy ran right through the summit. Victorian antiquarians had thought that an altar to the Phoenician Sun-God Belus had once been set at this spot. The very name seems to point to ancient rituals once enacted on this crag, for in its simple and literal meaning, Belstone would appear to be where a stone of Bel once stood. Bel was the Celtic Sun-God, Belenos the Brilliant, or Baal. Magnificent fires were lit on the hills of the ancient world to honour him at the high spots of the annual cycle, when his Goddess, the Earth, reflected his glory by the stages of her fertilization and fruitfulness. Such rites would have united the countryside in a common, sacred purpose in a way that has never been equalled. The fires were times of joy and celebration for everyone. No-one was excluded. It is practically impossible for us today to imagine the total sense of unity that such an experience would have held for each individual, not just at one with his neighbours but with the rhythms of the heavens.

Such thoughts naturally filtered into our minds as we sat squinting at the sun reflecting off the crystalline granite. The great fire festivals that were once universal seem to have combined processes of purification and fertilization with a recognition of humanity's part in the Cosmic process, cleansing the channels of the Spirit of the Earth, causing them to flow freely and arousing the planetary

Kundalini. It is hardly surprising that people love bonfires so much; gathering around an open fire is one of the deepest of all human experiences, dissolving artificial barriers and the cultural conditioning that separates us from one another. It also dissolves time, for the effect of hilltop fires on human minds is uplifting. The centuries disappear as the sparks fly upwards and a communication takes place between the land, the sky and the countless ancient people who participated in an act of synthesis and alchemy.

Walking, with heads still in the clouds, down the slopes of Belstone Tor, it seemed to us that a revival of the old Fire Festivals could be one of the most important ways by which we could restore our relationship with the Earth. The merest glimpse of a vision of great fires sparkling like a jewelled web across the countryside, recognizing the ancient sites and paths of the Earth Spirit, was exhilarating.

The stone ring known as Ninestones below Belstone Tor.

THE HOLY CROSS

JUNE 7th, 1987. Back in the green Devon countryside of small villages, country churches and, unfortunately, all the upheavals that the building of a modern bypass creates, we were led through South Zeal to the crossroads at Fire Stone Cross (yet another reminder of the old festivals), and on through Whiddon Down to the exquisite little church at Hittisleigh. This old building is situated on an ancient trackway called the Two Moors Way connecting Dartmoor and Exmoor, and is a visual delight, almost hidden behind weathered barns, and with architecture a Hobbit would feel at home with. Timbers seem to have been deliberately chosen for their qualities of natural liveliness. Those old carpenters would never use a straight bit of wood if they could choose one that was bent.

Norman in origin, the church possesses an interesting, almost secret feature. Hidden beneath the carpet in front of the altar is a most unusual granite slab, carved with an elaborate eight-foot cross standing on a hexagonal plinth. Its shape is striking, and while it is thought to be simply a fifteenth-century memorial, there is a strange feeling that it may be something more.

Towards Colebrooke, the path of the energy coincides with the road for much of its length, leading to the church, where it performs a curious angular turn inside. A similar change takes place at the gargoyle font in Lostwithiel. Here, it enters from the south and realigns to the north-east on an axis of the font, lectern and an ancient carved desk used as a priest's stall. It bears a carving of a 'green man' grotesque figure holding a shield with a serpent on it, believed to be the crest of the local Georges family.

The mid-Devon market town of Crediton is a friendly, welcoming place that bears its history with dignity. Its most famous son was St Boniface; 'A man who had a deeper influence on the history of Europe than any other Englishman who has ever lived'. Of Anglo-Saxon parentage, he visited Rome and travelled throughout Europe as a missionary during the eighth century, creating monasteries and uniting opposing forces. As an old man, he continued his work until he was murdered on 5th June 775.

His church is an impressive place. It was founded as a monastery during his lifetime and became the first bishopric of Devon and Cornwall. This helps to explain why the cathedral (now demoted to the status of a very lively parish church) has such a powerful presence. Its beautiful red Devon sandstone conceals a history of some magnificence even after Bishop Leofric moved the bishopric to Exeter about 1050. The present cruciform building dates from the twelfth century, with various additions over the years. Inside it has all the power of a cathedral with the intimacy of a parish church, a vibrant atmosphere that is inspiring. The central tower is Early English, and displays in kaleidoscopic mosaic a memorial to Crediton's most famous modern son, distinguished campaigner General Sir Redvers Buller. We tracked the line across the main road and into the south side of the building, where it went through a part known as St Nicholas' Chapel. Standing in front of memorial slabs bearing worn crusader crosses, we blinked at a brass plaque on the wall. It said that the chapel had been rededicated to St Nicholas in recent times. Before that, it had been the chapel of another saint. St Michael.

Talking to the chaplain, he mentioned that the original Saxon cathedral may have stood to the north, in what is now the car park. It had been originally dedicated to St Mary. Directly in the centre of the square Norman tower we found a node point.

From Crediton the current followed an interesting route. For over ten miles it

The Church of the Holy Cross at Crediton, with its central Norman tower marking the flow of the St Michael current.

was virtually coincidental with the main road to Tiverton, the A3072/A396 which for the last few miles runs parallel to the River Exe. At only one place did we observe it leave the road to travel to the atmospheric hilltop enclosure on the top of Cadbury Castle, over 800 feet high with a St Michael church on its slopes. This prehistoric hill is a truly magical place, with ancient woodland and a superb central enclosure through which the line runs. There was an indefinable impression of others being present, observing our arrival and meagre understanding of the original purpose of what is thought by archaeologists to be a fortress or castle. We were now, though, becoming used to the idea that these sites had a far greater significance, that they harboured secrets that were veiled by later, secular uses. This is particularly true of Cadbury Castle, where local folklore records that buried deep within the hill is a great treasure guarded by a dragon. Thomas Risdon, writing about 1626, recorded 'The Circuit of an antient Castle is here to be seen which stands aloft and overlooketh the Country about it; whereof men speak marvellous matters, that a Dragon (forsooth) should be seen there often . . .' Excavation in the nineteenth century revealed a ritual shaft in the centre of the hill, containing votive offerings and beads.

After spending some time within the enclosure, the mood was indisputably mystical. It seemed as though we were being given glimpses into another way of existence, a world where a mutual co-operation with Nature had laid the foundation for civilizations whose quality of life was almost unimagineable. These people, attuned to the requirements of their surroundings and their own inner natures, had been totally misrepresented by orthodox history. They experienced life on a far deeper level that we can possibly comprehend.

Following in their footsteps, with just a glimmer of understanding, was having a profound effect on our own characters. Neither of us were in a position to judge what these effects were, but we were certainly becoming more sensitive to atmospheres, far better at working on an intuitive level rather than following the dictates of the rational and logical, and coming closer to the Earth. We felt that in many ways it was a true pilgrimage, where the traveller is guided by the spirit of the enterprise to visit places which have an effect upon the innermost nature.

Walking back down the hill, we passed some old trees. There was a spontaneous shout of discovery as the dowser fell over a projecting stump. The tree was alive! It writhed and twisted in serpentine splendour, frozen in mid-motion. The startling shape of a dragon's head protruded in fiery defiance, its ears flaring and its mouth open. And in its mouth, a round object which could only be a dragon's egg. Astonished that such a natural formation should so closely reflect the legend of Cadbury Castle and our own strange quest, we laughed and spent some time appreciating this fine example of Gaia's sense of humour.

The Cadbury Dragon.

THE OBELISK

At Tiverton it was interesting to see that the current ran right through the elaborately-carved church of St Peter's, looking for all the world like an ecclesiastical wedding-cake with its white stones dripping with weathered icing, and carried on into the remains of Tiverton Castle, a ruin located a few feet outside the churchyard. It then headed due north for a couple of miles, veering well away from its usual direction of flow, to curve tightly round near Firebeacon Hill and suddenly point south. This was unusual, and we wondered why it should be.

We were standing in the shadow of Knightshayes Court, a Victorian mansion designed by the flamboyant architect William Burges in 1869. Set in one of the finest of Devon gardens, the house had been built directly in the path of the energy, which passed through the orangery and into its richly decorated interior.

A short chat with the administrator revealed that it had been built on a green-field site adjacent to the old main road. Sir John Heathcote-Amory had commissioned it as family home and centre of his business interests. As it seems unlikely that the actual spot was located by chance, the deliberate choice of such a site was apparently made by someone who understood the implications. The erection of churches, chapels, cathedrals and manor houses in Victorian times began to look increasingly like a concerted attempt to revitalize the energies associated with the St Michael Line. Exactly who was behind this impulse remains largely a mystery, although Archbishop Benson and John Heathcote-Amory were apparently linked at least by this common purpose.

Back in Tiverton, we were led to Blundell's School, into the school chapel with its memorials to notable Old Boys. The school itself is one of the most famous in the Westcountry, so it is interesting that its pupils have been educated within the benign ambience created by the energies of the earth current. Next stop was Halberton Chuch, with an indecipherable stone crest over the porch and the remains of ancient gargoyles.

Through the village of Sampford Peverell, the route led across the roar of the M5 motorway, an observation that delighted the dowser but alarmed the navigator. The dowser was delighted because he had for some years dowsed what he thought was the St Michael Line crossing at this exact spot whilst travelling up and down country. To come across such confirmation was the equivalent of giving the dowsing rods a good polish; enthusiasm was invigorated as he allowed himself a momentary bask in the efficacy of his strange talent. The navigator, however, was already experiencing symptoms of confusion as the ancient landscape had been irrevocably changed by the building of the motorway. In the next half-hour the current crossed it twice more, necessitating much reversing and back-tracking (not on the motorway, of course!) to negotiate the ceaseless stream of crazed traffic that thundered through the countryside.

Darkness descended. As the end of the day grew near, and as our capability of following the current waned, it occurred to us that we couldn't just stop in the middle of nowhere. On each expedition so far, there had always been a natural start and finish that had somehow given a particular character to that section. We had begun to look for these special places and wonder at the curious way they always seemed to turn up at the right moment. We got a little lost, and noticed a towering shape on the skyline.

It was Egyptian. The juxtaposition of a great Egyptian obelisk in the middle of the English countryside seemed tantalizing. Why such monuments should occur in considerable numbers across the land, built on hills as echoes of an ancient culture so far removed from pastoral Albion has often teased the minds of romantics and students of the landscape. They appear to harbour a secret significance. Enormous efforts have been expended in the past to remove the original stones from their Egyptian sites to modern centres of power and influence; when Christianity was adopted as the official religion of Rome, the Popes set great store by possessing many of them. Others have travelled far from the land of their creation, to London, Paris and New York. Many more are imitated on the summits of hills in the guise of memorials, especially in England. It is almost as if the influence of Ancient Egypt still hovers about the world, the relics of its formidable magical culture spread out to encompass a society that works on very different principles.

The tradition of obelisks is magical indeed. The Greeks saw them as 'celestial fire, solidified and made physical', as darts or arrows (*obelos*) of the Empyrean fire. The eighteenth-century Freemason Hargrave Jennings expressed this as a 'supersensual, superessential, divinely operative celestial 'fire'', a force which makes things grow, harden, and rise against gravity, fecundating the universe, producing all beings and life. It may be that all ancient obelisks, pillars and standing stones were originally raised for similar reasons that partook of a common philosophy, and that even the ritual of Maypole dancing is a memory of a time when the fire from the Sun, materialized into visible existence, is the centre around which the planets, or dancers, revolve.

As we approached the vast Wellington Monument, floodlit against the bat-black sky, its power could be sensed. Catching glimpses of its graceful shape through the rustling branches of the woodland path, it struck us as a particularly impressive remnant of ancestor worship, once so central in the ancient world. It was built as a memorial to the Duke of Wellington in 1817 by Thomas Lea Junior, and at 175 feet high is a dominating influence over the Black Down Hills and the surrounding Somerset country. 235 stone steps inside lead up to the dizzy heights that make one feel a great respect for steeplejacks, but do nothing to encourage one to emulate them. The positioning of this most impressive marker of the St Michael current on its way across the countryside of southern Britain must have been decided by someone who tacitly understood its existence. The only other explanation is that the landscape itself has an influence on the minds of those within it which results in the building of geomantically potent structures, continuing a tradition that seems to go right back to the earliest times.

The St Michael current in Devon: 1. Brentor; 2. Lydford; 3. Yes Tor; 4. Ninestones; 5. Belstone Tor;
6. Hittisleigh; 7. Crediton; 8. Cadbury Castle; 9. Tiverton; 10. Wellington Monument.

ST MICHAEL AND THE MUMP

NOVEMBER 15th, 1987. The serpent hugged the northern slopes of the Black
Down Hills as we tracked it down lanes resplendent in the deep golden colours of
autumn. Sunlight struck glittering pools of metallic leaves hidden in the woodland
twilight as we found ourselves sweeping right around the southern flank of
Blagdon Hill. This was a considerable departure from the rather gentle
meanderings of late, and the curving route through Prior's Park Farm and Wood
seemed to indicate its connection with the existence of an influential Priory in

Medieval times. At the tiny village of Corfe, the exquisite Neo-Norman church marks the flow. Inside, a powerful, almost electrically charged atmosphere envelops the visitor. The nearby church of St Michael at Orchard Portman is also situated on the current, which leads through Stoke St Mary and Henlade to the ancient site of Creech St Michael Church.

Here, we found it running through the tower and porch, the most ancient parts of the building. The vicar was a bit vague about precisely what the St Michael Line was. We had the impression he may have thought it was something to do with the Great Western Railway. However, it was very interesting to hear that he often walked into the old part of the church to catch the distinctive smell of burning incense. Curious, he commented, as he never used it.

Leaving Creech St Michael, we soon found ourselves at Durston, where the current again ran through the tower and porch. The whole place has the feeling of a monastic settlement, with its holy well, duckpond, ancient manor house and carved stones lying about. A mile or so away, we came across what must be one of the most secret St Michael churches in the country. Even many of the local inhabitants didn't appear to remember its whereabouts, or perhaps they were just naturally reticent in order to protect its mystery.

For a mystery there certainly is about the tiny St Michael's Church near the hamlet of North Newton. Secreted behind farm buildings, only the occasional glimpse of its squat Norman tower reveals its presence. The graveyard boasts some influential connections, for it appears to be full of baronets and dames. Just by the entrance is the memorial tomb of Herbert Adolphus Grant Watson, companion of the Order of St Michael and St George.

We enquired at a nearby cottage, where not only did its occupants keep the key, but the lady of the house offered a cup of tea and some intriguing information. It was the private church of the Slades of Maunsel, an old family whose seat, Maunsel House, is opposite the church and connected to it by a gate and footpath across the estate. She had worked for them in the past, when all the estate workers and locals would be married there, the floor strewn with flower petals. And there was a story attached to the place. Once a year, on a particular day, monks would come out from Glastonbury Abbey to sit and meditate in the old tower.

In the church, all is peace and tranquillity. The tower evidently once stood on its own in this remote position, until extended in Victorian times. An aura of strange mystery pervades the place. Stained-glass windows glow their vivid colours, dedicated to St Michael, King Alfred, St Mary and St Margaret, complete with dragon.

Across the levels, through the weird shapes of stunted withies, we could see the tumescent mound of Burrow Mump with its ruined church. As a St Michael site it is almost as prominent in the local landscape as Glastonbury Tor, which can be seen in the distance, and is in many ways as enigmatic. The red soil of which it is made is not found locally, a fact which has led to speculation that it may have been artificially constructed in some remote time. More orthodox opinion sees it as a natural hill, an island in the one-time marshes that possesses a long and interesting history. What may have been a sacred hill extending back into prehistory was

The ruined church of St Michael on the summit of Burrow Mump.

later occupied by the Romans and then King Alfred in 879, to protect the upper waters of the Rivers Tone and Parrett from Danish incursions. Later still, a Norman castle built on the summit was replaced by a chapel to St Michael which survived the dissolution but was partly destroyed during the Civil War. The evocative ruined church that now stands on the mound was built in the eighteenth century to reclaim the site in honour of St Michael after a turbulent past.

There was no sign of the serpent as we drove around the Mump. We were well aware that it was a crucial factor in the whole St Michael Line phenomenon, for it had been its instantly-recognizeable shape, seen from Glastonbury Tor, that had alerted John Michell to the possibility of an alignment extending across country. Yet nothing could be taken for granted.

The tension was mounting. We had gone virtually right around it, and there was still no sign. Then, we crossed the bridge and the rods crossed too. The current was coming in from the north-west, and going straight for the church.

In the empty ruin, the wind whistled through the grey shell as November clouds swept across the sky. It sounded vaguely of voices raised in strange, discordant harmonies. At the point where, presumably, the altar would have been located, there was a node point and the energy appeared to anchor itself into the centre of the hill. We stood at this spot in silence, lost in contemplation, and gazed out through the broken east end to the distant shape of Glastonbury Tor hovering on the horizon.

Chapter Four

AVALON, AND THE COILS OF THE SERPENT

'And the vast form of Nature like a Serpent play'd before them'

William Blake

FEBRUARY 19th, 1988. An early dawn start from Cornwall into a morning that was more like bright spring than late winter. As we followed the old route through North Devon, past Crediton and Cadbury Castle, places that were now becoming quite familiar, the unspoilt countryside seemed like something from another age. Nothing stirred, except the occasional farmer rounding up his cattle for milking. A hazy sun hung in the sky, and there was a romantic mood on this magical morning as we travelled towards Avalon while the world slept. Great banks of mist were rising out of the ground and hanging in the air like veils, half penetrated by golden shafts of sunlight.

Approaching Burrow Mump, we picked up the St Michael current running across an old ivy-covered bridge near Northmoor Green. For some reason, it appeared to be unusually weak, far less powerful that had been observed before. Previous experience had shown that the energies appeared to react to celestial events, and that the phases of the moon, solstices and equinoxes all affected their character and strength. Whilst there was a distinct lack of expertise to fall back on, it proved useful to keep a weather eye on the astrological *ephemeris* to see how the energies of the Earth reacted and resonated to the heavenly influences. As it happened, an unusual planetary configuration was in fact taking place at that time. The Sun had just moved from Aquarius into Pisces within the last couple of hours. Just a few days before there had been quite a remarkable astrological event; a conjunction of Saturn and Uranus as they had both moved together from Sagittarius into Capricorn, the fixed earth sign usually thought to have strong influence over Earth energies. As Uranus, the planet of sudden revelation, takes seven years to pass through one sign of the Zodiac, and Saturn, the planet of restriction (and initiation) takes two, this was quite a celestial occurrence. In a few days, Mars, with its fiery creative energy, was to join them, producing a three-planet conjunction in Capricorn, all within a degree. There was certainly something happening to the St Michael serpent as it approached Burrow Mump, passing right through the interesting old building of Manor Farm.

On tracking the line from the Mump, there seemed to be two distinct possibilities as to where it was heading. In the distance, the two church towers of Middlezoy and Othery stood out prominently from the Somerset levels, with the ever-present shape of Glastonbury Tor rising up from the landscape beyond. Around Middlezoy there was no reaction at all. But on approaching Othery church, the current crossed the road and ran right through the site. As we entered the churchyard, it became apparent that the entire building was precisely aligned on the energy flow. Turning the corner to enter the church, we were suddenly confronted by a striking image. Above the arched entrance was a most exquisite sculpture. St Michael was slaying the dragon, standing on the writhing body of the beast and thrusting a lance down his reptilian throat in a sculpted relief of considerable

St Michael thrusts his spear into the mouth of the writhing dragon over the door of Othery Church.

workmanship. We leaned on the porch gate with a certain amusement and delight. It seemed an excellent welcome to Glastonbury.

Inside the old building of Othery Church are many fascinating features. Tiles inlaid in the floor in front of the altar depict St Michael slaying a rather unusual dragon with a sinuous, scaly body and a human head, an image that is also echoed on one of the time-worn bench-ends. Other symbols include the Agnus Dei (the Lamb of God, a recurrent mystical symbol employed by the Knights Templar and others) and the Pelican feeding her young by pecking at her own breast to release droplets of blood. Others are the four elemental/alchemical signs, the Lion (Leo), the Bull (Taurus), the Eagle (Scorpio) and the Angel (Aquarius), Christianized and perpetuated as representing the four gospels of Matthew, Mark, Luke and John. A fifteenth-century cope, discovered in 1897 concealed under the pulpit, is displayed in a glass case, and the explanatory text reads; *'The imagery of the central figure appears to be that of Revelation XII,1,5. 'A woman clothed with the Sun and the Moon under her feet, and upon her head a crown of twelve stars . . . and she brought forth a man child . . . and her child was caught up unto God and to his throne''.* An allegory, perhaps, of ancient memories of the Earth Goddess, nourished by the energies of the Sun and Moon, and influenced by the celestial zodiac, the mother of Mankind.

The line was heading towards Glastonbury. It crossed the road at Greylake Bridge which carries speeding traffic over the King's Sedgemoor Drain, ran over

Priest Hill, through Walton Church and meandered casually around the approximate route of the main A39 road towards the Somerset town of Street. This town is notable for its long association with the footwear industry, and shoe shops crowd against each other in the main road. There was a characteristic flare of mercurial humour on the interesting discovery that the line passed right through the shoe factory.

Some conjecture as to why this should be led to the rather pedestrian conclusion that in some peculiar way, footwear was sacred. This has certainly been the case in the past, when sandals especially were thought to represent one's journey through life. The Egyptian symbol for the Life-force, the ankh, also represents a sandal-strap. With a flippant air, the imagination invoked images of pious monks engaged as cobblers and pedicures attending to the needs of all the pilgrims who had trod this way throughout history, and the modern shoe factory as a sort of vestigial memory. It was, at the very least, an entertaining diversion.

INTO AVALON

From anywhere in the surrounding levels, the extraordinary shape of Glastonbury Tor rises like a pyramid from the desert, its ancient tower dedicated to St Michael scraping the Somerset sky. Each glimpse of it seems to confirm the aura of other-wordly mystery that has made this small Westcountry market town such a potent symbol of human aspiration. Even the most hardened sceptic has to acknowledge a certain feeling of inexplicable awe descending on approaching the old sanctuary, undisputably 'a great prehistoric sacred site, comparable to Avebury, Silbury, even Stonehenge.'

It is interesting to speculate why such a remote part of the English countryside should have been sacred from the earliest times, and continue to become the national shrine of the Christian religion. In its heyday, the great Abbey church was one of the largest and richest in the country, and, despite the ruination of its buildings, the atmosphere around it is so impregnated with a heady spirituality that even today the town is a place of pilgrimage and a symbol of rebirth deep in the collective unconscious. There are not many places on the Earth that can boast such a remarkable continuity throughout the ages. Pyramids decay, their original purposes obscured by amnesia, deserts and jungles. Vast megaliths lie wrecked and desolate, inexplicably haunting. Temples across the face of the planet rise to prominence in accordance with the fashions of the time, and then deteriorate as the fashion fades. Yet Glastonbury has this peculiarly unique and timeless character. There can be little doubt that there are profound mysteries at this place which have been recognized and understood by successive ages.

'At Glastonbury a mighty pagan presence underlies Christianity' writes Geoffrey Ashe in *Avalonian Quest*. Archaeologically, we know that the area was important in prehistory, as an hour in the mellow building of the old Tribunal in the High Street, now the Town Museum, will confirm. Tor Hill, Chalice Hill and Wearyall Hill were islands rising out of the shallow watery marshes that isolated this region from the mainland. The practical problems of such an environment might have been expected to discourage settlement, but on the contrary, it was an important inhabited region, with the lakeland villages of the La Tène culture flourishing in the last century BC and first century AD. Proof of their considerable sophistication can be seen in their jewellery, bronze artefacts, decorated pottery and domestic arrangements, and there is evidence of widespread trading, with amber from the Baltic and tin from Cornwall. It is perhaps an interesting insight into their culture that no weapons of any sort have so far been found from this period, although artefacts from Glastonbury have been discovered in many other Celtic regions such as Wales, Ireland and Brittany. As a centre of culture it seems to stretch back into very remote times indeed, for tradition has always spoken of Avalon as a site of immense antiquity.

Perhaps it is a subconscious recognition of this continuity, as well as the refined atmosphere around the town, that strikes most people with a mystic potency that can have a powerful effect. The air around the old shrine is often strangely unnerving but uplifting, amplifying any latent convictions that may already be held. Confirmed cynics comment on the weird mood of the place, which, they point out, no doubt explains the superstitions that have given rise to its famous legends. Others often detect a powerful transformational energy that can induce strong psychic and spiritual effects.

The truth is that the strange magic of the place is so potent that all manner of uncanny things seem to have a certain amount of credibility when you are immersed in its atmosphere. There is no doubt that peculiar events and phenomena do take place around the town, and especially around the Tor. Everyone who has spent some time there has stories to tell, of strange meetings, dramatic weather effects, consciousness shifts and spiritual experiences. To ignore such experiences would be to deny the essential nature of the place, for

there can be no doubt that there is some definite, if intangible, energy present which has guaranteed Glastonbury's unique place throughout history, and apparently into the New Age, when its prophets claim there will be a great renaissance of spirituality and a return to the perennial philosophy, heralding a modern Golden Age.

THE HOLY THORN

On that almost spring-like February day as we tracked the serpent towards the legendary Isle of Avalon, there was no feeling of impending revelation accompanied by thunder and lightning. The landscape basked in the unexpected warmth of late winter sun and there was a mood of great gentleness in the air. On the outskirts of the town, the line led off up the old Roman Road which runs around the base of Wearyall Hill. It was evidently heading for the summit, towards the stark shape of a solitary thorn tree, bent eccentrically by the wind that blasts this exposed spot.

A few minutes later, we were standing next to this tree, traditionally a descendent of the original holy thorn planted by Joseph of Arimathea, the site of which is now marked by a broken slab of stone a few feet away. Finding that this thorn tree marked the exact centre of the line as it passed along the axis of the hill was greatly intriguing, and all of a sudden there seemed more significance in the Joseph legend than we had hitherto realized. Cornish stories had been told for centuries about how Jesus' rich uncle, a tin-merchant, had visited the West Country on perhaps more than one occasion. A foreman tinsmith in Cornwall was recorded early this century as saying *We workers in metal are a very old fraternity, and like other handicrafts we have our traditions among us. One of these is that Joseph . . . made voyages to Cornwall in his own ships, and that on one occasion he brought with him the child Christ and his mother and landed them at St Michael's Mount.'*

The connection between the Mount, Glastonbury and Joseph appeared to hold an inner meaning, a lost memory of powerful links between specific old legends and sacred sites. Later the figure of Jesus' merchant uncle was again to reappear, apparently affirming some obscure relationship between tradition and the natural energy of the St Michael Line.

On closer scrutiny, the entire phenomenon of the Joseph legend appears to underlie an ancient connection between these places, and even to have some interesting historical credibility. An intriguing little booklet by the Revd C. Dobson entitled **Did Our Lord Visit Britain as They Say in Cornwall and Somerset** quotes a fellow ecclesiastic, the Revd L.S. Lewis, as alluding to the actual discovery of Joseph's remains: *'The Vicar of Glastonbury tells us that Joseph's body remained buried here (St Joseph's Chapel—the old 'Mother Church') until AD 1354, when Edward III gave his licence to John Bloom of London to dig for it, and the Abbot and monks consented. There is the statement of a Lincolnshire monk in 1367 that his body was found. They placed it in a silver* *casket let into a stone sarcophagus, which was placed in the east end of St Joseph's Chapel, and it became a place of pilgrimage. There is a written record of the sarcophagus being still in position in 1662 when the chapel had become partially ruined. Owing to fear of puritan fanaticism prevalent at the time it was secretly removed into the Parish Church churchyard, and its identity was concealed by the pretence that the initials on it, J.A., stood for John Allen. In 1928 the present Vicar of Glastonbury found it half buried in the soil, and had it removed into the church, and its construction bears out the accounts of a silver casket which could be raised and lowered, and shows other marks of identity.'*

Joseph's arrival by sea on Wearyall Hill, as recounted by legend, has an intriguing plausibility about it. Traces of a Roman wharf discovered on the hill show that it was once used as a dock in the days of the lake villages. And as Geoffrey Ashe notes, 'Glastonbury's monks were not archaeologists. They knew nothing of the wharf or the lake-villages'. It would seem unlikely, then, that the monks invented the story of Joseph and his disciples, who came by sea and landed, 'weary-all', on the hill where the thorn still grows, unless it had some meaning. Although there cannot be any proof that he did in fact land here, or that he planted his staff in the ground which immediately came to life and blossomed, the legend has been remarkably persistent. The original tree was evidently tall and double-trunked, blossoming on Christmas day. Its mystique was unrivalled, famous across the land, with James I and other monarchs treasuring cuttings from it. It was evidently attacked by the Puritans, and ultimately destroyed during the Civil War. The original thorn, **Crataegus Oxyacanth Praecox**, now has many offspring in the area, including specimens at St John's Church and in the Abbey grounds, and every year as part of archaic ritual a sprig is sent to the reigning sovereign. This seems yet another of those peculiar Glastonbury coincidences that lead you to believe that there might be more to such legends than meets the eye, for this particular species grows in the region of the holy land and may well have been planted by a pilgrim or crusader, if not by Joseph himself.

There is little doubt that the site was an important place in the Middle Ages. Wearyall Hill once had monastic buildings on it, and the walls of both a church and a priest's house have been unearthed. The church was evidently 14th century, but others built within it were noted to be of materials from an earlier date. Several skeletons were found, and excavations by Philip Rahtz in 1967-8 uncovered material pointing to the 8th century. The antiquity and associations of the place show it to be something special, and the discovery that the line ran through the spot where the thorn and old mark stone are found may indicate a reason; the natural energies of the place were understood to be vitally important. But there was more. The flow of current did not just pass through the Holy Thorn, but changed its direction, as if this was indeed some sort of crucial point which affected the energies. Such an anomaly had been noticed on two previous occasions, at the weird gargoyle-headed font in Lostwithiel church and at Colebrooke, where there was a grotesque figure holding a serpent-shield. Now the same thing was happening at a tree, which had long been revered as especially sacred and miraculous. Later, we discovered that other researchers into the

The Holy Thorn on Wearyall Hill, an offspring of the legendary tree planted by Joseph of Arimathea.

Earth's subtle forces had noticed unusual energy formations at the Thorn, and Guy Underwood, the pioneer British dowser, refers to it in his book ***The Pattern of the Past***. He found that this thorn was precisely on what he termed 'a blind spring' or powerful natural energy spiral which is invariably present at ancient sites.

Standing on the hill, we gazed at the nearby Tor, with its terraced trackway picked out in relief by the noonday sun. Looking out from that high point, thoughts turned to the giant zodiac that lay spread across the landscape, the 'Temple of the Stars' discovered by the artist Katherine Maltwood in the 1920s. According to maps and aerial photographs, the signs of the celestial zodiac are imprinted on the area around Glastonbury, arranged in their correct sequence, with their shapes delineated by roads, tracks, rivers and natural features. In this great glyph of heavenly effigies, the shape of the Tor represents the Aquarian Phoenix with its head turned to drink the waters of Chalice Well, and Wearyall Hill depicts one of the fishes of Pisces. The hill does indeed look like a fish from aerial photographs, and it seemed an interesting coincidence that the Sun had just entered this constellation on its annual cycle. Down below, the serpent appeared to head off towards the town, through a building site where an ugly hypermarket was in the course of being constructed. We tracked the line running through a muddy corner of a field that was in the throes of becoming a car park. It flowed through the end of a cul de sac called Fairfield Gardens, by-passed the old Benedictine Church of St Benignus, continued on through the school and into the main car park at the rear of St John's Church. It was here that, whilst dowsing it running through the cobbled passageway behind the old pilgrim hostelry of the George and Pilgrim Hotel, one of those intriguing synchronicities occurred. The dowsing rods had been spotted by a fellow unloading his car, who looked up and asked casually 'How's the dowsing going?' This seemed a little curious as none of us had ever met before.

Jamie George is a well-known figure in Glastonbury, and co-owner, with his wife Frances, of Gothic Image, a bookshop with distinctive atmosphere that provides a focus for those of an esoteric turn of mind. Although we had never met, he was known to us as a publisher of books on dowsing, and so our chance meeting seemed perhaps a little extraordinary. Even more extraordinary, though, was the discovery that he had intuitively positioned his chair and desk right in the centre of the St Michael current, which was heading for the parish church of St John's. He received this news with some incredulity, but when he mentioned that he often found himself full of enthusiasm and right 'up in the clouds' or alternatively inexplicably 'down', it seemed to make sense, for the influence of such terrestrial energy flows has been noticed by others to have a similar 'upper' and 'downer' effect, amplifying any latent mood.

Leaving Jamie George perhaps a little bemused at the sudden appearance of two strange characters poking the air in his office with metal rods, the line passed through the tower of St John's, with its old carvings of the Agnus Dei and the Phoenix above the doorway. Inside, the building was deserted, and the twilight interior echoed with muffled exclamations of surprise on the discovery that the line performed another of its 'turns' between the columns adjacent to the entrance, as it had done at the Holy Thorn. The axis of the turn was in fact marked by an ancient oak chest, the angle being approximately 30 degrees, deflecting it through the Lady Altar and also, the small St George's Chapel on the right-hand side. This place has an alabaster effigy of one Camel of Campbell, who was a one-time treasurer of the Abbey. There is also a powerful atmosphere of sanctity. A notice reminds visitors that it is a place of worship, and its magnificent stained glass window depicts St Michael with his balance, St George slaying the dragon, Glastonbury and its legendary figures, and dawn rising over the New Jerusalem, all shining in ethereal glory. Perhaps it is no wonder that such a place should have a special uplifting effect, for the flow of intangible but spiritually potent energy would shine like the rainbow colours of the stained glass if only we could see it.

The present church was built by Abbot Selwood in 1485, erected on the site of an earlier Norman church which possessed a central tower, possibly where the line alters its angle. We wondered whether there could be something buried at this spot, for there was nothing visible to mark it, unlike previous occasions where a gargoyle font, serpent-shield and holy thorn had indicated the change of direction.

Following the line as it left the church, it ran through the corner of the High Street and Archers Way, across the pedestrian crossing and right through the Avalon Constitutional Club. Irresistable images of venerable Avalonians sprang to mind, drinking toasts and supping delicately from vessels shaped like chalices and Holy Grails. Still in slightly flippant mood, a walk down Silver Street revealed that the line curved round to head into the Abbey grounds.

Inside the cloistered sanctuary of the walled enclosure, the sun shone like a summer's day despite the fact that it was February. A few visitors wandered about, soaking up the atmosphere of the ruins of what was once the most famous monastery of medieval Europe. In its heyday, this quiet, tranquil scene would have been very different, full of bustling activity and all the clamour of a centre of pilgrimage and religious devotion. Hundreds of monks and students, staff and craftsmen would have crowded the place, the poor collecting alms at the gate, with vast influxes of pilgrims and the infirm on holy days, when miraculous cures evidently were commonplace.

The line ran in from Silver Street and swung round to suddenly reorientate and run towards the imposing remains of the great church of St Peter and St Paul, the vandalized ruins of which impress every visitor with a glimpse of what was once a truly remarkable building. It was 400 feet long and 80 feet wide, and its graceful and lofty arches struck observers as divinely inspired. In their desuetude, they still seem to be intimate with the heavens as the clouds race overhead. After the great fire of 1184, it was rebuilt by Henry II, who wrote in his charter about this date of the great significance of the place; *'Chiefly that the town of Glastonbury, in which the 'vetusta ecclesia' of the Mother of God is situated, which is truly reckoned to be the source and origin of all religion in England, should be free above all others, together with its islands...'*

Certainly, from the remains, it is not difficult to judge the extreme gracefulness and beauty of the building, and the richness of its decoration. In this place were the legendary tombs of King Arthur and Queen Guinevere, the English Kings Edmund, Edgar and Edmund Ironside, and many Abbots and others who were anxious to secure a last resting place in so sacred an edifice.

The St Michael serpent curved sharply to focus on the high altar, now marked out by a rectangle of turf and chained off to protect it from the ravages of modern pilgrims, within a few yards of 'King Arthur's Tomb'. This was the spot where the bones of Arthur and his queen were reburied after the monks had excavated them in 1190 from their original grave in the Abbey cemetery. At the altar we found a node point, accompanied by a distorted pentagram with two elongated arms pointing towards the north-west. The high altar and King Arthur's Tomb possess an interesting property: they are both situated on the axis around which the whole structure of Glastonbury Abbey is built, which leads, if projected across the countryside, towards Stonehenge. The altar thus marks the precise spot where the Michael serpent and the Stonehenge line cross.

Continuing on its way, the serpent swept through the corner of the building out into the Abbey grounds, right through an enormous oak, towards the corner of Chilkwell Street and Bere Lane. Blinking at the shape of Chalice Hill, and beyond

Glastonbury Abbey ruins.

it, the Tor shimmering in the late afternoon sunlight, we left to find a room for the night. We had been invited to Gothic Image to attend the launch of John Michell's latest book *The Dimensions of Paradise*. It all seemed extremely appropriate, even magical. Glastonbury can have that sort of effect.

THE COILED SERPENT

Another fine February day, and the weaving St Michael line leaves the Abbey grounds at a small roundabout on the road that leads to the Tor. At this point it measures 22 paces wide, as we walk in the sharp morning sunlight towards Chalice Hill. It leaves the road and sweeps around the lower slopes of the hill, through the rear gardens of the houses in Chilkwell Street, as though it is aiming for the Chalice Well gardens. All over the slopes of the hill the thorn trees are blossoming, sprinkled with a flurry of tiny white flowers.

In the cloistered serenity of the famous gardens, preserved for future generations by the seer and mystic Wellesley Tudor Pole, there is a pervading atmosphere of peace. The line passes through a box hedge and we allow ourselves a moment to speculate whether it will pass through the well-head, which caps an underground chamber built from vast megalithic-style blocks of stone, and whose cover boasts the mystical symbol of the Vesica Piscis. This, of course, is as usual an erroneous assumption. It in fact passes through perhaps the most tranquil part of the gardens, known as King Arthur's Court, where a waterfall brings the iron-rich waters from the well to form a rectangular pool. Everybody who enters this walled enclosure becomes aware of its soothing and therapeutic effect on mind and spirit. It is as if the energies we are tracking somehow combine with those of the healing waters, and, trapped and amp-

lified by the reservoir created by the walls, have an effect that is mentally and physically invigorating. Above the arched doorway is the Vesica Piscis, pierced by a sword. To us, it seems to be a physical expression of exactly what is happening in energy terms—the healing powers of the Goddess of the Earth, symbolized by the interlinked circles of the Vesica, crossed with the Sword of St Michael, or its Arthurian counterpart, Excalibur.

Outside the gardens, on the road that winds around the Tor, the line flows through a brick arched doorway in the wall and into the grey,solid edifice of a Victorian reservoir, now used as a café. This building was erected in 1872 to supply the inhabitants of the town with drinking water, and thereby hangs a tale. For the waters that it collected flowed from a perennial spring located not 50 yards from Chalice Well, and almost as famous. 'The White Spring', as it was known, had a rate of flow of between 5,000 and 7,000 gallons a day, and once formed part of a local beauty spot much frequented by visitors and pilgrims, who thought highly of its waters. The building of the reservoir had enraged local antiquarians, for not only was the spring that rises beneath the Tor obliterated, but buildings which were thought to be the last remains of monks cells were lost for ever. Some scholars think that it may even have been the abode of St Collen, of whom legend recounts how his hermitage on the slopes of the Tor was by a spring. The valley between the Tor and Chalice Hill, therefore, once possessed two springs, the Blood Spring and the White Spring, which may well have joined each other at what is now the Chalice Well Gardens. Some may well see in this an echo of the legend that Joseph of Arimathea buried the two cruets which contained the blood and sweat of Christ, miraculous relics brought from the holy land, at this very spot.

In recent times, the natural chambers that lie behind this spring have been tentatively explored. The tunnels and hollows that the waters have cut into the rock of the Tor were penetrated by cavers, who discovered that there was in former times access through them to the Tor itself. This lends some credibility to the persistent legend associated with the Tor that recalls it as being hollow. Various caverns were found, some large enough to hold up to a dozen people. Unfortunately, the subterranean passageways had collapsed further in, so whatever other secrets are hidden beneath the Tor will, for the time being, remain in the province of speculation.

However, if the two streams merged, it was likely that they did so at the place now called King Arthur's Court. If this was the case, then at least three streams of powerful natural energies merged and mingled, the two connected with Chalice Well and the White Spring, and the less tangible but nevertheless powerful serpentine St Michael line. Could this in any way help to explain the timeless associations of the place with miracles and myth, and its peculiarly potent atmosphere? Questions hung in the rarefied air outside the Chalice Well before we made our way to the field behind the reservoir, and the foot of the Tor.

In the shadow of the great conical mound with its distinctive tower to St Michael, the stream of energy was curving noticeably towards some old tennis courts, on the right hand side of the hill. Here it veered off before reaching the courts and instead went through a scrubby hummock of woodland before hugging the boundary fence, passing through a piece of ground riddled with rabbit burrows and continuing into a group of conifer trees.

It was running around the base of the Tor, and seemed to be deliberately avoiding it. It headed through an old derelict cottage, and then through a more modern one that was inhabited, to cross the old lane that leads to the base of the Tor from the south. Looking as if it was sure to carry on skirting the lower slopes, it swept into the field adjacent to the lane and there performed some extremely complex manoeuvres.

The curious modern maze at the foot of the Tor.

Half way across this field, it made a hairpin turn and bent back on itself in the most extraordinary manner. It ran parallel to its former course, at approximately 10 yards distance, and left the meadow. To our consternation it made another horseshoe turn very close to an intriguing modern 'maze' pattern, built out of small stones in the shape of a question mark. Whilst this was obviously quite recent, it seemed exactly to reflect our quizzical state of mind. We wondered who had made it, and whether they had been intuitively aware of the tortuous contortions of the serpent line. We sat down next to it with a feeling of vague incomprehension.

We had never come across anything remotely like this before. The line narrowed to about six paces wide and began to follow a series of paths which led through a scattered collection of trees growing on the southern slopes. It doubled up on itself again, and repeated the entire procedure a few yards further up, turning fiercely at three remarkably gnarled and twisted trees. The current had assumed the shape of a series of regular, rhythmical loops. Sitting down to make a sketch of what had been found so far, we plotted the sinuous path. We had stopped trying to rationalize it, but what was apparent was that it had suddenly become quite astonishingly serpentine.

Later, we discovered that the field where these strange contortions began was known as Fair Field, and was recorded with this name on an old tithe map. In past ages, this had been the site for an important fair held for six days every year in honour of St Michael. It commenced on the archangel's feast day of 29th September.

As it is commonly accepted that the first fairs were initiated by the gathering of worshippers and pilgrims around sacred places, and that many fairs whose origins are lost in antiquity can be traced back to a religious source, could this be a memory of a rite so ancient, and in some way connected with this energy, that it was only now remembered in terms of a medieval fair? After thinking that the line was avoiding the Tor, there was now no doubt that at least in our terms something very special was happening. The energies which up until this time had behaved reasonably organically, very much like a flowing river, now assumed a different character. We had come across node points and peculiar angular turns, always at anciently revered sites, but this was totally new.

Soon we were standing at a place on the terraced trackway that winds around the Tor. Above was what is known as a 'Tor Burr', a large boulder-like rock sitting in a natural sculpted hollow with old thorn trees clinging to it. The current now ran along the path to a certain spot, indistinguishable by physical characteristics, to one of those special points where a node was discernable. The actual spot was on a line between St Michael's tower and some distant playing fields, on the wide terrace of the south-eastern slope. We sat down and contemplated our findings, saying little. We were vaguely aware of the persistant story of a hidden chamber beneath the Tor, and speculated that there may be something buried at this, and the other places where nodes occurred. It was exceedingly difficult to imagine what could be the cause of these repeated anomalous effects.

It was at this point that, during a little light discussion while we rested to relieve the dowser's badly twisted ankle, the theory developed that places such as towers and prominent landmarks may sometimes have been specifically erected to draw attention *AWAY* from the 'true' places of power, which were deliberately 'hidden' from the popular gaze. Whilst this was more the product of idle amusement than serious speculation, it foreshadowed a later, supportive observation. After a talk in Devon almost a year later, a professional acupuncturist who was fascinated by the discovery of this particular spot on the side of the Tor offered an interesting comment: 'It's exactly the same in acupuncture technique' he said. 'The most powerful points are invariably a short distance away from the obvious places, as if they are in some way 'secret''. The plot was certainly thickening, as research also showed that the place where the node point occurred had been considerably changed by agriculture in the past. A tithe map of 1844 clearly marks this area as the 'Tor linches'—strips of land used for cultivation. If there had ever been some sort of structure or unusual feature at this spot, then any vestige of it would certainly have been obliterated by agricultural use.

The next couple of hours were spent painstakingly following the course of the line on its continuing journey around the Tor. On leaving the node point, it virtually completed a circle to enclose the great pyramidal mound, and turning sharply upwards, flowed around the hill in a totally unpredictable fashion, delineating a complex shape that seemed to have no rationale. Slipping and sliding as we scrambled up and down the terraces, it was obvious that the ever-increasing serpentine nature of this line would not fall into any preconceived pattern, for it had already occurred to us at this stage that it might be following the terraced 'labyrinth' that had been propounded as an explanation for the pyramidal step-like terraces that are so prominent. However, as was to be expected, the merest thought of such an idea was enough to make it evaporate into thin air.

As it completed its path around the circumference of the hill, the line led past some old stones that are thought to be the remains of a broken megalith known as 'the living rock'. Another stone a little further up seemed, along with this, to mark the beginning of a new pattern, as if what we had experienced so far had just been a preamble. It was at this point also that we discovered what appeared to be another line, completely separate, running alongside the one we were already following. However, meticulous dowsing showed that this was in fact our serpent line doubling up on itself as it wound its way back down the Tor. This could only mean that we were not finding a spiral-type maze, where the energy wound around like a clock-spring, but a true labyrinth design, with an entrance and an exit.

After making practically another complete circuit of the Tor, it then curved upwards and changed levels. We tracked the line across the main path, up to the summit and half-way around the north-western slope, where we were led to follow a most curious shape on the steep part directly below the tower. The energy now ran practically parallel to the main path before widening out to run around the tower, crossing over the summit directly in front of the modern concrete direction indicator. Its width narrowed to just four paces, something that was, in our experience so far, unique. As St Michael's tower marks the position of the ancient church which was demolished by a sudden earthquake 'between the first and third hours of the day' on September the 11th, 1275, this spot looked exactly like the place where the altar of the original church would have been. Collapsing wearily on the stone seat in the tower we rested, trying to take it all in.

The existing St Michael's Tower was erected in the 1360's, and a roof-crease shows where it joined the nave of the church. In a niche on the west side a damaged figure of St Michael, with his left foot pinning down a dragon, can be seen, and below, over the arch, two carvings, one depicting a soul being weighed in a balance by an angel (another function of the archangel), the other of St Bridget milking her cow. A similar 12th century sculpture is found over the entrance to St Mary's chapel in the Abbey, and the discovery of the remains of a 6th century chapel to St Bride found at nearby Beckery points to important Bride/Bridget associations at Glastonbury. Bride is in fact the Great Goddess of pre-Christianity, the 'Mother of Gods', the Virgin Mary and the Goddess of the Earth. Her day was the August quarter day (the 7th), to mark the beginning of harvest and the gathering of the fruits of the Goddess. Interestingly, this day (the Celtic Llughnasad) also provides a solar alignment in the same way as the rising sun at Beltane, thus creating an even more profound significance of this countrywide orientation of ancient sites. Both of these days were major Celtic festivals, with Bel's fires focussed on the energizing vitality of spring, and Llugh's on the fruitful bounty of autumn: 'One sending the spark of male energy to the Mother, the other receiving her gifts'. At both times, the sun could be seen to rise in the direction of distant Avebury, the 'mother-circle' of Britain, whilst fires were lit in a glittering countrywide alignment to draw in or return the solar energy in recognition of the cyclic integration of Earth and Cosmos. As a crucial component in the system, it is perhaps not surprising to find that the long, conical shape of the Tor is aligned precisely along this Beltane/Llughnasad axis.

Again we are confronted by the intimate connection between Michael and Mary, the God and Goddess forms of universal energy. In prehistoric times, the Goddess was often symbolized by the ox, whose horns resembled the crescent moon, and which was the motive power behind agriculture and the production of earthly fruits. The same symbol was used in Ancient Egypt as an aspect of the goddess Hathor, and is still observed in India, where cows are considered sacred animals. This symbolism recurs at Bury St Edmunds, a hundred or so miles up the St Michael Line, where a white bull led by a woman to the medieval shrine was considered to promote human fertility. Similarly, an Irish folk belief says that 'sometimes on the 1st of May, a sacred heifer, snow white, appeared among the cattle, and this was considered to bring the highest luck to the farmer'.

This connection between the landscape Goddess and the energizing vitality symbolized by the Christian St Michael is explored further on in the quest, when other significant discoveries are made. There seems little doubt that the interaction between the two polarities of energy was the basis of a universal cosmology in former times, and the reason for the enigmas of much ancient landscape sculpture. The appearance of St Bride and St Michael on the tower at the Tor may, in its own quiet way, point to a profound and ancient understanding.

In the 1930s the psychometrist Olive Pixley visited the Tor and 'saw' a host of people gathering before dawn to wind their way up the Tor in a celebration of singing, chanting and drumming. Evidently, as the people walked the maze their sound and movement created:

> 'an etheric serpent-like trail of energy, that became brighter as more people advanced to the top. Then the sun rose, and the raised serpent fused with the light from the sun through the circle on the summit, and the resultant energy shot out through the 'alignments' over the land'.

Another psychometrist, Iris Campbell, reported impressions of a ritual dance moving sunwise up and around the spiral path. The vortex of energy raised by this apparently stimulated regenerative forces which could be directed to the animal and vegetable kingdoms.

These clairvoyant impressions indicate that the Tor was a great ritual centre where the serpent energy, or Earth Kundalini, was raised to fuse with the solar energies on Mayday or Llughnasad sunrise. If this was so, then the whole thing was beginning to make some sense. We were evidently dealing with a system of energy fusion, where the forces inherent in the land itself were conjoined with the forces from the centre of the solar system. A technology of subtle energies so refined that it can only be described as spiritual alchemy. But how could we explain that the shape we were finding by dowsing was so dissimilar to the normally accepted 'Cretan' labyrinth design of the existing terraces around the Tor? Had the original design, shaped so many thousands of years ago, been irrevocably transformed down the centuries by natural and man-made changes, or was there some definite purpose behind it which we could not grasp?

There was no doubt that the Tor had undergone considerable changes in its shape. The terraces had certainly been ploughed up for agricultural purposes in the past. And if an earthquake had demolished the church on the summit in the 13th century, then it could have also radically affected the terracing. With thousands of years of natural erosion (which is visible in process on the southern flank today, where earth and stone are exposed), plus the archaeological fact that the summit was once used for defence in the 5th and 6th centuries, it was certainly possible that any prehistoric pattern could have been obscured. Or perhaps there were *TWO* labyrinths, an invisible, energy labyrinth created by a major terrestrial current, and a more mundane one for the perambulation of pilgrims?

It was impossible to conclude anything except that Glastonbury Tor, symbol to many of a dawning Golden Age throughout the world, was a unique place that had an accordingly unique effect on the terrestrial energy current that had been tracked from Land's End. Like a vast electrical transformer with its coils of wire wound around a central magnetic core, the volcanic mound seemed to be a generator and transmuter of natural energies that exerted a powerful effect on human beings. As we carried on tracing out its unpredictable path, the current that may well supply the natural energy for its operation widened out to create a rather bulbous shape that encompassed the site of the original church. Turning sharply to form a 'finger' pointing north-east, it returned to cross over the track for a few feet. It was exceedingly complex.

Wondering how we could possibly extricate ourselves from this truly labyrinthine tangle without crossing over the line that had already been dowsed, it was tracked back down the slope, where it pointed towards the Fair Field where we had started some three hours ago. The line neatly left the Tor within a few feet of the unusual modern maze pattern that had marked the start. The serpent had found the only possible way out, demonstrating to us the true labyrinthine nature of its course. We were back where we had started, at the edge of the Fair Field, breathing a sigh of relief that we were on reasonably level ground again. With blistered feet and bemused brains after three hours dowsing the Tor, we nevertheless were in mellow spirits following the last coil of the serpent as it wound back around the base, below the 'living rock', along the north-western flank and across the fields to the northern entrance to the Tor.

It ran directly over the crossroads at the junction of Stone Down and Basketfield Lane, and headed off into the countryside. Following it down into a valley, it led

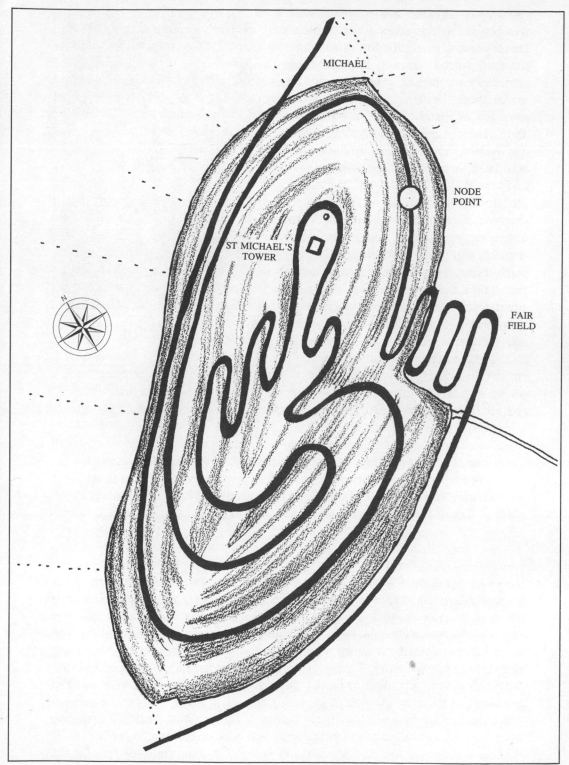

The labyrinth created by the St Michael current on Glastonbury Tor.

to two remarkable ancient oak trees, thought to be the remains of a sacred Druid grove. The quite astonishing shapes of the gnarled trunks and branches certainly indicate their great antiquity. We stood there, looking at the imposing presence of the old trees known as Gog and Magog, and wondered about our discoveries. There was both elation and confusion. What could be the meaning of this energy labyrinth we had tracked on the slopes of the Tor? Looking at the shape that had been sketched whilst following it round, it seemed strangely organic, and unlike any previous ideas of a labyrinth. Its purpose struck us as so profound and inexplicable that any attempt to frame questions seemed inappropriate. After Glastonbury, weary and weather-beaten, we had the distinct feeling that anything could happen.

One of the ancient 'Druid' oaks known as Gog and Magog.

At The Edge Of Prehistory

'The study of prehistory today is in a state of crisis. Archaeologists all over the world have realized that much of prehistory, as written in the existing text-books, is inadequate: some of it is quite simply wrong.'

Professor Colin Renfrew
BEFORE CIVILIZATION

As a centre of the Christian faith before the dissolution, Glastonbury ruled the piety of pilgrims and the attentions of Kings and Abbots, and its administrative influence on the surrounding countryside was total. A great network of churches and monastic settlements, the remains of which still possess a lingering atmosphere of the rural ecclesiastical life of medieval times, covered the district in a living web of religious devotion. That the churches and monasteries replaced existing places of power, sanctified in earlier days, is accepted; yet so fervent was the devotion that traces of those days are rarely seen. Old stones and other remnants of previous religions were lost in the waves of ecclesiastical building that took place from the twelfth to the fifteenth centuries. More tenacious, however, were the sites themselves and the legends and veneration that clung to them in the popular mind.

It is hardly surprising, therefore, that the St Michael current that is so intimately involved with Glastonbury's power passes through few places that exhibit artefacts from prehistory. They have been washed away in a tide of faith that replaced the old reverence for megaliths and raw Nature. It is not for quite a distance that stones begin to appear again, isolated in open countryside or half-buried in a tangle of undergrowth. Meanwhile, the current runs through a considerable diversity of beautiful old churches, each one with charms to delight the eye and spirit of those who enjoy such places.

The first of these is at North Wootton, an intimate little gem with a remarkable drunken font which leads you to consider that the holy water hereabouts must be a lively brew. A couple of miles away, the line passes at an angle through the huge flamboyant Victorian church at Pilton. Looking down over the bridge into the tranquil river below, it is difficult to imagine the intense activity that once filled the air; but tradition has it that it was once a busy port, with merchants from all over the world involved in trading lead from the Mendips.

Another tradition is more interesting to the current quest. Legend says that Pilton church was founded by Joseph of Arimathea, who stopped here on his way to Glastonbury and built a mud and wattle church where baptisms might take place. Accordingly, the dedication is to John the Baptist. Another story states that he brought the Christ-child with him, a legend colourfully depicted on the banner in the Lady Chapel. Interestingly, the whole place is built on solid rock and has no foundations, a classic site that may, like the many other rocky places that appear in connection with it, have once been dedicated to the Michael force. The centre of the energy runs through the ancient font.

In the twelfth century, Pilton was run directly by Glastonbury Abbey and was a powerful centre in its own right. In fact the Abbot of Glastonbury had a palace here, on the site of the present manor house. The old Tithe chest in the church contains rare books bound in wood and leather, preserved from the devastation of the dissolution when the contents of Glastonbury's famous library were given away, burnt or sold for a few meagre pence. On the tower are the recurrent symbols of the Lamb of God and the Phoenix, rising triumphantly from its flaming pyre, a potent image of transformation and rebirth. The symbolism and the story both indicate some mystery at Pilton. It is certainly curious that yet another site should point to a legendary connection with Joseph. Along with St Michael's Mount, Wearyall Hill and Glastonbury itself, could it be that the story of Joseph accompanied by the young Christ is a mythological interpretation of the sacred energies that connect these places, at a time when a new ethos was replacing a far older faith?

It was Sunday morning in Shepton Mallet. The organ resounded inside the parish church as if the second coming was imminent. Lusty and uncompromising, its great quaking sound vibrated through the stone floor and up through the skeleton to make the delicate bones of the inner ear tremble from within. As the current seemed very lively on its way through the north door and the south porch, it seemed like a good idea to measure it. A few days ago it had seemed weak and sluggish. Now it was transformed, and after some time spent in fine-dowsing the individual bands that made up the Michael current, we found it had grown much more powerful. It was currently twenty-two paces wide, with 280 separate channels each containing 64 individual streams a fraction of an inch apart. These bands flowed in alternate directions, presumably indicating that the current in its entirety was a two-way affair. The results meant little to us other than it had increased in strength by 40 x 64 bands. In matters of such baffling complexity, we could only fulfil the role of observers. Yet the energies had certainly multiplied within the last twenty-four hours. Some sort of behind-the-scenes change had apparently taken place.

In passing, this could be a good place to record details of a miraculous healing associated with the Tor. The dowser, suffering from a sprained ankle the day before, had experienced great difficulty in scrambling up and down the hill whilst dowsing the peculiar labyrinth shape, complaining bitterly about the excruciating pain. However, after a punishing time which would surely have incapacitated the most fleet-footed, followed by an evening of revelry and a sound night's sleep, there was not the slightest trace of discomfort. It seems that climbing Glastonbury Tor can be remarkably good for your health.

Doulting Church has an air of quiet magnificence about it, with its hexagonal spire and superb gargoyles looking down on more lowly creatures that crawl on the ground. The current runs diagonally across the building, which was originally a wooden structure until replaced by one in stone by the monks from Glastonbury. Over the interior arch, two dragons peer down from the walls in curious incongruity. Doulting was obviously once a place of considerable importance, for its buildings still possess a faded glory; carved stones lie about draped in moss, and a large holy well is to be found not far from the church. Less than a mile away, at the roadside near Chclynch, the current passes unusually through a pool of water, which has a mysterious eerie quality about it as if something strange lives in its depths.

Passing swiftly on through the ecclesiastical landscape of medieval Somerset, we came to Stoke St Michael Church, where the line passes through the south porch and north door. Unfortunately, the old church was demolished in 1839 leaving only the tower remaining. The Church of the Holy Trinity at Coleford, a Victorian edifice, is aligned on the flow, but with no ancient remains to remind us of its past.

The church at Mells, however, makes up for the previous two. Surely one of the most spectacular in the county, it is built in a dramatic perpendicular style, and has a very special atmosphere that extends to encompass the whole village. The axis of the building coincides with the flow of energy, and the mellow stones house ornate workmanship in many forms, most prominent to the blacksmith dowser being the exquisite ironwork. Although this church, like the previous two, was restored in Victorian times, the comparison is odious, like the difference between a motorway canteen and a Gothic cathedral.

One last church, at Great Elm, was to end the succession of religious buildings marking the current on its way through Somerset. Within the last twenty-five or so miles it had led through one abbey and no less than eight churches. Now we were driving towards the border with Wiltshire, and wondered whether the character of the sites would reflect its fame as a county of some of the most notable of prehistoric monuments. All manner of imposing remains from a lost world lie strewn across its countryside. It is the county of Stonehenge and Avebury.

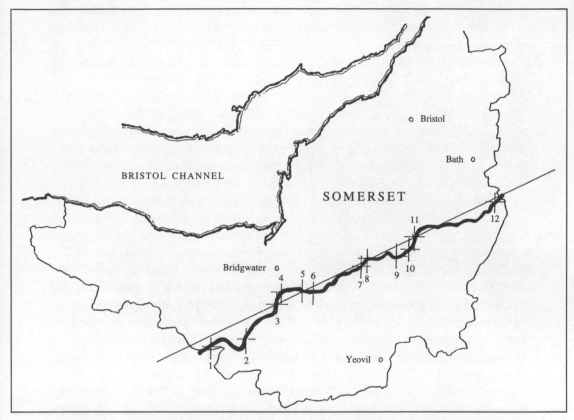

The St Michael current in Somerset: 1. Wellington Monument; 2. Corfe; 3. Creech St Michael; 4. St Michael's Church, North Newton; 5. Burrow Mump; 6. Othery; 7. Street; 8. Glastonbury; 9. Pilton; 10. Shepton Mallet; 11. Stoke St Michael; 12. Devil's Bed and Bolster.

BACK TO THE OLD STONES

Straight away, there was a change. We picked up the current running into Orchardleigh Park, an old estate on the outskirts of Frome. We chased it into some fields and peered over the hedge to see an intriguing sight. A few minutes later we were in the midst of a megalithic structure that seems to have been virtually forgotten. A huge monolith, at least twelve feet high, supports another, fallen, stone on a raised earth bank. Others lie half-buried in the ground. It is an immensely powerful site that seems to preserve something of its ancient importance despite the depradations of time. Suddenly, with the unexpected appearance of the Orchardleigh Stones, we were back in prehistoric territory.

The current ran precisely through the gatehouse to the park, situated at a crossroads near Lullington. Later we picked it up at Rode Church and noticed another prehistoric site marked on the map, situated in the right general direction. As it was a good afternoon for a bit of a stroll, we set off over the fields close to the Wiltshire border to take a look at the quaintly-named Devil's Bed and Bolster.

Having had considerable experience of diverse inns, hostelries and rest houses for the weary pilgrim, some of which remain vivid in the memory for their excellence or otherwise, we immediately christened this place the Devil's Bed and Breakfast. The site of a Neolithic motel, perhaps, where even the Devil himself took a jar of ale and a sacrificial sandwich. Over the fields, a grassy tump sprouted trees and boulder-like stones grew out of the undergrowth. It gives the impression of having been circular, with many stones concealed in foliage, and perhaps buried. Absorbing the atmosphere of what must have surely been an important ritual site, with the Michael current running through it, we noticed a peculiar effect which often seems to occur at these places. Above the large slab that marked the centre of the flow (presumably the Devil's Bolster), energy was pouring off, exactly like a heat haze on a hot summer's day. This is a clearly visible manifestation which can be seen by anybody to a greater or lesser extent, and even takes place during the depths of winter. Some interaction is occurring between the Earth, stone and air causing a shimmering effect which can be seen by the unaided eye.

Trudging through the farmyard we stopped to chat to the farmer. We commented on the air of tranquillity at the Bed and Bolster, and he replied that it was very popular with the locals. And not just for picnics or an evening stroll. It seemed that they preferred the Devil's place to the church, situated just a few hundred yards away, for paying their ultimate respects. It was invariably the spot chosen for the scattering of their ashes.

APPROACHING THE CENTRE

'The Serpent Temples thro' the Earth,
From the wide Plain of Salisbury...'

William Blake
JERUSALEM

Wiltshire is the least inhabited of all English counties, its lonely landscape largely untouched by urbanized society. Its wild emptiness is a paradise for those who love to have plenty of space around them to tune into Nature and the spirit of ancient peoples. Yet in prehistoric times, the reverse was true. It was acknowledged as a great centre of civilization which left behind monumental testimony to its sophistication. Where else could one find a Stonehenge, an Avebury? All manner of secret and inspiring places are scattered throughout its countryside, many unknown or forgotten, but alive with an energy that has been protected from the cacophanous discord of recent times. Even Avebury, saved from the gross insensitivity of modern building that afflicts Stonehenge, is still a secret and wondrous place.

The towns reflect this archaic dignity with a strange air of aloofness. Trowbridge, where we found ourselves next, was once the administrative centre of Wiltshire, with a castle and great wealth derived from the cloth industry. The magnificent spire of the church of St James disappears to a point in the clouds, growing out of worn and crumbling stonework. The interior is uplifting; a truly inspiring example of Victorian restoration. The Michael current runs right along the building, its centre aligned with the axis.

To the east, the level ground began to give way to a sudden escarpment that reared up and had a powerful presence about it, even from many miles away. The serpent was heading directly for a great ridge, jutting out over open farmland, and after a short walk we stood at the edge of this green precipice looking back across the countryside, picking out the distant churches that marked the flow and imagining the Michael current snaking its way across the country. Flanked on one side by Beacon Hill and on the other by a wooded scarp, Oliver's Castle, a prehistoric hill-fort with a huge central enclosure, is an exhilarating place. One looks down on the world like the Gods of Olympus, amused at the triviality of human lives. The entire hill is sculpted. Below is a large earthen platform, terraced by hands that used simple tools to add to Nature's art. Below that is a copse containing a holy well. Inside the enclosure, a rare prehistoric dewpond has survived the times when the place was used as a fortification, and the discovery that the current crossed the centre of the platform and ran into the enclosure to a node point approximately at its centre was enough to make us realize that it is a site of considerable significance. The effect of the place even today, with its sanctity overshadowed by memories of ancient wars, is inspiring.

A few miles away we crossed the Wansdyke, that enigmatic great earthwork in the form of a bank and ditch that stretches for some eighty miles across country.

In front of us was a landscape that had exercised great power over the hearts and minds of people who had inhabited the gentle downland five or six thousand years ago when it was heavily wooded. They had selected this area as a sacred centre, and followed trackways to it that stretched for hundreds of miles to the east and west.

A series of impressive monuments constructed from earth and stone were to be built by them, forever changing the face of the land. A vast mound was to be raised, the largest of its kind, taking generations to finish. Avenues of stone were to cut through the old trees, leading to the great circular earthwork that was to be carved out of the chalk, and later embellished by mighty megaliths. Chambered ritual structures and simpler mounds would be built throughout the area, often on the skyline where they stood out against the ever-changing backdrop of sun, moon and stars. The place was to become the most sacred site, a vision of a now vanished cosmology impressed into the very Earth. We were half way along the St Michael Line as it ran from Cornwall to the east coast, and had arrived at Avebury.

Chapter Five

THE SERPENT TEMPLE

'And this stupendous fabric, which for some thousands of years, had brav'd the continual assaults of weather, and by the nature of it, when left to itself, like the pyramids of Egypt, would have lasted as long as the globe, (has) fallen a sacrifice to the wretched ignorance and avarice of a little village unluckily plac'd within it'

William Stukeley
ABURY (1743)

THE FIRST IMPRESSIONS of the Wiltshire village of Avebury are striking. Turning the corner there is an immediate confrontation with a paradox of the past. A quaint jumble of assorted rustic architecture crowds an enormous earthwork, the largest in Europe, overflowing its great banks to include an old church and manor house. Amongst the grazing cattle and mature trees, startling elephantine shapes stand motionless in a mood of massive solidity. Many of these stones, weighing up to sixty tons, have remained rooted in the earth for at least four thousand years. The greatest temple of ancient Britain has, stretching over the surrounding countryside, other equally remarkable features; a mile away stands the artificial mound of Silbury Hill, a chalk pyramid higher than many of the natural hills around it; within two miles lies West Kennet Long Barrow, the largest of its kind in Britain; between them rises the Swallowhead spring which has for thousands of years suddenly bubbled forth during late winter to herald the return of spring, animating the landscape in some strange, cyclic manner ruled by deep water within the Earth; on a hill to the south-east is a site known as The Sanctuary, where concentric circles of standing stones once stood, linked to Avebury by a serpentine avenue of megaliths striding across the land. All around are the remnants of a time when life was ordered by the rhythms of Nature, when the Earth itself was adapted to harmonize with her secret forces.

Very few observers have seen in this extravagant array of ancient artistry anything other than the weathered bones of a prehistoric skeleton, the earthly remains of a savage and fearful society. Disconnected, eroded by time and changing traditions, the unseemly jumble reveals few clues to indicate the once-vivacious character of its life. Archaeologists hope to piece together fragments of bone and pottery to glimpse an idea of what this life was like, yet their counterparts in the future might just as well excavate a churchyard to understand the culture of the twentieth century.

Seven hundred years ago, the spectacle of Avebury looked very different. A complex structure ranged across the Wiltshire uplands made up of over six hundred huge stones which were still revered for their magical powers of fertility. Today only seventy-six remain. In the twelfth century, a Benedictine Priory was built where Avebury Manor now stands, discreetly placed outside the earthworks. The Church became ever more jealous of the attention paid to the temple, and determined that such a stupendous work of the Devil should be expunged. The memorials to a vastly different vision were diligently toppled, yet still a vestige of former veneration clung to them, for none of the stones were damaged, and they were all levered carefully into pits cut in the chalk, the surface smoothed out so that their position was undetectable. One by one they disappeared, swallowed by the earth that had produced them. The great Obelisk, the tallest of all, was felled to lie for four hundred years until broken up for building stone.

Why the work of despoilation was never completed is a mystery. It may be that the larger stones were just too cumbrous to dispose of in this way. Or the people engaged in the work may have felt they were invoking the wrath of ancient gods. In 1938 a thirteen-ton block was excavated and, trapped underneath, was the skeleton of a barber-surgeon, apparently crushed as the stone fell. It is not difficult to imagine the effect of such sudden retribution on those who had been told they were destroying the Devil's work.

John Aubrey, an early antiquarian and chronicler now famous for the wit of his biographical essays 'Brief Lives', accidentally came across the temple on a winter's day in 1649 and declared that Avebury 'did as much excell Stoneheng, as a Cathedral does a Parish Church'. It is a curious coincidence of fate that the seventeenth-century name of the place—Aubury—should so closely echo the name of the man who was to make it famous. He preserved in his sketches the position of many great sarsen stones which were soon to disappear, and noted that the earthworks could not have been constructed for defence because the ditches were inside the bank. He concluded that this, together with the 'antique rudeness' of the stones, was 'clear evidence that these monuments were Pagan-Temples, which was not made out before'.

Already, a new phase of destruction was under way. With a puritanical zeal, local farmers, encouraged by the Church authorities, embarked on their work to eradicate such a tangible memory of the old religion. Absolved from guilt and the restrictions of an ancient respect, people were freed to destroy the symbols of an idolatrous faith. The new owner of Avebury Manor levelled a great length of the bank to build a barn. Local preachers smashed up the stones, 'as hard as marble', to build a meeting house within yards of the site of the huge monolith known as The Obelisk. The tragedy continued; the monstrous sarsens were lowered into flaming pits, doused with water and set upon with sledgehammers. Farmer Stretch procured twenty cartloads of building stone for the Catherine Wheel Inn from just one megalith. 'Stone-killer' Robinson and Farmers Green and Griffin were responsible for the destruction of dozens of stones, often systematically working clockwise around the circles.

In 1719 the temple was a ruin. A young doctor from Lincolnshire called William Stukeley had, apparently by sheer chance, come across references to it in a hand-written account taken from Aubrey's record. Tantalized by the descriptions, Stukeley began an affair with the old temple that was to prove of immense value to later researchers. He made many visits to Avebury, meticulously recording the position of remaining stones and earthworks now long lost. Slowly he began to sense the true nature of the place, not as a disjointed collection of primitive idols but as a great instrument of Natural Science. No doubt he drew inspiration for this judgement from his membership of an aristocratic society that claimed to preserve the knowledge of the Druids. It certainly seems as though his inspired vision of Avebury was the result of a profound understanding of natural principles married to the archaeological exploration of an enthusiastic antiquarian.

There was heartache also in Stukeley's affair with Avebury. He angrily condemned the barbaric destruction, and knew as he sketched the stone circles at the Sanctuary on Overton Hill that his account of the monuments would be the last record for future generations. He was witnessing the last days of a centre of prehistoric culture that had no equal, a place which had taken generations of ancient Britons to construct in accordance with forgotten principles. Why should such enormous efforts have been made to sculpt the landscape in this way? Was such a place really the work of a 'people whose lives were brief, savage and fearful' as imagined by some modern archaeological writers? Is the simplistic image of the prehistoric savage an accurate one, as portrayed by the author Aubrey Burl, who writes 'Their imaginations, suspended between savagery and science, had images stalking in them of a primordial existence through which a terrible ancestor moved. . . To overcome him and other dreads these early people developed elaborate rituals designed to appease the malevolent powers of nature, and often enacted these rites in specially built religious monuments.'

The true reality of prehistoric life may well strike us as altogether different when we understand the evidence of our eyes, which must, one day, recognize in Avebury something far greater than we have ever previously imagined. Certainly, William Stukeley glimpsed a vision that was diametrically opposed to the images of barbaric savagery that currently mould our ideas of primeval existence.

> *'When I frequented this place, as I did for some years together, to take an exact account of it, staying a fortnight at a time, I found out the entire work by degrees. The second time I was here, an avenue was a new amusement. The third year another. So that at length I discovered the mystery of it.'*
>
> ABURY

What Stukeley saw modelled on the landscape at Avebury was an astonishing image. Symbolized in stone and earth was a monstrous serpent spread across the countryside, its sinuous body writhing over the gentle chalk hills. Its head was the stone circle on Overton Hill, romantically named The Sanctuary. Its neck was formed by an avenue of standing stones that led away to the southern entrance of the massive Henge, where, enclosed in the great circle were two smaller rings, one dedicated to the Sun, the other to the Moon. The snake's tail was represented by another stone avenue that led off to the west. The entire edifice was a marvellous image of Natural alchemy, the fusion of opposites. The raw energy of the Earth was the serpent, fertilized by the opposing cosmic forces of Sun and Moon, concentrated in the great circle, the generative organ of the whole complex.

Schooled in Freemasonry and a tradition of science that included Gnostic and Qabalistic concepts, Stukeley was perhaps more aware of the philosophy of the hermetic arts than many of his contemporaries. From his studies of comparative religion he also saw a continuity between different religious outlooks which recognized certain common principles. Thus he had no difficulty in synthesizing his Druidical notions with Biblical orthodoxy, and he took holy orders in 1729.

It is fashionable in academic circles to sneer at Stukeley's idea that Avebury was a vast temple built by the Druids. Modern dating shows the stones to have been erected at least two thousand years before their heyday. Yet antiquarians of previous centuries were not so much concerned with the precise classification of when an Iron-age priesthood reigned as with pointing out the immense antiquity of the ruins, which, in the classically educated 17th and 18th centuries, meant pre-Roman. In this climate, 'Druid' simply meant the priests of the Ancient Britons.

The notion that the ancient landscape was overlaid with remarkable effigies that represented natural energies seems similarly naive to many people today, yet the idea is remarkably persistant and appeals strongly to those of an imaginative disposition. Poets, artists and those sensitive to the concept of a living landscape appear to accept quite naturally such a vision, and some, like William Blake, are acknowledged for their images of inspiration. Others, trained in a more secular tradition of analysis and dissection see only the imagined fancies of hopeless romantics, impervious to reason.

Stukeley's vision of a landscape once covered with stone circles, the remains of a huge collection of serpent temples, is one that may yet have some encoded significance as we discover more about the hidden forces of the natural world. The most striking of these, at Avebury, seems to possess a particular attraction for those who can hear the Earth's archaic whisper echoing down the centuries. Despite the destruction, the enigma persists. As Stukeley observed: 'They have made plains and hills, valleys, springs and rivers contribute to form a temple of three miles in length. They have stamp'd a whole country with the impress of this sacred character, and that of the most permanent nature'.

APRIL 30th, 1988. There was an enchantment in the air. A gentle sun smiled on a rippling landscape that smelt sweet from recent showers. Heading towards Avebury the weaving St Michael line had crossed the Wansdyke and Bishop's Cannings Down and led to a lane not far from the chalk figure of the White Horse at Cherhill. This lane had a special charm, an ancient trackway bordered by old thorn trees which were flowering abundantly. The ground was covered with blossom like soft, pink snow as flowers fluttered down on the breeze. It was May Eve.

The track led to Windmill Hill, and exactly marked the current of energy. Through tunnels of trees and deep banks loaded with cowslips, there came a point where the path forked, and the serpent current passed through a patch of unkempt woodland. At the summit, as we stood on the top of the massive tumulus which had suddenly appeared over the horizon, the view was dramatic. Clearly visible was Avebury, the stone avenue leading to The Sanctuary, the uncanny pyramid of Silbury Hill hanging in a mist, and the West Kennet Long Barrow. Yet the immense earthworks at Windmill Hill, sculpted with concentric circles, pre-date all these. A thousand years before Silbury was built people inhabited this spot, recognized as the largest Stone Age camp in the world. Strangely, though, despite the fact that it is referred to as a 'camp', no evidence of a permanent settlement has been unearthed, indicating that the place was only used on certain occasions. The accepted notion is that it was used for seasonal rites for a population from a wide area with 'ceremonies performed to ensure agricultural fertility and celebration of harvest.' None of this seemed surprising to us, for it was now clear that ancient people were utilizing the invisible energies of the Earth in their rites as they venerated the natural world. The current passed right through the massive barrow, surrounded by a deep ditch, forming a node point at its centre.

The outermost of Windmill Hill's concentric ditches, before it was ploughed to oblivion, was three-quarters of a mile long, enclosing a remarkable twenty-one acres. Pottery from Cornwall has been found, along with more mysterious artefacts including chalk cup-like objects, plaques, and eleven stone discs with shaped edges. Even more intriguing are remnants of figurines, thirty carved balls of chalk approximately two inches in diameter, found in pairs, and four chalk phalli. There can be little doubt that this place was a centre for rituals associated with fertility.

William Stukeley had stood at this spot in the eighteenth century and observed 'a pretty round apex, the turf as soft as velvet. The air here extremely fragrant.' Deep draughts of it proved that a few centuries had not changed this, although the aroma was sharper as we tracked the line through the fields of East Farm, where a sign boasted that the regimented crops, with not a weed or insect in sight, were 'chemically protected'. The serpent's path followed another ancient track leading eastwards away from the summit of the hill, ran through the yard at Rutlands Farm, and crossed the road to enter the great earthwork of Avebury Henge within a few feet of the main road from Swindon, flanked by the enormous diamond shape of one of the most notable of the great stones, balanced delicately on one corner. The serpent had arrived.

REVELATION

Heading straight for the centre of the Henge, the normally broad band of energy tightened up to about ten paces wide and passed through the two remaining stones of The Cove, once a curious structure resembling 'a megalithic sentry box without a roof'. These stones are two of the most impressive of the entire collection, one squat, lozenge-shaped and heavily worked, the other smooth and pointed. The line just missed, by a few feet, the Avebury United Reformed Church, built from smashed megaliths in 1670, and led to the concrete marker that stands at the spot where the tallest pillar of all, The Obelisk, once stood. This exact point marked a node, with the usual pentagram shape, and also changed the direction of the flow, which now made for the most gigantic of the remaining stones, set at the southern entrance.

A few people wandered about the stones. Children laughed and dogs barked in the twentieth century, but we were wondering about other times. We were being drawn back to a world where this stupendous temple had been deliberately planned and constructed to take account of natural energies. Such a demonstration of how important they were in the ancient world suddenly seemed irrefutable. They must have been the motivating force behind society. The rites and celebrations were governed by them. Truly incredible effort had gone into building places which honoured and used them.

Paul Broadhurst seated in the Devil's Chair, the largest of the Avebury megaliths.

The most magnificent of all the stones of the outer circle indicate the passage of the St Michael serpent through the southern entrance. One, called The Devil's Chair, has a seat cut in it which is a favourite place for snapshots. This enormous sarsen is the greatest of them all, a huge square block sculpted with living folds that seem to animate it with a superhuman intelligence. A weird funnel arrangement traps rain and directs it down onto the head of anyone sitting in the 'chair', which some have thought may have been used for lustrations during sacred rites. These stones also mark the spot where the exact countrywide alignment of the St Michael Line crosses the circle, as well as the point at which the West Kennet stone avenue joins the Henge. It is a most significant place. In between the two towering stones is yet another node.

In a mood of exhilaration, we followed the current out of the circle. It led along the West Kennet stone avenue, with its curiously irregular rows striding away to Overton Hill. The stones marked with great precision the dimensions and flow of the energy. Stukeley's stylized plan of his serpent temple showed smooth, tapering avenues wandering gently across country, while John Aubrey's sketches were perhaps a more accurate indication of the curious irregularity of the structure. Where the avenue joins the Henge, it narrows and makes quite a sharp turn, which would seem out of place if a purely symbolic image had been the plan.

We had followed this serpentine energy for 150 miles. It had performed many strange contortions on its route across country. Here, for the first time, marked out by rows of standing stones, was a graphic display of how the energy actually operated. It was organic; it flowed without regard for human perceptions of symmetry and order. One minute it could be wide and gentle, the next narrow and

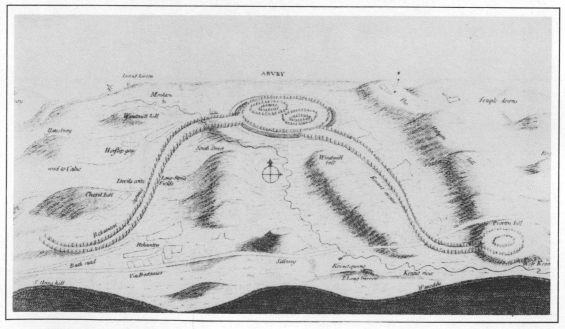

William Stukeley's Serpent Temple.

sinuous. Like a river, it formed curves and eddies, all of which were accurately laid out in stone. Many of the stones had been restored to their former positions before the War by the dedicated owner of Avebury Manor, Alexander Keiller, and such was the precision of their relocation that very few of them were more than a few inches away from the edge of the current. However, the results were unequivocal. William Stukeley had been right. Avebury was a Serpent Temple.

DAWN, MAY 1st, 1988. The clock at Avebury Church struck five as we approached the Henge. In the grey twilight weird shapes loomed like ageless observers that have seen astonishing sights. A wet mist seeped from all around. A mellifluous cacophany of birdsong filled the air.

Gradually, the grey lightened and then there was an impression of a great, gentle surge of energy pouring throught the spot where The Obelisk of Stukeley's solar circle had stood. No words were uttered. Thoughts were suspended. After half an age when intangible visions filtered in and out of the mind, everything seemed to have changed in some unfathomable way. There was a different quality of energy.

As we followed the old processional route along the West Kennet stone avenue, lambs sheltered under megaliths that seemed intelligent and alive, their features frozen in time. It is an interesting property of these stones that they occur in two

The megaliths of the West Kennet stone avenue lead away from the Henge, exactly marking the flow of the St Michael current.

distinct shapes, one the 'male' type of a tall, thin phallic pillar, the other a 'female' diamond shape, usually set on end in a quite striking manner. They are arranged in alternate fashion so that from whichever direction one observes the parallel stone rows, looking along or across, there is always a contrasting shape. There is an impression of petrified sexual balance that was evidently an important feature in the ethos of the megalith builders. At one particular place, the avenue and the St Michael current of energy that it contained veered off to cross the road and then rejoin the adjacent field leaving a couple of straggling, isolated markers. The rest of it ran practically parallel to the road, curving through a field of atomic yellow rape and up to the summit of Overton Hill, situated on the crest of the prehistoric Ridgeway. The Serpent was heading for The Sanctuary. Tracking the energy, we came across some outlying concrete markers which indicated the place where the original stones forming the serpent's neck had joined the Sanctuary, which had been destroyed in front of Stukeley's eyes: 'The loss of this work I did not lament alone; but all the neighbours (except the person that gain'd the little dirty profit) were heartily griev'd for it. It had a beauty that touch'd them.'

The serpent ran right through the circle. There was some confusion. Another current joined it, crossing in the centre. The reactions were checked. There was no doubt. There was another serpent. One that appeared to be a different frequency but just as powerful. It entered through a group of prominent tumuli over the road, ran through the gate and the only remaining original stone, and followed the path to the centre, heading off to the south-west. The St Michael serpent entered at the neck of the stone avenue and ran towards the south-east.

We stood surveying the scene. Showers and shafts of sunlight were producing extraordinary weather effects. Set into the landscape was Silbury, changing its mood by the minute. One moment it was a great green breast rising from a shifting, shadowy body, the next a golden cone glowing in the sun. Just when we had thought that we understood something of this mystery, another element had

Stukeley's drawing of the partially-destroyed Sanctuary, the last record of the 'head' of the serpent.

come into play. The head of the Serpent marked the crossing place of two major earth currents. What were we to do? There was only one thing. We had to find out where they went.

THE VEILS PART

There was confusion and clarity inextricably thrown together. The obsession of following the weaving St Michael line had temporarily blinded us to the wider understanding that this particular current was only one amongst many. True, it seemed to have a special significance and it had been necessary to avoid the entanglements and complexity of less powerful energy flows for the sake of coherence. But the experience at The Sanctuary showed there were other, similarly significant energies that were interacting with the St Michael current.

There was no mistaking that there was a different 'feel' to the quality of the second serpent, which crossed virtually at right angles, forming a 'Celtic cross' shape. It was just as potent, yet seemed gentler, smoother and altogether more feminine than its counterpart. In fact it was necessary to 'de-tune' from dowsing the St Michael energy to pick it up effectively, as if it were a different rate of vibration. It appeared we had only noticed it in the first place because of the especially sensitive frame of mind that existed after dawn at the Henge.

It led off towards the south-west, swinging north towards Avebury, and walking up an old farm track we saw the shape of old stones looming directly ahead on the horizon. It was the one hundred-metre West Kennet Long Barrow, the largest chamber tomb in Britain. The size of the stones at the entrance and in the geometrically laid out side chambers are of the same magnitude as those in the great circle itself, with one of the capstones weighing at least seven tons.

Inside the five stone cells there is an eerie but moving atmosphere. Standing in the womb of the Earth the old stones convey a purpose different from that of simple burial, and the jumble of bones that was discovered here may well have been of far later date than when the structure was originally built. Delicate drystone walling of limestone fills in between the huge sarsens showing workmanship of quite superlative quality. Spectacularly positioned on a hillcrest looking across to Silbury, it seemed that the choice of its situation could not be accidental. This was confirmed when the new serpent was found to pass right through the monumental megaliths of its facade at a diagonal angle, leaving to run down into the valley. There appeared little doubt that the 'long barrow' was much more than that, and may at one time have been an important ceremonial centre and a crucial component of the Avebury complex.

Many archaeologists now accept that 'barrows were shrines and temples rather than tombs.' The almost total absence of grave goods would certainly bear this out. There are deeper mysteries also, and the excavators of West Kennet found that the stone chambers were geometrically arranged inside a perfect isosceles triangle whose height was twice the length of the base. And every one of the 31 long barrows around Avebury is oriented between the extreme movements of the Sun and Moon, giving them an even greater dimension. One archaeological writer believes that 'because of the shortness and width of the megalithic passages... they must have been designed to 'catch' the sun or moon as an act of symbolism.'

Tracking the newly-discovered current down towards the tree-lined bank of the River Kennet, the feeling that it was closely linked with the St Michael line yet was of a different, more feminine quality grew stronger. The first place it led to after The Sanctuary had been a site of ritual significance within the Earth itself. This alone seemed to give it a particular character. What if we had discovered the female equivalent of the Michael force? If the Michaelic energies had an affinity with high places as dictated by tradition, then it was possible that their more feminine counterparts would seek out openings in the womb of the Earth. With this thought still hovering, we came across one of Avebury's most magical, secret places, which appeared to demonstrate that this theory could well be correct.

IMAGES OF THE GODDESS

Directly in the path of this new current lay a crucial element of the Avebury complex which must have possessed a powerful symbolism for the people who originally conceived it. In the autumn and winter, due to summer evaporation, the Swallowhead spring, source of the upper reaches of the River Kennet, is a dry hole in a chalk bank, its bed nowadays a neglected place of turves and grassy hummocks. It is likely, though, that in the past this was one of the most sacred places of the whole district, and was kept accordingly. For after the winter period, the underground reservoir which feeds the spring is full, and the sound of flowing waters is again heard within sight of Silbury and West Kennet as they trickle forth from the depths of the Earth. The time of this rebirth is appropriately the time of the revival of the annual cycle, during February-March, the ancient Spring. Michael Dames, in his inspiring book *The Avebury Cycle*, in which he sees the surrounding landscape as a great Goddess figure impressed on the Earth, explains the enigma:

> *'By Winter Eve, the Kennet goddess had swallowed her own river head (still called Swallowhead), and turned her river bloodstream into stone. At the same season, the Swallowhead is left dry as a bone. The familiar trickling sound is not heard. Nothing comes from the dark orifice in the curving rock wall. The natural semi-circle has been transformed from life-giving spring to barren womb, or skull; a memorable sight, and one which must be accepted, because it is natural.'*

This mystery, still operating as it did in remote times, is a striking example of the sanctity of the goddess of Nature, which can leave few people unmoved. The eighteenth-century name for the river, the Cunnit, makes it even more obvious that the connection of this spring with fertility was very special. The horseshoe-shaped head which fills with water on the return of the Goddess can have been nothing other than a sacred pool whose waters appeared miraculously to give birth to the dry bed, joining it to the stream which runs close to the Henge and around the base of Overton Hill. The fact that the distinctly feminine energies of the terrestrial current we were tracking pass through it is even more indication of its ancient sanctity.

It was now heading for the massive artificial mound of Silbury. Running across the Bath/Marlborough road, it swung round to pass through the western side. Silbury, of course, is a goddess image without comparison, its enormous rounded form projecting from the gentle curves of an otherwise rolling landscape. Antiquarians in the past, obsessed with sepulchral images, have thought it to be the burial monument of King Sil, yet successive excavations have revealed little other than some twisted snake-like strands of 'a sort of string', prehistoric ants and beetle wings, a few fragments of pottery, bone, plant material and some examples of pollen from a Neolithic summer. William Stukeley came across a farmer who claimed to have dug up some bones close to the surface, together with decaying remains including a rusty bridle, but such a find can hardly explain the original purpose of the hill. In 1849 an excavation into the interior was accompanied by 'one of the most grand and tremendous thunderstorms I ever recollect to have witnessed. (It) made the hills re-echo to the crashing peals, and Silbury itself, as the men asserted who were working at its centre, to tremble to its base.'

So far, no-one has put forward any plausible explanation for the vast conical mound, or why the people who constructed the Henge, West Kennet Long Barrow and Silbury, all at about the same time, should have expended such enormous effort. Precisely round at its base, occupying 5½ acres, and unlike other barrows, situated on a valley floor, it is unique. Flat-topped, with a circular terrace near its summit and surrounded by water, it remains one of the greatest of archaeological enigmas. The impulse that motivated a society to move thirty-five million basket-loads of chalk must have been overwhelming. And Silbury is not merely a heap of earth. It was constructed in a surprisingly sophisticated manner by people who understood the complexities of soil mechanics. Consequently, it has never eroded and has kept its original shape, the only artificial component of the Avebury complex to survive intact. Inside the smooth conical hill is a stepped circular pyramid built from a series of chalk walls linked together and infilled with layers of alternate organic material, chalk and gravel, with a core of clay and flint that was specially imported. Such is the scale of the project (compared by one writer to a modern space program) that it is likely that the people who started its construction did not live to see the completed monument. It is one of the great wonders of the ancient world to survive the depradations of millennia, and a remarkable testimony to the achievements of Stone-age civilization.

'Silbury indeed is a most astonishing collection of earth, artificially rais'd, worthy of Abury' observed Stukeley. Before him, Aubrey had recorded the legend that it 'was raysed whilst a posset of Milke was seething', a suitably esoteric tradition reminiscent of Earth Mother symbolism. Like the Henge, it had finely-cut ditches carved out at its base, making it virtually an island sanctuary, and although these are now silted up, water is still an essential element in the Silbury mystery. Why this great cone of chalk was raised in such an obscure position, on fertile, low-lying ground, has never been explained by archaeologists. Michael Dames' vision of Silbury as the pregnant Earth Mother in the landscape imagery of a great Goddess is perhaps the only explanation so far which offers a glimpse into its original purpose.

The great mound of Silbury Hill dominates the valley floor south of Avebury Henge.

An intriguing tailpiece to this episode was to surface later in the year. The summer of 1988 was notable for the many reports of 'crop circles' that appeared suddenly and inexplicably in cornfields across southern Britain. These tantalizing circular depressions, evidently created by some powerful energy which flattened the corn in a spiral-like fashion, created great interest in the media. As yet, still no reasonable explanation for their appearance has been offered: The geometrically-complex designs impressed into the growing crops is still as much a mystery as ever. In 1987, ten of these circles had been found at Beckhampton. In eight weeks during the summer of '88, however, an incredible 51 circles were found within seven miles of Silbury. Fifteen appeared within a few days of each other in the field opposite, close to the main road. The first five, which manifested during the night of 14-15th July, were seen and photographed by many people. When we saw the photographs there was astonishment; they were located exactly on the route of the 'female' current as it flowed between Silbury and the Swallowhead spring.

RETURN TO THE CENTRE

Crossing over the River Kennet again at a small bridge at the foot of Waden Hill, we were led across the northern tip, very close to, but not through, a tumulus. The view was overwhelming. The entire landscape was visible throughout 360 degrees. Behind, Silbury was alive, basking in an ever-changing display of sun and shadow. In front was one of the best possible vistas of the village of Avebury. Each stone could be picked out, and as we sat on the lush grass peering down to the old temple below, there was a quality of timelessness that is impossible to put into words.

The two enormous entrance stones, set where the West Kennet stone avenue meets the Henge.

1. Winter sun enhances the ancient terraces on the slopes of Glastonbury Tor

II. Writhing roots and a strange atmosphere at Menacuddle Holy Well in Cornwall

III. The Citadel of the Sun – St Michael's Mount

IV. The legends of Glastonbury, illuminated in the window of St. George's Chapel

V. A massive vertical stone guards the rocky promontory of Carn Lês Boel close to Land's End

VI. Boscawen-un stone circle, with its curiously angled centre stone

VII. The dramatic sight of St Michael's Chapel on Roche Rock

VIII. The great Norman Tower at Bury St Edmunds, precisely marking the St Michael current

Back at the Henge, another surprise awaited us. The recently-discovered current led directly to the two massive entrance stones that mark the end of the West Kennet avenue. It joined the St Michael current at the node point situated between them. It continued coterminously to the node at The Obelisk, carrying on to the stones at The Cove. Only at this point did it part company with the Michael serpent to veer off north-east, running through the only standing stone still remaining in this sector, to carry on over the earthworks and out into the countryside.

It had been quite a day. An entirely new facet had revealed itself which had profound implications. The crossing of serpents at The Sanctuary had demonstrated that there was another current of natural energy associated with the St Michael line that had a gentler, more female quality. This had led us to the greatest long barrow in Britain, the remarkable Swallowhead spring and Silbury Hill. There seemed little doubt that we were dealing with a distinctly feminine energy.

It had joined the Michael current within the Henge, and shared two nodes with

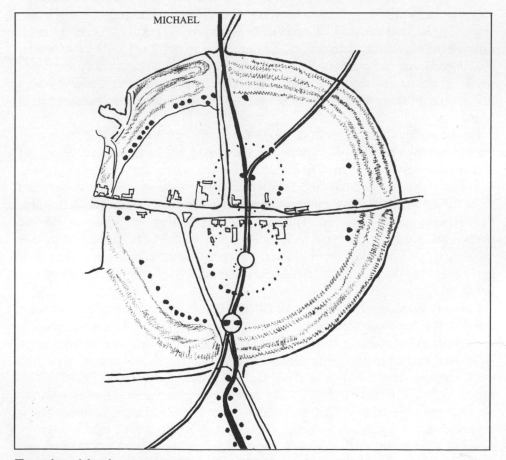

The male and female currents within Avebury Henge.

it. A fusion was taking place within the great circle, concentrated at the largest stones in the complex, the Devil's Chair and its adjacent partner, and in the two inner circles, at The Obelisk and The Cove, the remains of Stukeley's 'Solar' and 'Lunar' temples. There could be no other conclusion than that the great circle was a vessel for the interaction of the energies of Nature, directed and marked by the shapes of earth and stone so painstakingly contrived thousands of years ago. All the remarkable monuments of the Avebury landscape were linked by the flow of these energies, each one appearing to fulfil some specific function that was presently obscure. The energies themselves were apparently of different polarities. One type was Solar in influence, traditionally associated in the Christian ethos with St Michael, the other was Lunar, indisputably feminine and connected with the Earth Goddess whose Christian counterpart was St Mary.

In the dreamy atmosphere produced by the Avebury landscape and our recent adventures in it, there seemed little doubt that we had come closer to the meaning of these earth currents than had previously seemed likely or possible. If there were indeed two distinct forms of energy, one male and one female, then their natures should reveal themselves in the way they functioned. Galvanized by a great thirst to see if this theory could be elaborated, we strode off into the countryside to track the 'St Mary' current. It swept out to encompass the Michael serpent, leading to the nearby hamlet of Winterbourne Monkton. There, it passed through the old church, with a worn, recumbent monolith lying to the east. Inside, the magnificenly carved font displayed a superb chevron design, and the list of previous incumbents showed a strong connection with Glastonbury, whose Abbot had appointed many of them down the centuries. The church was dedicated to St Mary.

From the church, the current ran up to the summit of Windmill Hill, where we found ourselves standing in exactly the same spot we had been led to on our arrival in the Avebury area. The node point at the enormous tumulus pinpointed the place where the St Mary and St Michael currents crossed. The two serpents were fusing at crucial spots, always where nodes had been found: The Sanctuary, the Henge, now Windmill Hill. It was beginning to look as if the phenomena we were referring to as node points were in fact produced by this crossing of currents. Both types of energy appeared to concentrate to a fine point, enter deep into the ground and re-emerge. Something very intriguing indeed was going on.

Leaving Windmill Hill the St Mary line crossed Horslip Bridge and went straight for the Long Stones at Avebury Truslow. These two huge stones, sometimes called Adam and Eve or the Devil's Quoits, stand in the middle of a field over a mile away from the Henge, and are the only remaining stones of the Beckhampton Avenue, the vanished 'tail' of Stukeley's Serpent Temple. The greatest of these stones, 'Adam', is the sole survivor of the Beckhampton Cove, an arrangement similar to that which also existed in the Henge, as noted in the seventeenth century by John Aubrey. This stone is so large that when it fell over in 1911, enormous difficulty was encountered in its re-erection despite the powerful machinery employed. One can only marvel at the achievements of those who originally carried out the work, apparently using a far more basic technology. After the Long Stones, 'Mary' ran through a tumulus next to the Beckhampton Road and then through the Waggon and Horses public house! Sorely tempted, as pilgrims often are, to visit such inviting hostelries, we were, however, totally exhausted. Both brains and bodies had been overloaded with the revelations at Avebury. And the inevitable result of these was somewhat alarming. If there were indeed two separate serpents associated with the St Michael line that were interweaving and crossing at certain places, then it was necessary to track them both. Such a formidable task seemed overwhelming. It had taken well over a year to follow the St Michael current from Land's End to Avebury, yet it now looked as if the task was only half completed. And then there was another hundred and fifty or so miles up to the east coast.

But there was never any doubt whether such a quest could be left unfinished. The only answer was, with redoubled effort, to explore this new enigma to the best of our ability. We had to go back to the beginning.

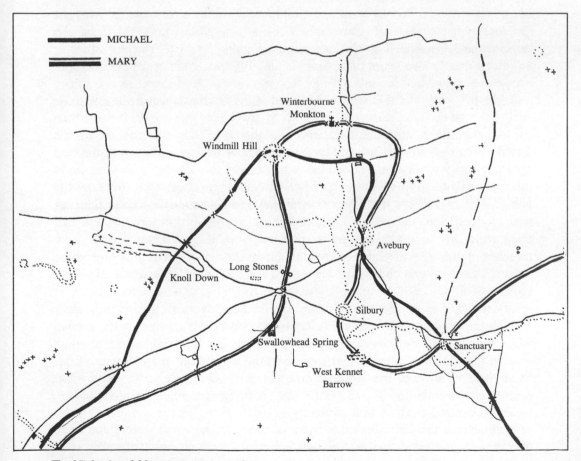

The Michael and Mary currents at Avebury.

Chapter Six

BACK TO THE BEGINNING

'There are in the earth's crust two different, shall I say magnetic currents, the one male, the other female, the one positive, the other negative . . .'

FENG-SHUI
The Science of Sacred Landscape in Old China
E.J. Eitel (1873)

JANUARY 1989. It was a strange feeling walking back over the cliffs to the rocky promontory of Carn Lês Boel. A poignant mood of *Deja Vu* accompanied the wheeling and screeching of gulls, for within a few weeks it would be exactly two years since first visiting this spot, right at the beginning of an adventure that had led into strange territory.

In the first days of 1987, we had been led to this secret, isolated place with no real idea whether the plan to follow the St Michael Line was anything more than the wild optimism of wishful thinking. At that time, vividly recalled by the approaching sight of the Carn and the surging sea below, we had been confronted by a great sweeping curve that had led us to the crag of worn rocks looking out to the western Atlantic. On drawing closer, it was impossible not to think of the great changes that had taken place within our own personalities since that last time, for following the energy of the St Michael current had in some way caused deep shifts in our understanding and the way we looked at the Earth. Like pilgrims of old, we had visited many of the great shrines of western Britain, some secret, others famous throughout the world, and as the sun picked out glistening patches of silver ocean, images of these places flitted through our minds: Dawn at Avebury, with its ageless stones towering in the grey half-light: Hours spent scrambling around Glastonbury Tor trying to decode the outline of the unique labyrinth-shape we had discovered: Standing at the Cheesewring, dwarfed by its vast weathered rocks in the last dying rays of the winter sun: A ringing bell from St Michael's Church at Brentor echoing across the countryside as we stood at the prehistoric earthworks below. They were like images snatched from some powerful dream, more vivid than reality.

Approaching the Carn, the huge flattened megalith that guards the place came into view. It is a cliche to describe such stones as 'sentinels' and yet in this case there can be no other valid description, for this great slab of granite, raised and deliberately perched on other smaller stones so that it is only just in contact with the earth, gives the distinct impression that it was erected to mark this spot as a place that is special and unique. It appears to be a singular example, for such standing stones are invariably earth-fast and usually sunk in the soil for a considerable depth.

It was the beginning of a new phase to the quest. Having discovered that there were two different serpent or dragon lines weaving around the central straight alignment found by John Michell, we had glimpsed an important aspect of the ancient and universal symbol of the Caduceus. It seemed that this great glyph of antiquity, still in use throughout the world as a perennial emblem of the healing professions, had other, more arcane meanings. Revered in the days of Ancient Egypt as the staff of Thoth, a magical rod crowned with the Sun-disk and encircled by two writhing serpents, it has come down to us throughout succeeding cultures as a potent symbol of the hermetic arts. Thoth had become Hermes, and later, the Roman Mercury. Considering the mercurial nature of the terrestrial currents which apparently flow like quicksilver through the surface of the

The Caduceus.

Earth, the conclusion seems inescapable. The serpent wand derives its power from its symbolism of energies operating in balance, the basic energies of existence mutually interacting.

Mystics throughout the ages have seen the Caduceus as a representation of how the subtle energies of the human body function. The central staff is, in the Eastern tradition, the Shushumna, the pillar which has its physical counterpart in the spine and the enclosing channel of the central nervous system. Around this spiral the twin energies symbolized as serpents, the Ida and Pingala, the former ruled by the Moon, the latter by the Sun. It is these powerful energies which are stirred into activity when certain disciplines concentrate on the raising of the Kundalini, the serpent power which starts at the base of the spine and rises upwards through the successive *chakras*, or subtle energy centres, to bring spiritual illumination and revelation.

So according to universal tradition, the staff of Mercury is a symbol of the natural energies working in the human body. If the Earth is itself a vast being, as understood by both ancient wisdom and the Gaia theory of modern science, the hermetic principle of 'as above, so below' should also apply to the living body of the planet. It is merely a matter of scale. It began to look as though the natural conclusion to draw on the discovery of the two serpentine currents reacting with each other was that this phenomenon was explained by the Caduceus. What we were observing as they led across the country was the Caduceus writ large across the landscape of southern Britain, a vast interconnecting network of natural energies that linked the most sacred sites in the land, both acknowledged and forgotten. Like the human *chakras*, certain centres existed where they were concentrated and which possess the potential for transformation. The node points of the Earth's body were vortices of multi-dimensional energy exchange which were capable of stimulation by the ritual techniques of a lost science, places where refined spiritual forces which underlie the physical world come into being. One of the properties of the *chakras*, according to mystical science, is that they can be activated by the use of certain tonal cadences, words of power and visualization practices. Such a concept, it seems, could perhaps throw much light on the actual principles involved in ancient ritual.

The two serpents entwined around the staff were of opposite polarity: There was the solar 'Michael' serpent, and there was the lunar 'Mary'. It all seemed lucid and obvious, quite suddenly, like a flash of revelation. Did places such as St Michael's Mount, Glastonbury, Avebury and all the other node points mark the *chakra* points along the staff of the St Michael alignment? Perhaps the shift of attention away from Avebury to later centre on Glastonbury in Christian times marked the developing evolutionary progress of humanity, as the cycle of time moved on and different Cosmic impulses came into play. Each place, like the energy centres of the human body, had its specific function according to the stage of development of the individual. And like the 'whirling vortices of brilliant energy' that clairvoyants reported observing at the human centres, this explained why psychics had often said they could see similar subtle phenomena operating at these sites.

Those involved in the Avebury rites at dawn on Beltane were taking conscious part in an extraordinary act of spiritual alchemy. Half-way along the St Michael Line, Avebury was the navel, the omphalos; the ultimate symbol of all birth. A meeting place between heaven and Earth, it was the cosmic centre from which the world was nourished. No wonder that such a ritual was thought to be concerned with fertility and renewal, an affirmation of the Cosmic and Earthly energies fused in a timeless acknowledgement of the way the Universe works. Today, the rationale of such an act is lost. But the place itself, and its spiritual successor Glastonbury, still stirs deep memories of its ancient purpose. And acknowledged or not, the Sun still rises to fulfil its endless task.

Our understanding of the principles involved had come a long way since the initial visit to Carn Lês Boel. Like the serpent swallowing its own tail, we had returned to the flat, horizontal rock that marked the most extreme westerly node in the country.

BACK TO BELERION

On dowsing around the granite outcrop, the response was practically instantaneous. The Mary current flowed in at an angle to the previously noted Michael current, right across the place where we had discovered the first node point. The significance of these mysterious centres seemed immensely inscrutable. As we had tracked the Michael current, we had discovered quite a number, which were always to be found at significant places. There were two very close together within the Henge at Avebury. We had observed that the width of the line gradually focussed to a point and disappeared into the ground before re-emerging, widening out and carrying on its meandering way. Now it had become apparent that not only did the two serpentine currents that had been christened Michael and Mary meet and cross at these precise points, but they both also obeyed this same curious function. If the theory that nodes were the planetary equivalent of the human *chakras* or energy centres was correct, it seemed that the energies were, amongst other things, concentrating to enter the earth for reasons that were currently beyond us. It looked as though they might be the nerve centres of the Earth's dynamic subtle energy system.

We both stood looking out to the distant horizon where shafts of brilliant sunlight cascaded through breaks in the cloud and created the strange effect of a distant land, glowing with some ineffable inner light. Beyond the isolation of the Wolf Lighthouse, out towards the unseen Isles of Scilly, we half-joked that lost lands were re-emerging, and talked of Lyonesse, and Atlantis.

Picking our way through the spiky gorse, treading carefully on the spongy multicoloured carpet of mosses and heather, we followed the line inland. A little quiet and introspective after the visit to Carn Lês Boel we trudged silently away from the sea, only breaking into conversation on the sudden realization that it was the day of the New Moon. The first New Moon of 1989! Traditionally, a New Moon meant a new beginning. Together with the start of a New Year, there certainly seemed to be some strange synchronicity at work as we began an entirely new phase of our quest.

THE HOLY WELL

A short distance away, the line passed very close to a white house which takes its name, Nanjizal, from the small bay it overlooks. The actual route led through the car park in front of the house, where for some reason the field behind had been excavated. It was interesting to note that large lumps of granite had been arranged behind this, as if to mark the place where it passed. It certainly wasn't the first time we had come across this sort of thing, and it was increasingly beginning to look as though people who live near these energies are in some way subconsciously attuned to the landscape, drawn into demonstrating this by marking their flow with stones, gateways, signs and other structures.

Heading off to pick 'Mary' up on the nearest inland road, we harked back to the time spent tracking her solar counterpart across this remote westerly tip of Cornwall. Then, the 'Michael' line had not passed through any of the major monuments with which the area is strewn, and this had surprised us greatly. In retrospect, however, this had its positive side, as those who may be inclined to accuse us of fabricating the entire adventure would surely naturally expect us to have made our dragon line pass through at least some of the impressive megaliths which abound in this intimate peninsula. Perhaps we could gain some credibility by default, we commented wryly. But the reality was that we could not make these lines do anything to fulfil our own ideas; the whole project had so far shattered our preconceptions at every twist and turn in the most uncompromising manner. The evidence for this is overwhelming from the written record so far. Throughout, the path of these energy flows has been merely observed. The earth currents and their preferred routes are beyond human caprice.

Taking out the dog-eared map of the Land's End district on which the previous line had been plotted, two new dowsed points were marked off on crossing the 'Mary', one near the turning to Trengothal Farm, and another a short way from Bosfranken. The map was already beginning to reveal a direction of flow. A large, gentle curve left Carn Lês Boel and was heading for Alsia Holy Well, marked on the map and located at the bottom of a field near the next lane. The excitement was mounting. Was the first place on the 'feminine' serpent line to be a holy well, sacred to the Earth Goddess and ruled by lunar influences? As we drove through the exquisitely beautiful countryside of stream-laden valleys and wooded glades, it was impossible not to be touched by both the magic of the landscape and of the moment. The landscape, completely undisturbed by the grossness of the twentieth century, has a charm which reaches right into the very depths of one's being. Memories of childhood, or secret, hidden impulses stir as you pass through it. It would not be at all surprising to turn a corner and see one of the Fairy folk languishing on a tree stump, surrounded by lush greenery and early flowers. Even at this time of the winter, cottages had vases of purple-blue irises and golden narcissi for sale at the roadside.

Turning down the road to the tiny hamlet of Alsia, it wasn't long before the Mary line appeared. Crossing an ancient stile, we walked through a field and soon found ourselves at the holy well, situated within a few feet of a stream. It is odd how so many of these old wells are to be found right next to water. The only conclusion can be that the people who revered them were not at all interested in procuring water for mundane purposes; they must have recognized that the waters from a holy well in some way were imbued with special properties, unique to the natural spring from which they flowed.

Old iron railings protected the well from cattle and an ancient thorn tree provided a picturesque canopy over the trickling spring. Faded rags fluttered in the breeze, tied to the lichen-encrusted branches by those seeking to create a magical connection with the spirit of the well and as offerings to invoke its healing powers. An atmosphere of utter tranquillity pervaded the place.

Then the secret of Alsia Holy Well was revealed. As the rods reacted powerfully to the 'Mary' energy flowing right through the womb-like chamber of the spring, we both felt humbled by this latest revelation. We tasted the cool, crisp waters and reflected on the many intriguing points that this raised.

'A wishing well once of great repute, and one of the most beautiful of the old natural springs to be found', Alsia was one of the most famous holy wells in the district, and people used to make pilgrimages to it from far and wide. Thomas Quiller Couch, who came across it in the nineteenth century, before the old ways were almost entirely forgotten, writes evocatively of its ancient, but fading, use as a centre of hydromancy:

> *'Of a summer's evening scores of maidens might be seen around it, eager for their turn to see what sweethearts would be united or parted, which they discovered by the fall of pebbles or pins. As the articles sank near or apart so their future was foretold; and the number of the bubbles raised bespoke the number of years before the happy or unhappy issue could befall.'*

As with many holy wells, there can be little doubt that these quaint customs from Victorian times are in reality a dim memory of powerful rites that once took place at this spot. With the potent energies flowing through it, it certainly seems the case that Alsia's fame was a recognition that it was very special indeed, a shrine to the natural energies of the Earth which were used for mystical purposes including that of penetrating the veils of time to see into the future.

Then there was the fact that the 'lunar' serpentine line should make its first call at a place that was totally attuned to Moon-type energies, with all its associations of healing, prophecy, visionary trance states and psychic rapport with elemental entities. The 'Michael' line had never passed through a holy well, although it did run very close to Menacuddle Holy Well near St Austell further up into Cornwall. The only place where a similar state of affairs had occurred was at the Swallowhead spring near Silbury Hill, a holy well *par excellence* where the newly-discovered 'Mary' line had passed right through it. This latest discovery thus linked Alsia Holy Well with the Swallowhead spring in both theory and practice, something that seemed to have considerable implications that we could not yet fathom. We wondered how many more holy wells we would come across as we followed 'Mary' up country.

THE OLD STONES

The winter dusk was gathering quickly. Back at the road, the tattered Ordnance Survey map was produced and scrutinized. There seemed little doubt that if the very gentle curve that had been tracked so far was projected, it would lead straight to St Buryan Church, sited at the crossroads in the village, and visible from practically the whole of the south of the Land's End peninsula.

As yellow lights began to illuminate the windows of the Penwith cottages, we arrived at St Buryan and drove around the church, silhouetted on its circular raised mound. We were taken aback. There was no reaction. We stopped the car and walked all the way round it. There was no doubt, there was not a sign of 'Mary'. It was as if we were being taught yet again that it was impossible to indulge in preconceptions about how these energies worked, no matter how obvious the next place on the line appeared to be. Encouraged by the events of the day, and perhaps because of a tacit agreement that the next location would be the last before heading home for welcome refreshment, we had jumped to conclusions and paid the price. We had lost the line.

Along the main Land's End-Penzance road, one last attempt at locating it was made just in case it had made a sweeping detour, something that seemed unlikely. It suddenly appeared on the curve of a tight bend just as the great shape of an enormous upright slab of rock became visible above the level of the hedge. It was the Blind Fiddler, a magnificent menhir over 11 feet high and one of the finest in the county. It is also exceedingly powerful, and the energy field that surrounds it is so potent that it can be detected a very great distance away. Standing at its base, with the quartz crystals embedded in its ancient granite picking out the flashing headlamps of cars hurrying home from work, we squinted at the map and suddenly realized why the line had made such an unexpected detour. It was apparently heading for one of the most remarkable stone circles in the West Country, one of the great meeting places of the Druidic bards, which was still known by its proper old Cornish name of Boscawen-un.

To approach Boscawen-un stone circle is to be drawn back to an earlier time. Hardly a telegraph pole is visible along the granite-bouldered hedgerows, cattle rasp at the rough grass and skylarks sing their perpetual melody. To pass the delightfully rustic but ancient farmstead of Boscawen-noon is to follow in the footsteps of the ghosts of prehistory, for the old trackway is the processional route taken by those who used this place for now-forgotten purposes. As recently as during what historians refer to as 'the Dark Ages', ceremonies were taking place at this, one of Cornwall's finest stone circles, for the ancient Welsh Triads refer to 'Beisgawen yn Dumnonia' as one of the three great gorsedds of the island of Britain, where the old Bards met. The continuity of this has been re-established in this century, when in 1928, the Gorsedd of the Bards of Cornwall was inaugurated here, even though this is perhaps a far cry from the sages of old gathered for their mystical purposes.

From this direction one comes across the stones suddenly. Hidden by the tall hedges, their appearance can be startling. One may marvel at the sheer perfection of their setting, or at the effect created by the ring of smooth granite enclosing the sacred space. One can be transfixed by the sight of the remarkable centre stone, angled sharply to the north-east like the aerial of a modern radar dish, or the realization that the stone adjacent to the western entrance is an enormous block of almost pure quartz. One cannot fail to be aware of the distinctly numinous quality of the place.

The morning was brilliant. Standing and staring, as the poet recommends, we soaked up the spiritually invigorating atmosphere. We attuned to the site before dowsing to see if the 'Mary' line did in fact visit this spot. It didn't take more than a few moments to establish that this was so: The current entered the circle in between the first and second stone to the left of the quartz block (standing within the circle), with its opposite extremity passing between the third and fourth. This delineated its width. The centre of the line continued to the base of the great angled monolith that gives the impression of pointing to some specific spot in the sky.

Then we discovered something utterly intriguing. For where the line joined the base of the stone it quite suddenly changed its angle to correspond with the ridge of the leaning monolith, and headed off through the gap by which most people enter the circle. Compass readings indicated that 'Mary' entered the circle at an angle 13 degrees east of north, turned at the base of the centre stone and left, heading off into the countryside, at 53 degrees east of north. It had dramatically shifted its flow by approximately 40 degrees.

According to our observations this stone, erected in the Bronze Age or earlier, actually caused the energy flow to reorientate or it marked the precise spot where this happened naturally. Either way, this could throw light on the argument that has raged between antiquarians about whether the stone had originally been upright, and subsided, perhaps through excavation, or whether it had been meticulously set at this angle many thousands of years ago. If it was raised with this intention, then it must surely mean that there is a long shaft of stone buried beneath the ground in order to counteract natural subsidence. The implications are plain: It is beginning to look more and more as if we are dealing with a megalithic technology of such sophistication and precision that its scope is entirely beyond us at present.

Although we normally made it a rule not to investigate other aspects of the energies present at such sites for the simple reason that we would never actually move along the line, it was felt that a short time spent at Boscawen-un would perhaps give a clearer picture of what was going on. It had long been apparent that whichever line was being followed, 'Michael' or 'Mary', they were only arteries ✓ of a vast interconnected system. Main arteries, perhaps, and with enormous significance. But like a great river, tiny tributaries and large streams join the main flow in a way that is totally synonymous with the organic metaphor of the planet's waterways. Major sites marked by prehistoric remnants always seem to be places where these streams of energy merge and interact, often in a way unique to that particular spot.

Twenty minutes or so later, other information was being interpreted. The situation was complex. Another serpentine line entered from the north, headed for the central stone and stopped just short of it. There was no tapering to a point. It just stopped dead. Yet another, roughly the same dimensions as the 'Mary', entered from the south-west, its centre passing through the quartz block, and performed precisely the same function. A much smaller line emerged from this point and flowed off to the east. The impression was of a nerve ganglion, a crucial point of exchange and interaction in a nervous system that was alive and functioning irrespective of whether Homo Sapiens comprehended it or not.

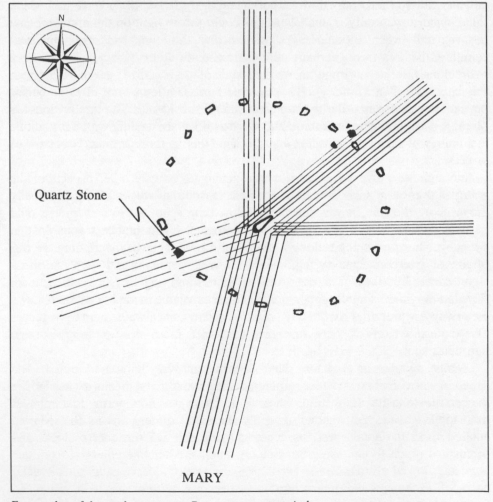

Energy plan of the earth currents at Boscawen-un stone circle.

Not for the first time, and certainly not for the last, we walked back to the road somewhat bewildered. Boscawen-un had given a glimpse into the rationale of such places. Were they really the nerve centres of the landscape, where major flows of terrestrial energy pulsed and streamed to harmonize and resonate with each other and where certain types of 'surface' energy actually entered the ground to interact with other, subterranean forces deep within the Earth? Did the discoveries of the geometrical and astro-archaeological properties of such sites indicate that extra-terrestrial, cosmic energies were also involved? The scenario was tantalizing. Yet there was a feeling that somehow, we were slowly beginning to grasp the truly holistic nature of these old sacred places.

Taking the road to Sancreed, the next point was soon tracked. It was running across the car park of the Drift Reservoir which supplies the Penzance district with its mains water supply. Ten minutes later, it had been found to cross the river that is now the outflow from this reservoir at Buryas Bridge. It also flowed across the same river a short distance away as it followed its meandering course down to Newlyn and out into Mount's Bay. Within a mile, 'Mary' had crossed the same waterway three times. It was difficult not to imagine some sympathy between the tidal, lunar energies we were dealing with and their physical counterpart in the rivers and streams of the countryside.

Tracking the course of the line into Penzance, we found ourselves at the great towering edifice of St Mary's Church. The whole building was exactly aligned on the flow. The last time we had visited it, unconnected with this project, its blackened windows had been boarded up after an arson attack had totally gutted the interior. Since then it had been completely refurbished at considerable expense, and the atmosphere of utter desolation had been replaced with one of benign presence. The phoenix had risen from the ashes.

'Mary' left her church, which is second only to St Michael's Mount in visually dominating the bay, ran the length of Quay Street, passing within feet of The Quay Bookshop, and right through a Victorian harbour master's office at the docks. It also ran across the edge of the berth belonging to the *Scillionian*, the marine lifeline that connects the Scilly Isles to the mainland. A chance meeting with Mark and Marga Thomas from the bookshop, out for a morning stroll, revealed that there was a legend of an ancient chapel at this spot which in the dim past had been important when this area had been considered especially sacred. The very name *PENZANCE* is apparently the modern equivalent of an old Cornish title that means *HOLY HEADLAND*.

Leaning on the sea wall, we looked across the bay to the Mount. It was illuminated by the winter sun low down in the southern sky, and picked out in sharp relief by the deep shadows. Dramatic grey squalls were drifting over Mount's Bay from the west creating Turneresque lighting effects that seemed other-worldly. We were heading back to the island sanctuary of St Michael's Mount.

CITADEL OF THE SUN

As we approached the Mount, we recalled how we had been a little disappointed on the first morning of the quest to find that the St Michael current did not go through the castle itself, with its rock-cut church on the summit. We had been led to the most prominent natural feature of the island—a great rock, balanced on a horizontal platform on the western side, looking out across Mount's Bay to Penzance. This time, on climbing up to this quite dramatic spot, we became conscious of its immense power, which we had been unaware of on the previous occasion. Set like a huge rocking stone at the edge of a crag, it was draped in straggly green lichen, and had curious niches set into it, as if to accept candles or flaming torches. Across the bay was the ugly sight of Pendeen Quarry, through which the Michael current passed. Also visible was the tower of St Mary's Church which marked its feminine counterpart. 'Mary' ran to the rocky platform and there, joined with the Michael energy to form a node.

Up at the castle, the Mary current headed towards the summit, and to our surprise, did not pass through the rock-cut church, but through the eastern part of the building known as the Blue Drawing Rooms. This wing of the castle had been converted into accommodation about 1750. Previously it had been the site of the ruined Lady Chapel.

Below the terrace, an ancient cross was positioned exactly on the centre of the flow, which overlapped the present building by a few feet on the northern side, but otherwise was perfectly aligned. Here was an impressive testimony to the ancient sanctity of the Mount, with its chapels to St Michael and St Mary built right next to each other. The crucial point, though, as had been observed before at Brentor, Glastonbury and other sites, was 'secret'.

The sun was now appropriately beating down as we looked out over the bay from the Mount. Before it was associated with St Michael it had been venerated as a sanctuary of other Solar gods, and had possessed a singular importance. This, we were later to discover, was fully justified. Not only does it mark the flow of the English St Michael currents on their way across southern Britain, but it is unique in that it is also the place where even greater currents of energy flow in from the continent, the energies of a 'European' St Michael Line.

This other St Michael Line was originally rediscovered by the French researcher Jean Richer, who noticed an alignment of sanctuaries dedicated to the Greek Sun God Apollo which included Delos, Athens and Delphi. His brother, Lucien, found that this line, if projected westward, crossed the east coast of Italy at Monte Gargano, where a vision of the archangel had been recorded centuries before the one on St Michael's Mount. It continued through various other sites in Italy and France dedicated to St Michael, through Mont St Michel, St Michael's Mount in Cornwall, and also the remote island of Great Skellig or Skellig Michael, situated just off the west coast of Ireland, where there is a ruined monastery named after the saint.

This great line across Europe demonstrates clearly the close connection between St Michael and earlier gods of Light, and the way that important sites became centres of veneration for whatever the God of the moment happened to be. The 'God' is merely a symbolic interpretation of a form of natural energy, which persists whichever mythology is current. Later work on the island of Rhodes was to show that the European Michael Line had its solar and lunar components in exactly the same way as its English counterpart (dubbed 'Apollo' and 'Athena' to differentiate between them and 'Michael and 'Mary'). These energies passed through the sites of ancient temples and fortifications once controlled by the Knights of St John, who went to Rhodes after their expulsion from the Holy Land at the turn of the fourteenth century. According to Greek mythology, the island was especially chosen by the Sun God Helios, or Apollo, whose giant Colossus figure stood astride the harbour of Mandraki.

It seems a long way from Cornwall, yet the places are linked by these powerful energies which run for thousands of miles. Tracking them on the Mount, the crucial importance of the place became apparent: The currents of both the European and the English lines fuse at a node point of great significance. It is tempting to consider that the Normans understood this, and that when William the Conqueror invaded England on St Michael's Eve, 1066, and gave Cornwall to his half-brother Robert de Mortain (who rode into the county flying a banner of St Michael), they were guided by more than the material considerations of conquest. The tangible link between St Michael's Mount and Mont St Michel that resulted from this, and the establishment of a Benedictine monastery, was to last for centuries.

IN THE FOOTSTEPS OF THE SAINTS

Back on the mainland, we soon found ourselves at the beautiful little church at Perranuthnoe, a small village just around the bay from the Mount. Those who have spent summer afternoons seeking out Cornish churches will be aware that they have a special quality, unlike any others in Britain. Occasionally, they give the impression of having been lifted from another landscape entirely, perhaps that of Cornwall's French equivalent, Brittany. The remaining two hundred or so are ancient and uniquely Cornish. They emphasize that until very recently, Cornwall was a separate land from Britain, practically an island, with its own distinctive customs and language. Its peculiar atmosphere is still preserved in an almost tangible way at places where the wandering nature mystics and Celtic saints impressed their personalities and legends.

Perranuthnoe Church is dedicated to the two saints that have served as Cornwall's patron saints in strange succession, St Michael and St Piran. Cornwall has the unique position within the British Isles of being protected and watched over by the archangel Michael, and in the old days there were many hilltop chapels and shrines to the one who, in the Book of Revelation, is to clear the way for the second coming. He was only supplanted officially in relatively recent times by the itinerant figure of St Piran, who was supposed to have shown early miners the secrets of tin extraction, and who had been immediately adopted as the

new patron. A symbol, perhaps, of the change of emphasis from the old spiritual
to the new material values. But there are those who claim that St Michael still
presides over the land, and has been, like Merlin and King Arthur, merely
slumbering. Some, like the clairvoyant and visionary Wellesley Tudor Pole, are
of the opinion that he is at this present time awakening, stirring ancient memories
that are hidden in the land itself.

Our next port of call was just a little different from the weathered and worn
beauty of Perranuthnoe Church. At Rosudgeon, the line passed through the first
Methodist chapel we had ever come across that was directly associated with either
'Mary' or 'Michael'. Ecclesiastical intrigues abound! Did the chapel replace an
older structure, or was it sited intuitively by a 'sensitive'?

As if to provide the maximum contrast, we then found ourselves standing on the
green outside Germoe church. There cannot be many places like Germoe. It has
preserved its purity, its simple character, against all the onslaught of the age of the
machine. A crystal stream trickles past the venerable church, which welcomes
you with its warm embrace of old familiarity. Hens and geese cackle away from a
plot opposite, sandwiched between the delightfully rustic architecture of make-do
and mend rather than pull-down and rebuild.

Outside the church, St Germoe's chair, a peculiarly pleasing ancient building, is built into a wall, with its carved stone head, presumably a representation of St Germoe himself, gazing out across the scene in moody meditation. Inside, the atmosphere is so special, so primitive and pure, that it is beyond words. It makes this building one of the most uplifting of all Cornwall's superb collection of country churches, and in some way one of its most secret. The 'Mary' line passes right along its length and within a couple of feet of the saint's chair.

As if caught in a dream, we had to wrench ourselves away from the soothing abstractions of Germoe, to continue the quest in tracking this decidedly feminine terrestrial current. On the horizon loomed the great rounded shape of Tregonning Hill, 194 feet above sea level despite the fact that the sea was only just over a mile away, surmounted by a cross and once a centre of prehistoric culture. The cross was erected to mark the old hill as a war memorial, and it is curious just how many of the Cornish sacred hills have been so protected, as if in some way fallen warriors are intimately connected with the landscape much as they were in ancient times, when their bodies were often interred in barrows and mounds venerated by local tradition. Carn Brea, Roughtor, Trencrom, Tregonning, perhaps the spirits of those who died protecting their land still hover amidst the sweeping clouds that float over them, and often descend to veil them from human eyes.

'Mary' curved around the seaward side of the hill, and after driving as far as possible, wellingtons were needed before we could follow her further. Cattle stood in ankle-deep mud and watched as we squelched up the lane. In a quarter of an hour we were standing in a beautiful earthwork on the eastern slopes, raised up from the surrounding land with a circular ditch enclosing it, and marked on the map as a 'settlement'. The line passed through the topmost quarter, and the impression was that it had originally been a ritual site of some importance. Germoe Church tower was visible to the south-west, with the sea beyond.

Godolphin church marked the next spot, although the line does not pass right through it; it keeps to the porch side, where there is an extremely ancient stone cross, much worn and with a round shaft. This could be explained by the fact that the church is Victorian, and may have been inaccurately erected instead of directly on top of the old foundations. The church of St Crewenna, a female saint, at the village of Crowan was next. Travelling around so many churches one becomes extremely sensitive to their atmosphere, and it is a sad observation that many of them today, whilst exhibiting a certain picturesque neglect, give the psychic impression of gloomy sepulchres rather than the uplifting structures which they must have been in former times, when they were the centres of the local community. Some send a shiver up the spine instead of a warm glow to the heart, and it is no wonder that people often shun them as depressing relics. However, to walk into one that is obviously loved is a rewarding experience, for the energies apparently react to the human emotions that are released within their walls, amplified and attuned by both priest and congregation when operating harmoniously.

Crowan church certainly exhibits this almost electric feeling of being beautifully balanced. This atmosphere is complemented by more tangible splendours. Ancient columns are carved with dozens of angels bearing shields with intriguing designs, serpentine chevrons, crosses and other symbolic devices. The 'Mary' line passes right along the length of the building, and a deeply-coloured stained glass window depicts St Crewenna flanked on either side by the dragon slaying saints St Michael and St George. The tombs of various members of the St Aubyn family are located here also, the famous Cornish family who have had charge of St Michael's Mount for many centuries. All this seems to point to this particular church as being special. We were even more fascinated by all this on the discovery that the Revd Robert Law was the incumbent. We had come across him first at Leedstown chapel at the beginning of the adventure, when he had been aware of the energies associated with the St Michael Line, and had given us much encouragement. As the exorcist of the area, he spent much of his time dealing with disharmonious energies, and was naturally initiated into their significance. No wonder, we thought, that the place was so spiritually alive.

However, after this the line reverted to more prominent points in the visible landscape. It ran through Black Rock, a granite outcrop over 200 feet above sea level, and then across Crowan Beacon, a focal point when the fire festivals were a part of the annual cycle. It appeared to head off through another 'settlement' on the side of Calvadnack Hill, and then to Stithians reservoir. This in itself seemed intriguing, as it had already passed through the Drift reservoir which supplies the water for the Penzance area. Was it coincidence that water kept cropping up in the path of this apparently 'lunar' energy flow?

The increasingly decrepit map with which we had started the project now began to show an interesting shape, with the two lines we had dowsed contrasting with each other. The original 'Michael' ran from west to east in what was practically a straight line, curving near the Land's End and away from the population centres of Camborne/Redruth. Otherwise it was remarkably straight, indeed, the straightest we had found it in approximately 150 miles. 'Mary' seemed more contrary. In a great sweeping 'S' shaped curve, she flowed through Penzance to the north of the Michael current, crossing it at St Michael's Mount and then carrying on to the south. The two lines therefore possessed their own distinct character in the vicinity of the Mount, with the solar 'Michael' virtually straight, and the lunar 'Mary' far more serpentine. It seemed to make a certain amount of sense.

On with the chase, and we soon arrived at Stithians parish church. Then we were led a merry dance as the line became ever more sinuous, winding through the countryside until we wondered if we had somehow lost it. But then, we tracked it crossing a lane just outside Stithians, stopped the car to check it, and were amazed on looking over the hedge to discover the most exquisite Celtic cross standing alone in a field, with the centre of the line running right through it. One side had a worn carving of a 'crucified' figure on it, the other a cross with elongated lower arm, like a staff or sword. Such moments of sheer unexpected pleasure continually revitalized us with enthusiasm as they demonstrated to us the palpable reality of tracking the energy, even when disoriented in a strange landscape.

Through the gates that led to Roskrow Manor, on to the beautiful church at Perranworthal, built high up on a mound, and then to Devoran Church we followed it. All of a sudden we were on the banks of the river Fal, high above the estuary in a wooded promontory belonging to the National Trust. Leaving the car behind, we headed into the trees, glimpsing water through the bare branches that filtered the January sunshine. Inside was another prehistoric 'settlement', this time with a different personality than the others, as Nature had preserved it with undergrowth and venerable trees. Leaves crunched underfoot around the impressive earthworks, with a great circular moat or ditch and raised central enclosure. The natural beauty of the place was inspiring, a place, we felt, where the old gods still ruled.

Another delight was in store. A mile or so away, we were led to yet another spot of profound tranquillity, the site of Old Kea Church. Situated in a creek of the Truro River, a ruined tower gives shelter to birds and other wildlife amongst the ivy-draped walls and old arches, all of which are in a dangerous, if picturesque, condition. A unique stone, thought to be pre-Christian, stands in the churchyard. The smooth, round shaft with strange circular markings was discovered beneath the foundations of the old church when it was demolished in 1802, and is reputed to be from the time when a monastery was founded here by St Kea, probably one of several monks who came from Glastonbury in about 500 AD. The monastery grew large, eventually covering a total of 7,000 acres, making it the most influential in the area. Today, the crumbling pinnacles of the tower and precariously balanced window tracery betray little of its former glory. But the *genius loci*, the spirit of the place, is strong, and the line passes through the tower which still marks this particular spot as being quite special. It has the effect of imbuing strength and spirit, which before long, we were soon to discover, was to be most welcome.

AN EERIE ATMOSPHERE

To find the next point it was necessary to shake ourselves out of reverie and face the reality of the modern world. To get to the other side of the river, we drove through the cathedral city of Truro, with the main road quaking with juggernauts and heavy traffic. Before long, though, we were down near the Tregothnan Estate, the seat of the Earl of Falmouth and the largest landowner in Cornwall, back amidst the rural charms of this wooded, watery landscape and its quieter way of life. It was not long, either, before we located the line. It was running into the imposing church of St Michael Penkevil on its raised mound, at the edge of Lord Falmouth's estate with its Victorian cottages and busy rustic lifestyle.

This church was dedicated to St Michael by Bishop Bronescombe in 1261, who had, only two years before, consecrated the old St Mary's Church at Truro, now part of the cathedral beside which runs the St Michael current. The restoration in 1862 left a large and unusual structure, with a massive western tower. The

St Michael Penkevil in the 19th century.

original stone altar was at one time removed for a tombstone, but is now back in
use as one of the four altars in the church, a most unusual state of affairs in a
Cornish church. The interior includes an array of memorials, notably to various
members of the Boscawen family, to which the present Lord Falmouth belongs,
including Admiral Edward Boscawen who survived various perils to die of fever
in 1761.

However, on entering the church, such details seemed to us of secondary
interest. The first thing that struck us was the depressing, burdensome atmosphere
that pervades the entire place. The memorials seem to exude a melancholy that
makes the spirit utterly despondent. We wondered whether this was just
subjective; however, we both felt this sense of gloom so strongly that we

concluded that the place itself was in some way unharmonious, affecting anyone inside. In all our travels, which had taken us to so many churches and ancient sites, we had never met such a feeling of black depression. The peeling paint on the walls, the patches of damp and air of total neglect added to this. It reminded us both of some creepy set for a Gothic horror film, ready for the appearance of vile and obscene creatures from a warped imagination. Even the figure of St Michael himself in a stained glass window looked depressed. We couldn't wait to get back outside in the fresh air of the gathering dusk.

The implications of the black atmosphere of St Michael Penkevil could be thought of as worrying. A similar feeling of sheer despondency had existed at Lydford castle, a place notorious in the past for torture and incarceration. But at least that had been a castle, even if it was built on an ancient mound. Here was a church, which should be a place of inspiration, that was so inharmonious that it dragged the spirits down into a slough of despond. And a church where there were memorials to members of one of Cornwall's most elite families.

The traditional use of places where the terrestrial currents are at their strongest suggests that the multi-dimensional nature of the energies involved can inspire revelation, as acknowledged in the legends of the Celtic saints who reputedly founded their oratories at such spots. Yet the days of such attunement have long gone; neglect and ignorance is more apparent in the modern world, and the opposite is also true. The Spirit of nature reacts to the refined vibrations of human emotion, sometimes causing blockages or pollution of the energy flows when this emotion is intensely negative. On one occasion in Cornwall, a lady who was experiencing a morbid dread of death which prevented her from going outside was found to be living on the site of an old abattoir. She had apparently picked up the fear of the animals about to be slaughtered, which had somehow been trapped in the energy field of the site, ready to affect anyone who was sufficiently sensitive. This situation, happily, was resolved by a process of healing where the negative energy was transmuted to a different vibrational frequency. This technique seems in many ways preferable to the more physical method of countering such 'black lines' or 'black streams' by hammering metal spikes into the ground and redirecting the infected energy flows into the earth, where they are presumably dissipated and healed naturally. Using the opposite emotion of love to counteract fear seems to work wonders.

In visiting old churches, it is impossible not to become sensitive to their psychic and spiritual atmosphere, focussed and amplified by the structures themselves and the natural properties of the places on which they are built. Many are like mausoleums, possessing a grey, leaden quality that afflicts the soul. Others, lovingly tended and venerated by people with their minds attuned to higher things, are aglow with a spirit of harmony and peace. It is obvious that the human component in the harmonious operation of such sites is essential. However, because the energies resonate with those invoked, a terrible blackness descends if, through ignorance or accident, negative emotions are allowed to build up and become trapped. There can be little doubt that today, many of the churches across the land are in need of healing. It is not surprising that people shudder as they walk inside, and do not wish to repeat the experience.

Whatever caused the black gloom at St Michael Penkevil may never be known. But its effects on the energies of the place, and its transference to those who visit it demand considerable attention. It could be that the blackness not only affects the immediate vicinity, but that it is spread right along the natural flow which weaves its way over the landscape, in precisely the same way that a polluted stream affects a river. Perhaps, given such an example as this, which must be repeated many times across the countryside, it is not surprising that our sensitivities are blighted and our finer feelings are in abeyance; the spirit on which we all unwittingly feed is suffering from poisoning. We need a new awareness, guided by an inner understanding, which will help to heal a diseased landscape of the shadows of the past.

CROSSING AT THE WATERS

A few weeks later we found ourselves back in the verdant countryside through which the great River Fal snakes its way to the sea. The church at the remote village of Ruan Lanihorne marked the flow of earth current, passing through the porch and tower. The day was fresh and the mood enthusiastic, yet the neglected church on its ancient mound, picturesque in its decay, still had a vague feeling of the desolation of St Michael Penkevil, and we wondered whether this was in some way communicated by its proximity, just a few miles down the line. However, the sight of glorious peacocks strutting about below helped us to shake off any feeling of sadness.

The current crossed again at the bridge over the river at Tregony. In the past this place had been an important port, with boats coming all the way up the now-silted Fal, and it still retains the charm of its former glory. Its church, again raised up on its circular mound, marked the place where the serpent passed. Its affinity for water was unambiguous, for it was following the course of the River Fal, diverting only to visit churches in the valley such as Tregony and nearby Creed. It also crossed at Golden Mill, right on the bridge, where we came across a quaint sign above the door of an old building: *'Vicar Priddle is permitted to dispense alcoholic beverages to persons of quality only'* the legend read. Wondering briefly if we fulfilled this lofty ideal, we noted the padlocked door and departed, much amused.

Yet another bridge was crossed at Grampound, and then two more marked the flow below a vast railway viaduct near the Trenowth Estate. The fondness for water that the 'Mary' line demonstrated was quite remarkable, with a particular penchant, it seemed, for holy wells, reservoirs and rivers. This was familiar territory for us, for we had chased the 'Michael' line through this countryside almost two years ago, where it had gone through the estate where a ruined Celtic chapel exists somewhere in impenetrable woodland.

A few minutes later we stood at another place we remembered. Indeed, we could hardly forget the ancient earthwork of Resugga Castle. It had occurred to us last time that it was one of Cornwall's hidden beauties, looking out over wooded countryside that must have changed little down the years. Hardly a building to be seen, just the railway line down in the valley. It is a secret place.

It possesses other secrets also; for right in the middle of the central enclosure is a node point, strangely undetected by us before. At this point, the Michael and Mary lines cross, with the Mary running north-south, and the Michael east-west, forming a Celtic cross and pointing to the great significance that this place must have had in the past. Mary had hitherto remained aloof from her opposite counterpart, crossing it the last time at St Michael's Mount. This second crossing indicated the original importance of Resugga Castle, despite archaeological opinion that it was some sort of fortification. It was clearly an important ritual centre where ancient ceremonies had once invoked the Earth Spirit at crucial times of the annual cycle. One can feel a presence at the place as if it is somehow protected. We had the strangest feeling we were being observed by eyes that were not physical, not of this time. They welcomed us in recognition of our understanding that this place was no mere fort. We were both extremely wary of what could easily be a subjective delusion, yet the impression was so strong that we both had to admit, in all honesty, to an experience that struck a deep chord within.

THE CHAPEL ON THE ROCK

St Stephen Church was the next place, locked, but curiously displaying a fine example of the Glastonbury Holy Thorn, planted in the churchyard by a Canon Gilbert. This seemed intriguing, as it was the first time we had come across a descendent of the famous thorn outside Glastonbury itself. Could it be that Canon Gilbert was in some way inspired to create a physical tie with the Isle of Avalon, to echo the more spiritual link that existed in the world of subtle energies between this remote parish and the holy centre up in Somerset? Other examples of this strange echoing tendency to demonstrate a connection had been noted in the past; like the miniature 'Abbot's Kitchen' on St Michael's Mount, a fine replica of the original to be found within the grounds of Glastonbury Abbey.

We were deep into the clay country now, and everything seemed bleached a ghostly pallour by the fine white dust that covered the landscape. The line meandered through a shattered land, ripped apart with its unprofitable residues dumped in great pyramids as memorials to a ruthless god. Yet the earth seemed weirdly unmoved, and its subtle artery of energy carried on as if its essence was not on the surface but deep inside. Tracking it through a wasteland is not a gratifying experience, though, and we were faintly depressed as we headed north. Stopping to check the line at a huddle of squat dwellings cowering amongst the spoil-heaps, we were greeted by a striking image. There, beyond the modest homes lining the road, not more than half-a-mile away, was one of the most dramatic sights in the whole of Cornwall.

To come across Roche Rock by accident is a humbling experience. In a flat

Roche Rock and hermitage.

landscape, moulded into hills and valleys by heavy industry, a great crag of black rock rises over a hundred feet into the air. Its startling, stark shape makes you catch your breath. On its summit, built into the living rock, is an ancient chapel dedicated to St Michael, its eyeless vaulted window gazing out across a devastated country. Massive pylons stride away into the distance; factories belch out their white smoke. Yet the place itself is timeless. An archaic magic hangs in the air, amongst the strangely-contorted rocks that inhabit the place and which cause the wind to howl weirdly through weathered crevices. Constructed by expert hands from superbly-worked granite, the hermitage was built to defy the centuries. This it has done admirably. The imagination is stimulated by its raw solidity. The spirits are uplifted by its imposing presence.

Ancient legend attached to the place tells of an early Celtic saint, St Conan, who piously took refuge here to commune with his god. He was a formidable character, achieving fame and distinction as one of the first Bishops of Cornwall, and eventually he left the Rock to install himself at that other romantic sanctuary of the archangel, St Michael's Mount. Perhaps he had followed the earth-current we had been tracking, making a pilgrimage that led ultimately to the Mount.

The Rock itself is nature's markstone for this channel of energy, intimately connected with St Michael. Clambering up the iron ladder to the eyrie above, we found that the current passed right through the chapel with its lower room sculpted into the rock, yet not levelled so as to disturb the natural qualities, a feature of all early rock-fast chapels. In the eastern quarter of the windswept room exists a powerful energy centre where presumably the altar would have once stood. The line passes through the east window, after making a turn of approximately 45 degrees, demonstrating a powerful rapport between the human hands that constructed this place and the hand of nature that preceded them. Not far away, at the foot of the crag, a peculiar holy well that is said to ebb and flow with the tide exists in a hollow boulder. Whether this refers to the tides of the sea or the subtle, psychic tides of the earth is open to question. Either way, Roche Rock is unique and impressive, remaining forever in the mind as a place of enormous power.

We were leaving the clay country, and quite suddenly found ourselves in winding, wooded lanes. Soon we were standing outside Luxulyan church on its circular elevated site, where an old Celtic cross marked the line as it ran diagonally through the building to the altar, as if the old stone was influencing it. As the building was enlarged and restored in the fifteenth century, it is quite possible the original chapel referred to in a document of 1162 stood in a slightly different position.

Inside, a superb carved Norman font is decorated with a menagerie of mythical beasts, including an exquisite winged dragon with serpentine tail. Looking at the map, we were struck by the realization that at Luxulyan, the Michael and Mary lines were running amazingly close together, within a few hundred yards of each other. We recalled how the Luxulyan valley was famous as one of Cornwall's most beautiful, and wondered whether the interaction between the two could possibly affect the visual qualities of the place. Driving away from it, we could see the tall tower of Lanlivery church in the distance, and noted from the church guide that the two places had been under the Benedictine Prior of Tywardreath. Traditionally, the Benedictines had been initiates in the mysteries of the earth's energies, and like the Knights Templar who were charged with the protection of the pilgrim routes that were the physical counterpart of the terrestrial channels, always seemed to crop up in exactly the right place. They had also been in charge of St Michael's Mount.

RETURN OF THE GARGOYLE

Mythical beasts were again in evidence at Lanlivery church, prominent on its raised mound, along with gargoyles and angels carved on its great tower. The line ran right along the building, after leaving the local hostelry called The Crown. Fortunately, perhaps, it was closed, otherwise we might have been tempted to explore the interior for evidence of geomantic sensibilities within the licensed victualler's trade. There was a feeling that something was about to happen. The lines had been running very close together now for some miles. Would they cross? If they did, then it was sure to be at a very special place. Driving towards the old Cornish capital of Lostwithiel, we could see the graceful lantern spire of St Bartholomew's, unique in the county, dominating the roofscape of the town.

It was good to return to pay our respects to the amazing gargoyle font in the church. The striking grotesque head still peered out, with its weird pineal spiral and twin serpents wriggling across its strange skull. This now seemed to us an extraordinary symbolic representation of what was happening in energy terms, for the two serpents, the Michael and the Mary, did indeed cross at this very spot. On the opposite side, an interesting blend of the early Christian and the Pagan amalgamated into the head of a 'Green Man' with a bishop's hat. All around were animated scenes of hunting—a perennial mythological scenario that dates back to prehistory. On our first visit, we had not noticed that the font was a node, so perplexed were we that the Michael current suddenly changed its angle. It is also sometimes difficult to dowse properly inside churches without creating understandable interest from others. However, here we had another crossing point, this time at a Christian 'holy well', or at least its equivalent, for a font is nothing less than a 'well' constructed from a raw block of stone and taken inside a church. It is still common practice to use the waters of any nearby original sacred spring.

Out in the town, heavy rain beat down as we tracked the energy flow to the ancient Guildhall, once the site of a royal palace. It passed directly through, and, squinting at the rain-lashed building, we noticed something intriguing. The stained glass windows were in the form of six-pointed stars and the square and

Lively hunting scenes animate the gargoyle font in Lostwithiel Church.

compasses, the familiar devices of traditional Freemasonry. What was a royal palace had been commandeered as a Masonic Lodge. It has long been claimed that the Masons have access to knowledge which is 'occult' or 'hidden' and that they understand certain principles not generally acknowledged. Here, it seemed, was evidence that such claims might well be based on truth.

Down the end of a tiny lane at St Winnow was an obscure little chapel that had once been quite an important place, with old stones lying in the churchyard, and Beacon Hill rising to the east. Much damaged during the Civil War, it has been restored in a rather plain and ugly style which, however, does not affect the atmosphere or the energy as it runs at an angle through the building.

'Mary' was now running south of 'Michael', and within a short while we were driving through the beautiful old estate of Boconnoc. Ancient oaks stood in the parkland, with small groups of deer grazing in the distance, and the Mary current ran through the small private chapel near the house. A few miles away, it also passed diagonally through St Pinnock Church, where the dampness brought out the sweet smell of new-mown grass and enveloped the village in a cloud of evocative richness.

MEGALITHS OF THE MOOR

The moorland village of St Cleer is but a stone's throw away from some of the most tantalizing remains of prehistory. Within the village itself are two important sites, one now occupied by the beautiful church, with a curious stone near the door that seems to possess a pair of eyes, the other a holy well that was particularly sacred. It was in ruins until the year 1864, but the locals still muttered tales about its miraculous virtues and powers of healing, and visitors were approached by the 'keeper of the well', a poor old woman, bent and tottering with age, who recounted its magical properties in reverential tones. Rebuilt as a memorial to a local vicar, it now stands in Gothic splendour in the midst of soulless bungalows, its architecture echoing its once-powerful presence in the lives of past people. A few feet away stands an imposing Celtic Cross, marking the outside of the Mary line as she flows at an angle through the well. A similar effect exists at the church, where the 'eye' stone this time marks the centre of the line on its diagonal route through the building.

The Gothic building over St Cleer Holy Well.

The light was fading fast, and on pulling into a small hamlet a massive shape appeared on the horizon, black against the distant glow of sodium lamps from a village on the edge of the moor. Trethevy Quoit is the greatest of the Cornish quoits, and, at night, raised on its earthen mound, is an impressive sight. It is impressive by day, but at night observation is mellowed by the imagination. A Neolithic 'tomb' with six enormous stones supporting a seventh, the great capstone leans at such an alarming angle that one would have thought it would have slid off a thousand years ago. The realization that the Mary line flows through this remarkable structure, though, would appear to indicate that its original use was far less prosaic than that of mere burial.

Trethevy Quoit, the largest megalithic structure in Cornwall.

FEBRUARY 16th, 1989. The sun glinted on the TV mast that crowns the summit of Caradon Hill, 369 feet above sea level and the site of ancient villages and deserted mine-workings. 'Mary' seemed to be in a contrary mood, and headed off up the hill only to change her mind half way up and go straight for the Hurlers.

In the middle of the three circles, she 'mated' and crossed with the Michael current at the node point. The places of entrance and exit are marked out as special; two female squat 'diamond' shaped stones precisely align with the centre of the flow, whereas the other stones are more like pillars. She changed direction slightly at the node and swept out to the open moor, past the Cheesewring, through a group of tumuli on the summit of Langstone Downs and then on across Bearah Tor.

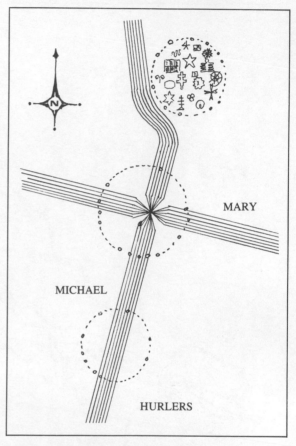

After an exhilarating stroll across the moor, North Hill Church came as a nasty shock. Walking around it, we became aware of a quite disgusting atmosphere emanating from something within. Inside, we immediately saw that the source of this blackness was a tomb. A grim figure stood with one foot on a scaly dragon, the other on a skeleton. The entire edifice was surrounded by a pallour of gloom and despondency, and we had the distinct impression that one of its occupants objected to letting go of his only connection with the material world. He had been hanging on like grim death for centuries, and the tomb had become a focus for other unbalanced energies which reinforced it as a source of fear. Its effect on the church was certainly not conducive to thoughts of divinity. Before leaving, we did our best to help.

At Trefrize, we were led to the site of All Hallows Well, an old holy well which had once been greatly venerated. Within a hundred feet of it had stood a large chapel to St Mary, where the famous Treffry family were married, baptised and buried for generations. Before this, Sir Reginald Bottreux had a medieval mansion there. A few years ago, a local historian unearthed old stones of considerable antiquity and workmanship, remnants of a time when this place was the centre of local life. Today, there is nothing to remind us of its past fame except the well, now rebuilt as a sad box of concrete blocks, and a curious atmosphere that pervades the place. One last church marked the Mary current before we were to cross the River Tamar, at Lezant, where it also passed through an adjacent house with the esoterically potent name of Tredragon! In the east, the hazy hills of Dartmoor beckoned once again as we drove into Devon.

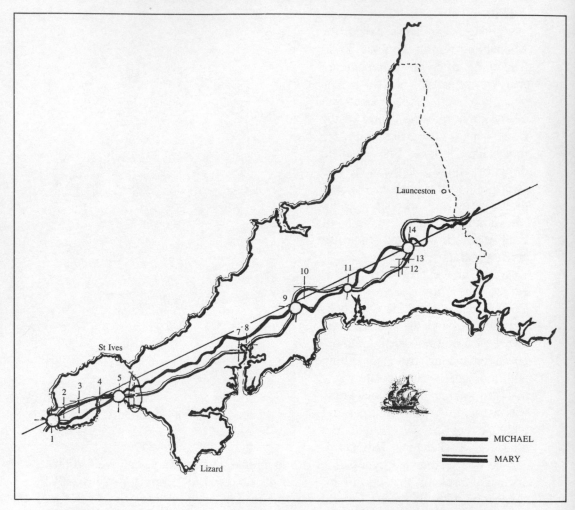

The Michael and Mary currents in Cornwall: 1. Carn Lês Boel; 2. Alsia Holy Well; 3. Boscawen-un; 4. Penzance; 5. St Michael's Mount; 6. Germoe; 7. Old Kea; 8. St Michael Penkevil; 9. Resugga Castle; 10. Roche Rock; 11. Lostwithiel; 12. St Cleer; 13. Trethevy Quoit; 14. Hurlers and Cheesewring.

Chapter Seven

LOST CHAPELS,
OLD CASTLES,
ANCIENT CHURCHES

'Things that accord in tone vibrate together. Things that have affinity in their inmost natures seek one another. Water flows to what is wet, fire turns to what is dry. Clouds follow the dragon, wind follows the tiger... What is born of Heaven feels related to what is above. What is born of Earth feels related to what is below.'

Commentary on the hexagram ch'ien
THE BOOK OF CHANGES
translated by Richard Wilhelm

THE FIRST CHURCH in Devon visited by the Mary current on its way up from Cornwall is a lonely sort of place. In previous times, it was the centre of a village that sat on the sloping hillside; now only the church remains. The rest of Dunterton has been washed away by time, or concealed by the shifting earth.

Close by is an equally lonely standing stone, isolated in the middle of a field on the outskirts of Milton Abbot. Glimpsed by motorists as they flash by, it only reveals its secrets on close inspection. Erected exactly on the centre of the current, it possesses a powerful energy centre of its own. Its irregular shape, weathered into lively anthropomorphism, suggests a female face when viewed from various angles. From one direction, it assumes the image of a Madonna.

After Milton Abbot church, whose name suggests a significant centre of ecclesiastical administration, the realization of how the megalithic system was apparently operated harmoniously alongside the network of medieval churches that sprang up during the religious revivals began to form. Of course many of the old stones were destroyed, and those that remain today are the merest fraction of what was once an enormous array spread all over the countryside. Yet not all were lost. The Church appeared to realize that to keep the currents flowing freely, the stones performed a crucial function. Many of them, thousands of years old, were allowed to co-exist with the waves of church building that took place at various times. At Milton Abbot, two churches situated very close together were linked by the earth current that passed through a standing stone that had been erected long before. It would have been a simple matter to root it out. But some tacit understanding miraculously preserved it even in the midst of times of religious fervour. Can we be left in any doubt that this, along with many other examples, indicates that the early Church had a deep understanding of the natural energies that guided their predecessors?

A short distance away is a forgotten earthwork on the brow of a hill, marked on the map as an 'enclosure' and now a haven for tall, wild grasses and nesting birds. The Mary line passes through it and points across Quither Common to a distinctive shape on the horizon, the 'Church on the Rock', the most prominent feature on the edge of Dartmoor.

The lonely church of St Michael perched on the volcanic mound of Brentor.

It would perhaps seem obvious to a poet's eye that Brentor has an effect upon the surrounding landscape. Its great volcanic crag dominates the area in a physical sense, and yet there is a deeper aspect. The node at the prehistoric earthworks below the rock marks the place where the Michael and Mary lines cross for the first time since leaving the Cornish border.

As the two lines part, one heading up to Lydford, the other straight out across

Dartmoor, they both run across wild country. Before the wilderness, though, 'Mary' makes one last call at the beautiful little moorland church at Mary Tavy. Set on the banks of a trickling river, Medieval and Norman relics mingle with Victoriana to create a singular atmosphere. William Crossing, the well-known writer on Dartmoor, spent his last years here, and is buried at the top of the churchyard.

Ahead is the moor. Hazy tors and invisible bogs stretch away in the direction of the Mary line, which says a temporary farewell to civilization near a weir at Wapsworthy. After that, the line can only be tracked on foot, an adventurous undertaking.

It occurred to us at this point that it might be interesting to leave a section of the route untracked, in order to give others the opportunity of entering into the spirit of the quest. There is a special sense of discovery about following these energies when their path is unknown that involves a rewarding intimacy with the land. It is not the same when the route is known. So we decided to leave the exploration of wild Dartmoor and the Mary line to others, giving them the opportunity to participate in the adventure and us the opportunity to take the easy way out and pick up the line where it leaves the eastern fringes. It will prove interesting to see what those of a more rugged disposition discover. . .

FEBRUARY 22nd, 1989. The silver streams on the edge of the moor were glinting in the sharp morning light. Early flowers splashed their colours across the deep greenery of the sheltered valleys, occasionally poking their heads through isolated patches of white snow. We located the Mary current at Throwleigh Church, which was appropriately dedicated to St Mary the Virgin. She left to head south, and was lost for a short time in the winding lanes. She reappeared suddenly on turning a bend, and looking over into the field, we saw an ancient building down below, with a group of old oaks sprouting from its interior. The place had a mysterious air about it, desolate but delightful, and was placed directly in the path of the line.

On our arrival at Gidleigh Church with its adjacent ruined castle tower, both of which mark the current, the interesting story of this building was recounted in the local guidebook. It had been a very ancient brookside chapel dedicated to the Blessed Virgin Mary, which appears to have preceded the church itself. It told a sad tale. A clerk named Robert de Middlecote had evidently raped a local girl, the miller's daughter, in the chapel. He was also accused of the murder of the

Old oaks grow from the ruined chapel of the Blessed Virgin Mary at Gidleigh.

child she was carrying, and when accused had fled only to be caught at Haldon near Exeter and be dubbed 'the Mad Monk of Haldon'. His eventual fate is unrecorded, but the tiny chapel in honour of the Virgin was afterwards scorned by local people. It became a cattle byre until, in the 19th century, the owner thought it a sacrilegious use for a previously sacred building, and planted five oak trees within it to prevent further abuse. The picturesque ruin, practically hidden in the valley, is nowadays difficult to find. Unless one happens to be dowsing the Mary line, that is.

The area around Drewsteignton has long been associated with the Druids. The 'Druid's Town on the Teign', as antiquarians used to consider its derivation, certainly has connections that indicate some importance in the past. The quoit or cromlech known as 'Spinster's Rock' stands on high ground well within view of Dartmoor. Its 15ft by 10ft capstone rests on three supports and is reputed to weigh more than sixteen tons. Previous chroniclers noted that the structure was once part of a larger complex, consisting of stone avenues and circles lying to the west. Polwhele described it as 'overlooking a sacred way, and two rows of pillars and several columnar circles', which were later removed for building purposes. Its legend says it was erected by three sisters before breakfast, an herculean task on an empty stomach.

The meaning of this tradition, though, may conceal a clue to its ancient use, for the Mary current passes right through the old stones. And in the old Celtic religion, the 'three maidens' or 'three sisters' were a symbol of the Goddess in her three distinct phases of Virgin (new moon), Mother (full moon) and Crone (waning moon).

Passing the rather gaunt shape of Castle Drogo, built by Lutyens on a green hill to irritate the aesthetic sensibilities of lovers of beauty, the current leads through

Spinster's Rock near Drewsteignton on the edge of Dartmoor.

its grounds, just clipping the formal gardens, on into the wooded valley of the River Teign and across the southern end of Fingle Bridge. This place is one of the most popular beauty spots in the area, with its rushing waters and tree-covered slopes, and attracts many thousands of visitors. One wonders whether the energy of the spot contributes to the natural attractions in some subtle way to draw such numbers of people, who subconsciously wish to immerse themselves in its atmosphere. Then, it is up to Prestonbury Castle, a towering hill-fort that looks

out to a landscape peculiarly rich in such prehistoric 'fortifications'. Across the river is Cranbrook Castle, and further along is Wooston Castle, standing on the side of a wooded cliff. The extensive earthworks at Prestonbury, however, make it quite special, and an ancient track follows the course of the energy to lead to a very unusual feature. On the brow of a hill overlooking the conifer-covered valley is a spring-fed pond, full of water-weeds. The Mary current goes right through it.

Through Wooston Castle, we are led to St Mary's Church at Dunsford, which is aligned with the current and in which there is a beautiful Jacobean monument to Thomas and Ursula Fulford, which sports playful dragons as well as the strangely-moving sculptures of their seven children. The real treasure of the

The striking 'dragon chair' in Dunsford Church.

church, however, is ignored in the literature. Whether this is through embarrassment it is difficult to say, but near the altar is a magnificent ancient chair made of black oak. A pagan 'Green Man' spills greenery from his mouth. Dragons and serpents writhe all over it. And a Celtic 'Bishop' or early Saint thrusts his cross down the throat of a large dragon in a style that indicates great antiquity. It is very odd that such a rare treasure is left unmentioned amongst the lesser relics which are recorded as being of interest.

THE HOLY CROSS REVISITED

The Mary serpent now swung north to cross the main A30 road. It led to the ancient church of St Mary the Virgin at Tedburn St Mary, and ran through a worn and battered moss-covered cross to pass diagonally through the porch and tower. Inside the building is a feeling of immense age, and curious square columns are surmounted by carved angels and naked male figures carrying pitchers of water.

A few miles further into the Devon countryside and we were in familiar territory. Mary was leading into the outskirts of Crediton, where we had previously found Michael flowing through the Norman tower of its one-time cathedral. Inside, all was silence, and Mary entered at an approximate angle of 45 degrees to join the node point, and the Michael line, in the centre of the tower. It suddenly struck us. The Holy Cross. The name of the church itself indicated its function. And there had been an adjacent Anglo-Saxon cathedral to St Mary before the Norman Building.

The Mary current curved gently away over the recreation ground where the centre went precisely through St Bonifacc's Holy Well, a restored building over a spring that goes back to very early times. Over Chapel Downs it travelled in a north-westerly direction, something we had not come across before. It seemed to be going well out of its normal way for some reason. We soon discovered why. It went to a place called Beacon Cross, through a tiny church in the middle of nowhere called Beacon Church. The hill behind it was where the fires were lit in the old days, and it still has a voluptuous beauty about it that makes it seem special.

MARCH 3rd, 1989. Well off the beaten track, a few houses and a church constitutes the village of Upton Hellions. Its chief claim to fame would appear to be that one of its inhabitants was the eighteenth-century composer John Davy, famous in his time but now forgotten, who, being a blacksmith with a smithy down by the river Creedy, practised his art on an instrument made of horseshoes.

The quaint, primitive little church (dedicated to St Mary the Virgin) has a rustic royal crest of some charm, and the Mary line running right along its length.

Mary also aligns with St Mary's church at Calverleigh, just outside Tiverton, where there is a memorial to Lt.Col. Sir William Heathcote-Amory, from the same family who built Knightshayes Court on the Michael current over the other side of the Exe valley. Before crossing the river Exe, one other church marked the flow, at Washfield, where it passed through the porch and tower. Here there is a serpent or dragon carved on the porch and other, quite remarkable dragons on the rood screen inside. Foliage spills from their mouths in great profusion. It is dedicated, of course, to St Mary the Virgin.

The church at Cove broke the run of St Mary churches that seemed to be becoming almost predictable. St John the Baptist's Church was in a very neglected state, despite its one-time fame as the Gretna Green of the Tiverton area. Apparently there is just not the demand these days. Huntsham Castle was a prehistoric 'settlement' on the side of a wooded hill not far away, and then we were at the village of Holcombe Rogus.

Sheltering in the lee of a hill with its Tudor mansion and ancient church the place takes its name from the Fitzrogus family, who lived there for seven generations from about 1100. They lived in a stronghold on Watchtower Hill, a Norman site in the grounds of the present court, where the whole village used to shelter in emergencies. Today, the old church along which the current runs is surrounded by solid, weathered buildings that lend an air of aloofness to the place, and inside there are many fascinating memorials and other remnants of its long history. It is dedicated to All Saints, a later change from its original patron St Michael. The church guide says this may be 'possibly because the church lies on the lay-line (*sic*) between Glastonbury and St Michael's Mount, but this is speculation.'

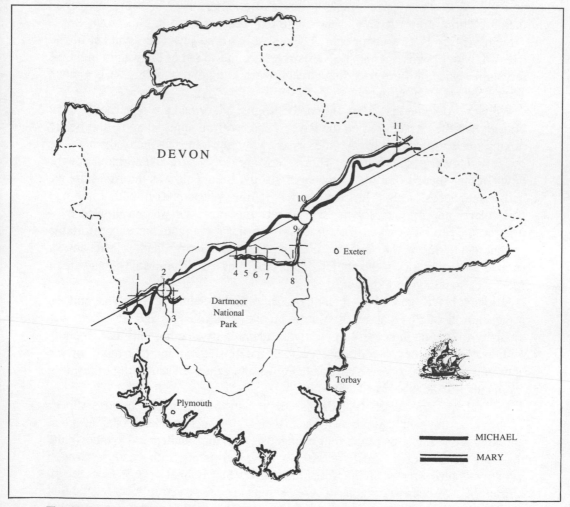

The Michael and Mary currents in Devon: 1. Milton Abbot; 2. Brentor; 3. Mary Tavy; 4. Throwleigh; 5. Gidleigh; 6. Spinster's Rock; 7. Prestonbury Castle; 8. Dunsford; 9. Tedburn St Mary; 10. Crediton; 11. Holcombe Rogus.

A SURFEIT OF DRAGONS

There can be little doubt that a quest such as this is one of the best ways to see the English countryside. The element of surprise sharpens the wits and the sense of adventure is always present; not only does one find oneself in the most exquisite backwaters of rural England, saturated with history and a mellow, unhurried peace, but the intimacy and atmosphere of the landscape affects the perceptions. It is easy to forget, while jostling with juggernauts on the motorway, that half-a-mile away a different world exists. In our frenetic folly, we ignore the beauty around us simply because we do not allow ourselves the time to slow down and soak up the tranquillity that is always present in Nature.

Old churches have this effect. Impregnated with the lives of countless countryfolk right back to the earliest times, they are a focus for the finer perceptions that recognize simple beauty and another order of being. Some, in their isolation, preserve an ancient magic that reaches deep into the soul.

Such a place is Greenham church. Set like a spired jewel in a thicket of old trees, the door opens out onto a riverbank where the sound of the waters immerse the whole place in a never-ending stream of trickling and bubbling. It is a place where Nature is in harmony.

We were in Somerset. After Holcombe Rogus, Mary had swept across Beacon Hill to visit the tiny church on the River Tone, with its unusual spire and belfry poking out above the trees. A mile or so away, she ran diagonally through the porch and tower of the church at Thorne St Margaret, where an enormous rough-hewn goblet-shaped font marks the centre of the line. This was the first time we had come across a St Margaret church in the Westcountry, and it seemed particularly appropriate, for her legend recounts how she was swallowed by a dragon, only to kill it when she miraculously burst forth from her uncomfortable containment. She is the feminine counterpart of St George and St Michael. A stained-glass window in the church depicts the Blessed Virgin Mary alongside St Margaret standing on a dragon.

Stopping briefly to call at Runnington Church, All Saints at Nynehead and the large church of St Giles at Bradford-on-Tone, it looked as though Mary was virtually following the course of the river, again exhibiting her curious sympathy with water. St Giles, we discovered, was a late dedication, like many of the churches whose patronage had changed down the centuries according to fashion. Its original dedication was to St Mary.

In Trull parish church (All Saints, previously St Michael), besides superb carvings on the pulpit and bench ends, there is some remarkable stained glass containing the emblems of the four evangelists (the four alchemical symbols) and the holy grail. But the real treasure of the place is its 15th century 'dragon window' which shows St Margaret flanked by St Michael and St George, all killing their respective dragons. These exploits are preserved in local legend that goes back to an earlier time, for nearby Castleman's Hill is said to be the actual site of the dragon's death.

A curious effect was noted at St George's Church at Ruishton. Immediately upon entering, the visitor is struck by the mis-alignment of the chancel, which is at a completely different angle from the nave. No explanation for this strange aberration on behalf of the builders is given, yet we found that it may not have been a mistake after all. The Mary line enters the tower, which, even in a county famed for its church towers, is strikingly elaborate, and changes angle at the arch in front of the organ. It then aligns precisely with the angle of the 'misaligned' chancel. Also interesting is the fact that the piscina, according to the church guide, marks the site of an ancient altar which may have been dedicated to the Virgin Mary, whose guild or brotherhood flourished in Ruishton shortly before the Reformation.

St Margaret in the fifteenth-century 'Dragon window' at Trull Church.

RETURN TO AVALON

Creech St Michael Church had struck us as quite a special place as we had tracked the Michael current through its south porch and into the most ancient part of the building. It has some interesting features, including traces of an arch at ground level, indicating perhaps a one-time subterranean crypt or vault (legends speak of underground tunnels), and a set of 7-holed village stocks that must be unique. There is no doubt, on examination, that they were specifically made like this, and the only conclusion can be that at some stage in Creech St Michael's history, a one-legged reprobate must have been a regular customer.

The church guide states that 'It is very likely that the present building was erected on a site of pagan worship'. Our findings showed that this was more than likely, for what was revealed made this ancient church so far unique. Right in the centre of the main aisle, situated a few feet to the right as one walks through the fine old oak door, was a node point, which we had missed before. Mary came in through the west and ran right across the altar, crossing the Michael current at a 90 degree angle—a 'Celtic cross'. This was the first time we had found a node in a humble parish church.

North Curry church, with its impressive octagonal tower, is built along the flow

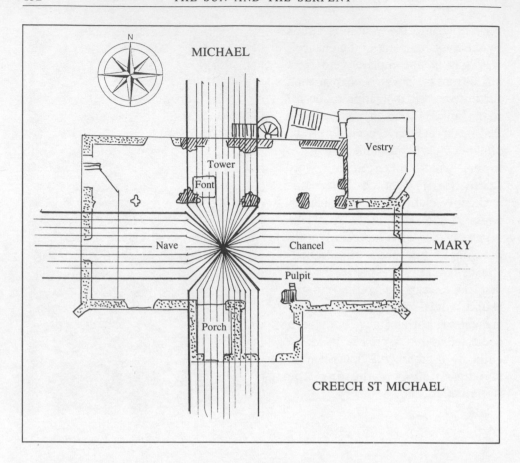

of the Mary current, and has a St Michael chapel and a fine reredos by Frederick
Bligh Bond, who astonished his archaeological colleagues earlier in the century
by discovering the remains of various buildings in Glastonbury Abbey through the
medium of automatic writing, apparently from a 15th century monk. He naturally
thought they would be interested to know how he could pinpoint ruins long buried
and forgotten, and in the spirit of true scientific enquiry, divulged his sources.
However, he underestimated the stifling rigidity of the academic world of the day,
and found himself dismissed for 'dabbling in the occult', despite the fact that he
had made the most important discoveries at Glastonbury for centuries.

Stoke St Gregory Church also marked the flow of the Mary current, and we
were back on the Somerset levels. To the north, the distinctive shape of Burrow
Mump protruded from the flat landscape.

A short time later we were standing in the ruins of St Michael's Church on its
summit, peering eastwards to catch a glimpse of the distant Tor. The node point,
situated at the place where the altar would have been, marked the crossing of the
Michael and Mary currents. The Michael line came in from the north-west
corner, changed its angle at the node and left through the ruined east window. The
Mary line came in from the south-east, likewise changed its angle, and headed
off to the north-east. We speculated that the original Norman church that had

occupied this spot may have been built at a different angle, and not aligned east/west, as was the general practice with later churches. However the actual energy was marked by the buildings on the summit, though, seemed a later embellishment. It appears to be the mound itself that anchors the energy and causes it to change orientation.

Middlezoy Church, its tower visible for miles around, marks the Mary current on its way towards Glastonbury, as does the Church of St Mary the Virgin at Moorlinch, which is built at the foot of 'Knoll Hill' and looks out across the levels below. The line passes right over this hill, which has a certain magical feeling about it. At St Mary's Church at Shapwick, the wide band of energy takes in the whole building, which is aligned on its flow. As we drove across Glastonbury Heath, the familiar shape of the Tor magnetized us and drew us irresistibly to it. The last time we had been to Avalon, we had found the Michael current passing through the high altar in the Abbey to head for the Chalice Well gardens, and then create an extraordinary 'energy labyrinth' on the Tor, for which we could find no satisfactory explanation. Perhaps, we thought, tracking the Mary current would help us to understand what it could all mean, as the fragments of this most perplexing puzzle came together to give us a glimpse of its ancient purpose.

THE GRAIL

MAY 24th, 1989. A cemetery was the unlikely place for the first mark-point as the Mary current entered Glastonbury. The first of two identical Victorian chapels on the side of Edmund Hill was aligned directly on the flow, which swept through the outskirts of the town to the northern side of the Tor. Here, it crossed at the junction of Maiden Croft Lane and Stone Down Lane, its centre running through a wooden seat strategically placed to view the Tor directly ahead. We sat there in the sweltering sun and looked at the heat haze shimmering over St Michael's tower. It had been the driest May since records began, and today was the hottest day of the year. Weeks of continuous good weather had created a totally relaxed atmosphere over the English landscape. The few people who were out and about moved unhurriedly as if in a dream, and the place seemed unusually quiet.

We had never even come close to understanding the weird labyrinth-shape formed by the Michael current as it wound its tortuous way around the Tor. We vividly remembered the three hours spent tracking it, and the great difficulty we had in negotiating the damp and slippery sides of the hill. This was not going to be such a problem today, but the heat would bring its own discomfort. A sense of anticipation mingled with a slight trepidation about what we would find, and whether it would be as exhausting as before.

As it was, there was little cause for this. The gods (or, perhaps more accurately, the Goddess), exhibited a benign influence over our task. The Mary current flowed around the base of the hill to the south side in a beautiful regular curve. The remains of the curious stone maze-pattern that had been noticed last

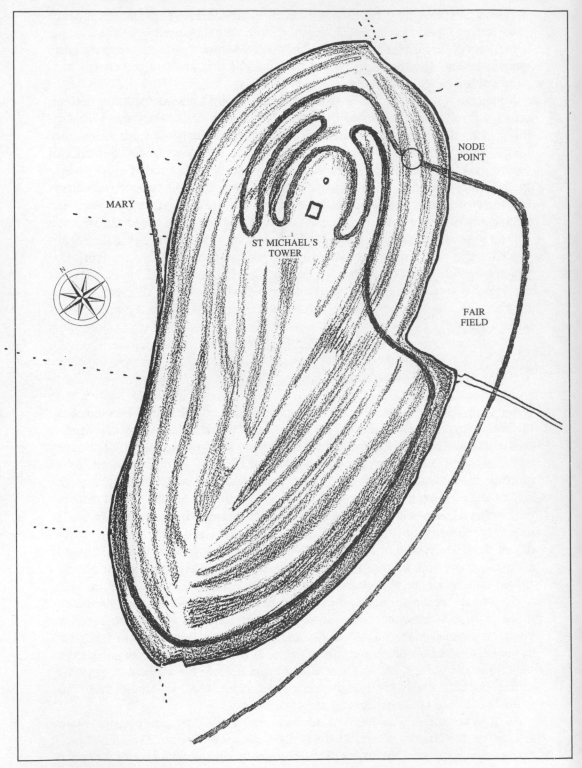

NODE
POINT

MARY

FAIR
FIELD

ST MICHAEL'S
TOWER

N

The Mary current on the Tor.

time marked the place where she ran up the side of the Tor. Mary was now inside the 'Michael' labyrinth that had been meticulously plotted the last time.

An hour later we lay in the shade of an old thorn tree, perspiring freely. The sun beat down and tiny figures moved dreamily about in the landscape below. There was a sense of quiet revelation.

The current of energy had wound around the north-eastern section of the Tor in the most exquisite manner. As gentle and regular as if it had been constructed by a pair of giant compasses, it had delineated a shape that had remarkable implications. Suddenly, the inexplicable shape we had found before was explained in terms that had never crossed our minds.

The Mary energy formed a container which encompassed the Michael current and its bulbous projection around the tower. The symbolism was graphic. The female force enclosed the male energy in the form of a double-lipped cup. It was a chalice or Grail.

FUSION

It would be honest to admit that we were somewhat stunned by this. Within an hour the secret purpose of the Tor had been revealed. It was a place where the male and female energies of the St Michael Line were ritually mating, the actual point of fusion apparently located at the site of the altar of the old church. There seemed little doubt that this had been divinely inspired to create an instrument of sacred science that had always been recognized as a place of transmutation. Yet the symbolism was so explicit that we recoiled from the implications. Such a discovery was explosive. We knew that to reveal our findings would be to invite scorn and derision from some quarters.

What were we to do? The interacting polarities of earth energy and the forms they adopted obviously conformed to a universal archetype. Ever since Avebury we had been aware of the male and female forces and their intimate relationship with special places where node points were found. We were confronted by the inescapable conclusion that what we were really dealing with was nothing less than the sexual energies of the Earth. Such a concept was bound to invite hostility from those who may not perhaps see that these energies are the basis of life itself, sacred forces that are the creative impulse behind existence. Yet we felt that this may have been revealed for a profound reason, and that we had to pass it on, come what may. It was not for us to judge the significance of such a revelatory concept, or to censor it from those who may find inspiration from the discovery.

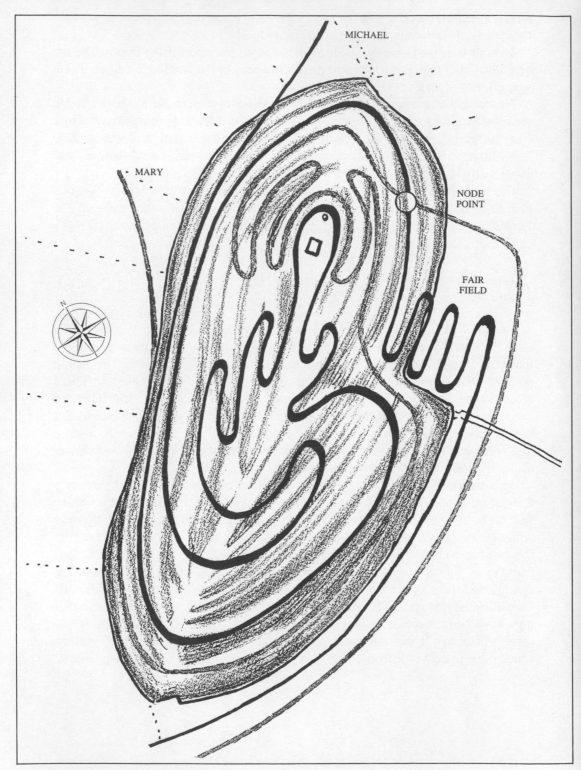

MICHAEL

MARY

NODE
POINT

FAIR
FIELD

FUSION: The labyrinthine energies of the Michael and Mary currents on Glastonbury Tor.

THE CHALICE

The cool, tranquil atmosphere of the Chalice Well Gardens was very welcome after the heat of the Tor. Sitting in the dappled shade, sipping the chalybeate waters that poured from the spring, we allowed ourselves a few moments to soak up the gentle mood. Mary had crossed the Michael current at the node on the south-eastern side of the Tor, flowed around the serpentine convolutions in Fair Field and led into the walled enclosure of King Arthur's Court. There, it had

crossed again at a node, which had not been observed on our last visit, situated at the top of some steps that lead down into a shallow pool. She followed the course of the stream, through the cascading waterfall, led through the Lion mask from which gushes a continuous flow of distinctive-tasting water, and carried on to the famous well-head. From there it turned sharply across the summit of Chalice Hill, heading towards the town.

The chalice symbolism connected with the well and hill struck us as particularly appropriate. The function of the Mary energy on the Tor was

The Chalice Well.

indisputably that of a container or grail, a vessel of alchemical fusion. This knowledge had apparently been preserved in the name of the spring and the hill from which it issues, a memory of the essential femininity of the quality of energy that links them with the sacred Tor itself.

THE MOTHER CHURCH

In the town, the Mary line crossed Chilkwell Street and ran into the Abbey grounds. A few people wandered about in shirt sleeves and thin dresses, moving unhurriedly in the soporific heat. The place seemed virtually deserted.

The current curved to align exactly with the axis of the Abbey buildings. It passed through the eastern end at the ruined Edgar Chapel whose foundations were discovered by Bligh Bond, and focussed on the site of the high altar, where it crossed the Michael line at the node. At the site of King Arthur's Tomb, something quite extraordinary was observed. The energy divided into two separate streams, flowed around the 'tomb' and rejoined to continue its route, running precisely down the centre of the Great Church. Here, this highly unusual phenomenon was repeated between a pair of brick squares, two rows of which mark the site of vanished columns. The actual spot was mid-way between the third pair of columns from the great arches of the chapel of St Peter and St Paul. Although there was nothing to mark it, we both felt that this place concealed some profound secret. Along with King Arthur's Tomb, it was unique. This, and its position within the Great Church of Glastonbury Abbey, seemed to indicate a deep mystery.

The energy flowed right along the axis of St Mary's Chapel, across the altar in the below-ground crypt and out through the west wall.

This was yet another revelation. St Mary's Chapel has always been acknowledged as the 'Mother Church' of Britain—the earliest site of the first Christian church, founded, according to legend, by Joseph of Arimathea and his twelve disciples shortly after the crucifixion. Its subterranean crypt, now open to the sky, contains an altar, one of the most sacred places in Glastonbury, and a holy well. Its dimensions preserve in stone many indications of its ancient function and significance, and the ratio of its length and width bear a mathematical relationship with the symbol of the *Vesica Piscis*, the mystical symbol that adorns the cover of the Chalice Well. John Michell explores the numerical symbolism of the chapel in *City of Revelation*:

> *'The circle of the original foundation (on which the chapel is built and which preserves its mystical dimensions) has a diameter of 39.6 ft or 14.56 Megalithic Yards, and its area is 166.5 Megalithic Yards. 1665*

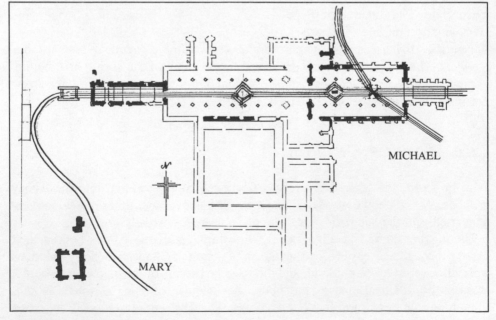

The Michael and Mary currents at Glastonbury Abbey.

is equal to 555 x 3, so it is the supreme number of the Earth Spirit, the microcosm represented by the number 5, and by Gematria (the ancient science whereby the meaning of words and numbers are interchangeable), 1665 is the number of the Greek name for the Spirit of the Earth. This is the true dedication of the Glastonbury chapel of St Mary.'

Leaving the chapel, the Mary serpent curved sharply near the wall of the Abbey grounds and meandered about with no apparent design, passing within approximately twenty feet of the Abbot's Kitchen and running right through the fishpond. A sacred fishpond? It was beautiful, full of flowering water lilies and teeming with small fish. Finally, she left the sanctuary of the Abbey grounds to enter the hurly-burly of everyday life, running across Bere Lane and off into the outskirts of the town.

FROM AVALON TO AVEBURY

The mysteries of Glastonbury are profound. We felt that there was good cause for Avalon's legendary status as a planetary power centre and its effects upon those who claimed it as a place of inspiration and revelation. Besides the striking energy forms of the Tor, it seemed remarkable that the Mary current coincided with the axis of the Abbey, which, projected in a straight line across country, leads across Gare Hill (with a St Michael church on its summit), and through the site of a ruined Priory, to Stonehenge. After the current project was over, we resolved to investigate this enigma further in order to begin to piece together other facets of this tantalizing esoteric jigsaw. We recalled the prophecies of Albion, the persistant tradition that a Golden Age would again visit the ancient isle. Austin Ringwode, the last of the Glastonbury Abbey monks, spoke of this on his deathbed:

> 'The Abbey will one day be repaired and rebuilt for the like worship which has now ceased; and then peace and plenty will for a long time abound'.

For the time being, though, we had to continue the quest. It was less than 50 miles to Avebury, and then we had to head east. Some of this eastern section had already been dowsed and recorded on occasional weekends over the previous year, and the things we had found had been equally as interesting as the route of the Michael/Mary currents between Land's End and Avebury. However, it was necessary to move at a faster pace than previously, mainly because we were working so far away from home. This did not detract from the adventure, rather it sharpened and focussed the discoveries into a more succinct picture. We had already learned many of the lessons in the early stages, and were now more familiar with the way the terrestrial energies operated. The sheer delight at tracking them, though, never waned. The unfamiliarity of the landscape provided a continuous procession of surprises and unexpected encounters which are lodged deep in the memory.

After leaving Glastonbury, the Mary current passed through a wooded glade near Edgarley, across the earthwork known as Ponter's Ball, and took in the large church at West Bradley. Over King's Hill near East Pennard, Beard Hill near East Compton and Maes Down, we were led to another of those secret places that appear to have been all but forgotten. On the map it is an earthwork called Small Down Knoll. On walking up to it, though, it is neither small nor really a knoll. It is a sculpted hill, 222 feet above sea level and shaped like a giant arrowhead. Mary runs through a small pond and right along the centre, through three tumuli and a long barrow at the sharp, western end. From there is one of the most impressive sights in Somerset. Down below in the far distance, the shape of Glastonbury Tor hangs in a veil of thin haze, glinting green like an emerald in its gilded setting.

Through St Mary's at Batcombe and Barrow Farm a few miles away, we

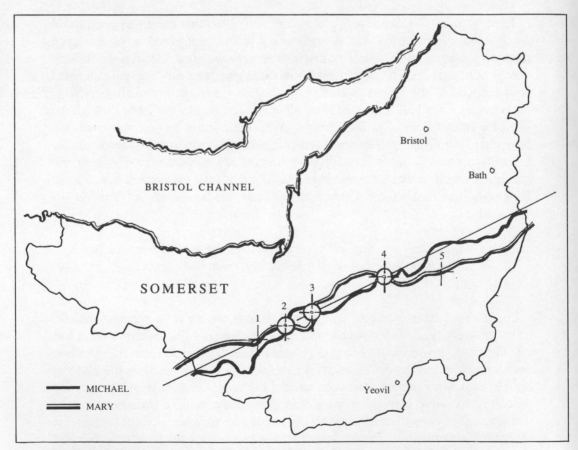

The Michael and Mary currents in Somerset: 1. Trull; 2. Creech St Michael; 3. Burrow Mump; 4. Glastonbury; 5. Small Knoll Down.

crossed the River Frome a short way from an ancient, lost village at Marston. There seemed to be few churches or other mark-points in this area, as the current weaved about the countryside unrecognized and forgotten. We were now in Wiltshire, remarking on the unusual nature of this, when we came upon a tiny chapel at Yarnbrook, which immediately responded to our comments by showing us that it was aligned directly on the current. However, this was an isolated occurrence, and the line soon reverted back to meandering about, passing through the village of Semington and open countryside to lead to a modern housing estate on the outskirts of Melksham. It was called Bowerhill, an evocative name that belied the sprawl of twentieth-century dwellings. Beyond the houses, at the edge of unspoilt countryside, was a node. The two currents crossed at a small spring overshadowed by trees. It was half-filled with bits of old timber, utterly neglected. Yet it was unique, the only spring that marked a node in the entire quest. It must have been a particularly holy place in the past.

At Bromham, in between Melksham and Devizes, is a church with the most astonishing gargoyles crawling all over the outside. They leer lasciviously, animated by the skills of the same sculptor who adorned the church at Trowbridge. Other points of interest are the superb Lady Chapel with a memorial effigy of Sir Roger Tocotes, controller of the King's Household in the reign of Henry VII, and a towering Celtic cross, hidden behind the church, in memory of the Irish poet Thomas Moore, decorated with impressive Celtic knotwork often terminating in griffins' or dragons' heads.

We were then led back to the spectacular Oliver's Castle, where there was a node just yards from the prehistoric dew pond, in the middle of the central enclosure. A few miles away we were led to one of the finest churches in Wiltshire, St Mary's at Bishops Cannings, where the heads of bishops and kings peer regally down from their lofty heights and Mary runs right along the axis. Remembering the discovery of the Mary line and the fact that the first church she had passed through after Avebury Henge had been St Mary's at Winterbourne Monkton, there could be little doubt that the Church understood something of the energies of the earth that had animated the Serpent Temple. The vivid image of an early bishop trampling on a serpent, carved on the worn font in Avebury church, and the old tradition that 'there are no snakes at Avebury' seemed well enough to indicate the Church's recognition of the nature of the Earth's subtle forces.

On crossing the Wansdyke we found that within a short distance of the main A361 road, both Michael and Mary ran within 60 yards of each other. Over the other side of Bishops Cannings Down, the Mary line ran through a tumulus high on the ridge. As we stood on the top, surveying the wide sweep of the Avebury countryside, we could see Silbury in its giant grandeur, inscrutable as ever. The last time we had been here, everything had changed. The project itself had instantly doubled in magnitude on the discovery of the Mary current, and we had now come full circle. Now, however, we had a far greater understanding of how the terrestrial energies operated.

There was still a great amount of work to do. We were back at the Serpent Temple, and about to pay our respects to the great stones that immortalized a vision of the Earth as an intelligence that responded to the energies of the heavens and the understanding of humanity. It was time to continue our quest tracking the energies between Avebury and the east coast, a hundred and fifty miles away. Various expeditions had already been undertaken, and had led through an unfamiliar landscape full of strange memories. Some of the special places along the route had revealed the reasons for their ancient veneration, and we were still to discover the role of many other famous and secret centres within a cosmology that had recognized the hidden forces of existence from the very earliest times up to the present. It seemed to us that a rediscovery of these principles could be an essential feature of the realization that we must be more concerned with the health and well-being of the planet. It was not a question of exploiting these forces simply for the good of humanity, but of a harmonious co-operation between the Earth and its creatures.

Chapter Eight

A LAND OF DRAGONS

'The dragon was originally a concrete expression of the divine powers of life-giving, but with the development of a higher conception of religious ideals it became relegated to a baser role, and eventually became the symbol of the power of evil.'

THE EVOLUTION OF THE DRAGON
Sir G. Elliot Smith (1919)

T HE PEOPLE OF East Anglia are familiar with dragons. For many centuries the countryside has, according to popular legend, been exceptionally well populated with them. The eighth-century epic poem of Beowulf recounts how he was mortally wounded by a fire-breathing dragon which was guarding a hoard of buried treasure, and medieval monks record in their manuscripts all manner of exploits attributed to the fabulous monsters.

If one is to believe the accounts, rural life was inextricably linked with the habits of these capricious beasts. Occasionally, they were in docile mood, basking languidly on hills and rocks of a summer evening. At other times they caused havoc amongst the populace, mauling and devouring cattle and sheep and terrorising villages. The local dragon, it seems, was an essential feature of life in the old days.

Even when most of them had been slain by heroic knights and saints, they were still the focal point of ancient festivals celebrating the return of spring. Their fearsome qualities often belied a genuine affection amongst the population of town and village alike, and in places such as Norwich, large wicker effigies paraded through the streets amid great revelry, echoing ceremonies that date back to prehistory. Church officials and inhabitants of the town would walk the parish bounds, stopping at specific points supposed to be a lair of the dragon, to pray for the blessings of the Earth and protection from evil. In the Middle Ages, these artificial dragons (many of the original beasts, it seems, having been killed), became highly sophisticated, incorporating flapping wings, noisy sound effects and the belching of smoke and fire produced by gunpowder. Two of these formidable creatures can still be seen, adorned in faded green and gold canvas, in the Norwich Castle Museum.

The cult of St Margaret, the female dragon-slayer, was particularly active in Norfolk and Suffolk, where churches often show her subduing one of a great variety of lurid reptiles. In this task she is frequently helped by St George, who also tames the raw dragon energies of the Earth. The root of all these persistant traditions is a deep memory of the understanding of natural forces that become particularly active in spring, the ancient Beltane. This understanding appears to have recognized that in a flat landscape such as East Anglia, the energies could become sluggish and stagnant, causing foul concentrations which affect cattle, sheep, crops and people. The answer to the dilemma was to build churches on the currents, where human minds, attuned to the needs of the Earth, could co-operate to ensure the free flow of the forces that guaranteed fertility and resilience against disease. Interestingly, the most striking feature of the landscape is its enormous number of country churches, often totally isolated from village or habitation. The regularity with which they appear cannot fail to impress anyone driving through the countryside. Sometimes one can see half-a-dozen church towers punctuating the flatlands, and this in an area that shows little evidence of great population.

The character of the quest to track the currents of the St Michael Line across eastern England reflected the nature of the landscape. Intensively cultivated districts or busy towns alternate with areas of rural solitude, where the beauty of the buildings, constructed of chalk, flint, clay and timber, blend harmoniously with the seclusion of a largely rustic country. Picturesque windmills, round-towered flint churches and ancient cottages with thatched roofs delight the eye, whilst the surprises that lie in wait for those who chase dragons can be equally enjoyable.

THE LAST LAIR OF THE DRAGON

OCTOBER 29th, 1988. The St Michael alignment, when projected eastwards, leaves the east coast between Great Yarmouth and Lowestoft. Trying to find a dragon in such circumstances calls for a particular alertness, and so driving along the coast road, minds were focussed inflexibly on tracking the place where the Michael current might cross. We had just passed the Suffolk/Norfolk border when the rods reacted strongly. There was definitely a dragon in the vicinity.

We were at the seaside village of Hopton on Sea. Just off the main road was the evocative ruin of an old church, clad in ivy and set amidst an oasis of greenery. The church had been dedicated to St Margaret.

It had been destroyed in January, 1865, when a gale fanned an over-heated stove into a fierce fire. It roared through the tower like a chimney, licking up seats, books and all the treasures of an ancient church in its fury. The heat peeled off a dozen coats of whitewash to reveal brilliantly painted patterns, which can still be faintly seen. A brave attempt was made by fishermen to save the organ, which, however, had to be abandoned in the porch as the doorway was too small to allow it through. A few hours later, nothing remained of it but a lump of lead.

In the roofless and ruined shell, elegant in its decay, was a large wooden cross planted where the altar once stood. It marked a node point, the last one before the

Michael and Mary currents swept out to sea. We were both taken aback that such a dramatic place should mark the last crossing of the two currents in England. White doves fluttered in and out of the decaying tower, and the atmosphere of the place was supremely moving. The flint and yellow mortar crumbled under the touch, and the history of the church stated that some of the material from which it was built was taken from another church at Newton, before it disappeared beneath the sea.

The ruined St Margaret's Church at Hopton, the last lair of the St Michael dragon.

In 1866 the villagers of Hopton built a new church to St Margaret a short distance away, and it is a lovely example of Victorian architecture, with fine octagonal tower and belfry. The chancel window was designed by Sir Edward Burne-Jones and made by William Morris. But most intriguing of all is that it was built directly on the Mary line before she passes through the old, ruined, church.

The Michael dragon left English soil incongruously at a breakwater on a beach behind a caravan park; the Mary parted company a short distance away. A wrought-iron beacon cage, raised on a tall post, had been erected directly in her path, one of a countrywide network that had recently been established to commemorate the defeat of the Spanish Armada.

STATUES AND SHRINES

Further inland, the Michael current led to an isolated church on the edge of Somerleyton park. This is the estate of Lord and Lady Somerleyton, whose beautiful stately home is regularly open to the public. Across a field behind the church we saw an interesting sight. An isolated statue marked the line after it passed through Somerleyton Hall. It was in Greek style, of a Hermes-type figure holding a spear, situated at the end of a straight avenue of old trees. Some of them had been lost in recent gales, and the avenue led down to a temple-like fountain in the gardens of the hall. The whole arrangement was geomantically laid out. We concluded that a past owner of Somerleyton Hall must have been aware of the Michael current, and had erected the statue in its path. The Hermetic form of the statue could surely be no coincidence.

The statue, connected by a tree-lined avenue to the grounds of Somerleyton Hall.

Across the Somerleyton marshes and the River Waveney, we came to Wheatacre Church, dedicated to All Saints (previously St Michael). Besides being quite small, it was quietly spectacular in its flint and brick structure. Unfortunately, it was locked, so we could not investigate why the current performed a surprisingly sharp turn inside. At the fine Early English-style St Mary's Church, Aldeby, it ran through the Lady Chapel. This place was both a monastic and a parish church, for it had been a Benedictine priory from about 1100 AD. Its other claim to fame was in having a parish clerk called James Futter, the oldest and longest-serving in the kingdom, who had been present at over 1,000 baptisms, 250 weddings and 500 burials.

In Saxon times, the market town of Beccles was a place of considerable importance. The sea reached into the town and it was a centre of trade and commerce. When the Normans arrived they erected a large stone tower, 97 feet tall, in the centre near the market square. Wherever the Normans left their mark, they appeared to leave evidence of their knowledge of the Earth's forces, and were responsible for the building of many grand cathedrals as well as thousands of churches, often richly-decorated, on previously sacred sites. Esoteric tradition points to the fact that such knowledge was learned during their crusades in the Holy Land, an idea that also extends to include their fellow-crusaders the Knights Templar, with whom they had strong connections. At Beccles, the tower, appropriately standing alongside St Michael's Church, exactly marks the Michael current, and dominates the surrounding countryside with its massive solidity.

Tracking the energy inland, we were led to St John's Church near Mettingham Castle and St Peter's at South Elmham, where there used to be a Chapel to St

Mary on the north side. A couple of miles away it passed through a moated Bishop's Palace where a wide moat enclosed old buildings surrounded by trees, and then ran through the remains of an ancient Minster to the isolated medieval church of St Mary's at Withersdale. This place is one of great beauty and antiquity, with its rare wooden beehive-shaped belfry and an air of delicious quaintness. It stands in front of a fine medieval farmhouse which was once moated, and in a county of superb churches, is one of the most memorable. At nearby Weybread Church, the next point on the Michael current, thirty churches are said to be visible from its round tower on a clear day. Another lovely St Mary's church near Syleham Manor was stunningly situated in a wooded dell on the banks of the River Waveney, and then we were at the Suffolk village of Hoxne, the legendary place of the death of the Saxon King Edmund, a figure whose life had been associated with many miraculous events.

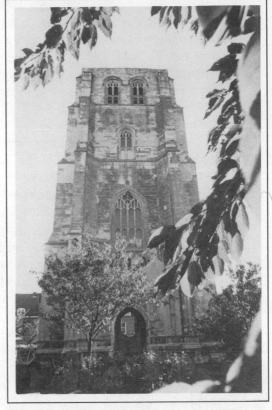

The Norman tower at Beccles, built on the St Michael current.

Edmund was crowned in 855, and became a revered monarch, but his East Anglian kingdom was devastated by Danish marauders, who defeated him in 869 at the Battle of Thetford. Edmund sought refuge at Hoxne, then an important town with a cathedral, but was betrayed as he hid under the bridge over the Goldbrook. Legend tells how a passing wedding party saw the sun glinting on his spurs, and gave him away. In the village until 1848 stood an ancient oak tree, reputed to be the one to which Edmund was bound as his Danish foes executed him with bow and arrow. It was 'entirely demolished on September 11th, without any apparent cause; the trunk shivered into several pieces and the immense limbs with the branches lay around in a remarkable manner. The dimensions of the tree were 12 feet in length, 6 feet in diameter and 20 feet in circumference.' Perhaps the most curious thing about this 1,000 year-old tree was that an iron arrowhead was found projecting from the inside of the hollow trunk.

Not content with his martyrdom, Edmund's murderers cut off his head, which went mysteriously missing when the time came for burial. It was found in a nearby forest being guarded by a wolf, which, however, willingly relinquished it and followed the procession to the King's grave in the village. Here, the body and head were miraculously reunited. Later, the remains were disinterred and reburied at Beodericsworth, which became Bury St Edmunds, and pilgrims from all over England would visit the illustrious shrine of St Edmund, whose story lives on in many church and cathedral carvings up and down the land where a wolf guards a man's head between his paws.

At first sight, one of the most famous of English legends having a connection with Hoxne church, through which the Michael current passes, would appear to be nothing more than coincidence. Yet these traditions often appear to have an almost secret mythology hidden within them which is difficult to pinpoint. St Edmund was to become one of the most notable saints in England, and both his life and his relics were reputed to be attended by miracles. The first of these is said to have been a white light descending from the skies. The last is perhaps one of the best-documented in English history. On Monday, 23rd November, 1198, whilst renovations were being carried out on the shrine of St Edmund, the uncorrupted body of the saint was examined by Jocelin of Brakelond. After three layers of cloth had been removed from the coffin, a foot-long relief in solid gold was exposed. The relief depicted St Michael. At the dead of night between 25th-26th, he found that the body was 'similar to that of a man lately dead.' This was the last time the body of the saint was beheld by mortal eyes. Stories such as these, especially when recounted by scholars and first-hand observers, often appear to be something more than mere fanciful imaginings.

THE EYE OF THE DRAGON

Eye is a rather strange name for a town. But then, Eye is in many ways a rather strange place. The first image is of a curious earthen mound, surmounted by a ruined castle, rising from a cacophany of ancient and modern houses. Adjacent to it is Eye Church, an equally surprising sight, for its magnificence would seem to be incongruous in a place of this size.

The Normans originally built their castle on the prehistoric mound when it was an island. Many centuries later a windmill was erected on the spot, to be replaced by a Victorian mock ruin which today lends an air of faded romance to the place. Aerial photographs show that this steep mound looks very much like an eye when viewed from above. The Michael current runs right through it, taking in the impressive church and also the remains of a nearby Priory which was, in Norman times, attached to a Benedictine Abbey in Normandy. It could be that the ancient mound was originally a sacred island, surrounded by the flood waters of what is now the River Dove, and that the church and priory took over its role as it was utilized for more secular purposes. There is also a part of the town called The Devil's Handbasin, where, perhaps, the Devil, supplanted in his domain by the Church, washed his hands of the whole affair.

The current also passes through one of the local pubs, where we spent a most entertaining evening. 'The Horseshoes' is a lively sort of hostelry, one of those inns where there is never a dull moment. This is not the place to record the quite astonishing antics of some of its clientele, however. Suffice it to say that after a

Eye castle on its prehistoric mound.

somewhat raucous evening, when we were hospitably treated to a fine meal in front of a large, blazing fire, we were warned not to venture from our room for any reason whatever during the night, on pain of serious consequences. One glimpse of a pair of slavering Rottweilers, teeth bared and saliva flowing, was enough to ensure that this advice was taken very seriously indeed. Throughout a rather sleepless night, full of strange scratching and snuffling noises outside the door, nightmarish visions invaded the dreams which were only dispelled by the clear and welcome light of morning, and the incarceration of the two fearsome beasts in their compound behind the pub, from where they reacted violently to anyone passing within a hundred feet.

St Mary's at Yaxley was the next stop, a fine old church with much to interest those of an antiquarian disposition. This includes two wild 'woodwose' figures fighting beasts above the porch, ancient symbols of pagan fertility beliefs and old May Day celebrations, and the faded remains of a Medieval 'Doom painting', where horned devils torment sinners in an attempt to intimidate those whose minds might be tempted to stray from the straight and narrow.

The beautiful little thatched church of St Mary's at Thornham Parva possesses a magnificent retable, one of the greatest treasures to be found in any English church. There are only two others like it; at Westminster Abbey and Norwich Cathedral. As the eyes become accustomed to the dim light, the striking image of St Margaret appears, spearing a writhing dragon with knotted tail. Just down the road, and marking the Michael current, were St Mary's at Thornham Magna, with its square thatched tower, St Andrew's at Wickham Skeith, St Andrew's at Cotton and St Mary's at Wetherden.

A strange story is attached to St Mary's at Woolpit, which, whilst having little to do with the fact that it marks the Michael energy, is worth recounting for its bizarre nature. The chroniclers Ralph of Coggeshall and William of Newburgh, who admits that his initial scepticism was overwhelmed by the evidence of so many credible witnesses, record a weird tale. During the reign of King Stephen, two children were found wandering through cornfields in a confused and perplexed condition. What astonished the villagers was not so much their unintelligible speech or strange clothing but the fact that, from head to toe, their skin was green. The news of this remarkable event spread fast, and although they were obviously famished, they steadfastly refused any food offered them. The only thing they would consume were fresh beans.

With the passage of time, their skin lost its green hue and they learned to speak English and eat other foods, but the boy, who became melancholy and morose, died. His companion, though, a girl, adapted to a normal life, became a servant and was eventually married in King's Lynn.

The children told how they had lived in a land where everything and everyone was green, a twilight place where the sun never rose. One day, while tending their flocks, they saw a land of light beyond a wide river, and, enchanted by the sound of bells, found themselves at Woolpit, where the bright sunshine almost caused them to faint. Failing to find their way back home, they were discovered by peculiar people with pink skin . . .

Three other churches led us in fairly rapid succession to the outskirts of Bury St Edmunds. They were All Saints at Drinkstone, Bradfield St George and St Nicholas at Rushbrooke, where a dragon is to be found on the royal arms of Henry VIII, the only example in the country. It is a surprising place, looking very plain on the outside but extremely elaborate within. The Jermyn family are buried at this place, the barons and baronesses of Bury St Edmunds. Then we were at Bury, one of the greatest shrines of Christianity in Medieval England, second only to Glastonbury. It was time to go back to the east coast and see where the Mary current would lead us.

MARY, QUITE CONTRARY

It was becoming apparent that the dedication of the various churches through which the Michael and Mary currents passed did not necessarily reflect the classification of the two types of energy as might have been imagined; it was just not that simple. Sometimes St Michael and St George sites fell on the Mary line, but mostly, St Mary sites were in great prevalence on both. This seemed, on reflection, quite a natural state of affairs, as while the earth currents might be considered to be 'male' or 'female', they were both channels of the Earth Spirit, the nervous system of the Goddess of the Earth, or St Mary. Add to this the great changes in ecclesiastical fashions down the centuries, when churches were often rededicated to the saint of the moment, and any continuity going back to early times could, at the very least, be confusing. However, the large number of St Mary sites we were encountering did seem to be a memory of places that were, in ancient times, dedicated to a female spirit of the Earth.

From St Margaret's at Hopton, we were led to St Mary's at Ashby, a striking long, thin, 12th century building with an octagonal belfry on top of a round tower. It had a thatched roof and was in the middle of nowhere. A short while later, the deep crimson rays of a dying sun shone on the chequerboard flintwork of Haddiscoe Church's round tower, set on high ground above the low-lying marshes, and by the light of a rapidly-fading torch, we noted that the centre of the energy passed right through the old font. The church was dedicated to St Mary.

The following morning, the sun shone and we were at Maypole Green near Toft Monks, where sepia memories of quaint village festivities peopled our minds as we drove through the quiet hamlet. In the centre of the Raveningham Estate was a sombre, neglected church with an octagonal tower built on a round base, a feature that seemed to be cropping up regularly in association with the Mary energy. Fonts were often octagonal, we recalled, perhaps because of some symbolic imagery associated with the Goddess. The font in Raveningham Church marked the centre of the current as it curved through the rather sad building, with its grandiose memorials to the Bacon family, including Sir Edmund Bacon, the famous actor, who was also involved in the building of many churches and cathedrals. An interesting crest (of the Bacon family?) is emblazoned on a flag over the font, consisting of two pentagrams with white circles in their centre, and a hand between.

At nearby Hales Church (St Margaret), a magnificent Norman doorway beneath its thatched roof had other symbolic devices, and the sun symbols and 8-pointed stars seemed highly unusual. Its round tower was echoed at its opposite end by another unusual feature, for the east wall was built similarly round to create a most surprising effect. The current passed through the tower and the two Norman doors.

St Michael's Church at Broome, a large square structure at the end of a lane with not a habitation in sight, marked the next point, where the line ran diagonally across the building. At St Mary's at Ditchingham, shafts of sunlight filtered through the stained-glass windows to pick out the magnificently painted ceiling, and the air was heavy with the scent of roses, freshly arranged around the font which marked the middle of the line. A memorial window to the author Rider Haggard contained many interesting images, including St Michael holding a flaming sword, the pyramids of Egypt, sacred Druidic leaves, a chalice, serpent, and six-pointed star. The other churches that marked the route of the Mary current on her way towards the south-west, were found to be:

St Mary's at Denton, which has another of Norfolk's 119 distinctive round towers, this time with a square one built on top of it, a most peculiar feature.

All Saints at Alburgh, which may at one time have been a St Michael church, in a remote position.

Pulham St Mary. A huge church, similar to the last, but this time at least it has an excuse for its size, as it is located in a village. The building is aligned on the current.

St George's, Shimpling, with a round tower, octagonal belfry and steeple all built on one another! The village sign is a dramatic representation of St George engaging in a bout of dragon-slaying.

St Andrew's, Scole, near a crossroads on the banks of the River Waveney.

St Nicholas, Oakley, a large church in an isolated situation. St Nicholas often seems to have replaced St Michael during a wave of re-dedications.

St Mary's, Brome. A delightful church, with round tower, topped by octagonal belfry. Heavy stained-glass, carved columns, knight's tombs and memorials, an uplifting atmosphere. Site of a timber church in the 8th century.

Burgate Church, close to a moated hall.

St Mary's, Rickinghall.

St Margaret's, Wattisfield.

St Mary's, Walsham Le Willows. A dignified and graceful building with many features of interest.

St Mary's at Castle Ditches, near Langham. Surrounded by old trees, in the middle of a private estate. Stained-glass windows of St Mary and St George.

St George's, Stowlangtoft. A grand Medieval church built on a mound, with many treasures, including gargoyles, mythological bench-ends, and quite a few dragons lurking in the woodwork. Dragon-hunters will also note the large and colourful stained-glass window of St George despatching his prey.

St Mary's at Pakenham. Locals call the church 'the synagogue' because of the unusual shape of its tower. A large cruciform building with interesting font displaying phoenixes and elemental emblems.

Holy Innocents, Great Barton. Aligned on the current, it is an imposing place, very different from the other churches, reflecting its proximity to Bury St Edmunds, just a couple of miles away.

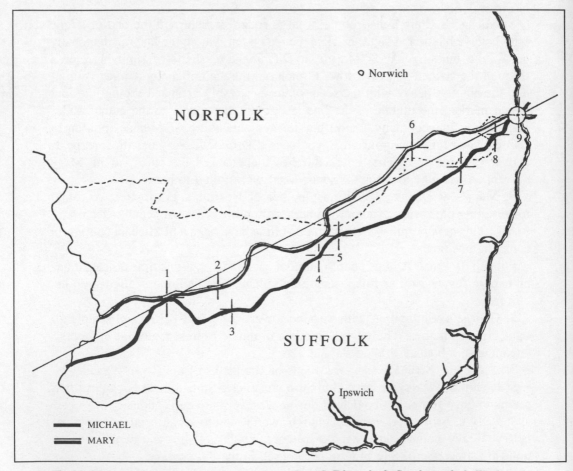

The Michael and Mary currents in East Anglia: 1. Bury St Edmunds; 2. Stowlangtoft; 3. Woolpit; 4. Eye; 5. Hoxne; 6. Ditchingham; 7. Beccles; 8. Somerleyton; 9. St Margaret's, Hopton.

A JEWELLED SHRINE

Perhaps if Henry VIII had not so desperately wanted to divorce his first wife, the grandeur that was Bury St Edmunds Abbey would still exist. In his crazed destruction of the monastic system in an effort to divest the old Church of its power, all the great centres of learning were obliterated. The great libraries of Glastonbury, containing many rare works of extreme antiquity, were lost. Throughout the length and breadth of the land, priceless treasures and buildings were smashed without mercy.

But something was also happening on a deeper level. The monasteries and abbeys were situated on previously sacred sites, reflecting their role as important components in the subtle energy system of Britain. The dissolution of this system, and its subsequent neglect, may well have had consequences about which we can only conjecture. There has never been such a time in English history when the ancient places of the Earth Spirit were abandoned so ruthlessly.

Centuries after the burial of St Edmund, Bury St Edmunds Abbey had become one of the largest, richest and most famous in Europe. Its abbots went to extraordinary lengths to enlarge their collections of holy relics, and pilgrims royal, noble, ecclesiastical and common brought such treasures with them that the glorious shrine within the heart of the abbey glittered with gold, jewels and all manner of precious artefacts. In the twelfth century, the Normans added their

The ruins of the once-magnificent Abbey at Bury St Edmunds.

own glories, erecting a magnificent tower to serve as the main gateway to the great abbey.

The place also left its stamp on the common law of England, for within its walls the barons of the land gathered on the saint's feast day in 1214 to plan their opposition to King John, an act which led directly to the granting of the Magna Carta.

Today, the magnificence has vanished, and the ruins convey little of their former importance. Over the centuries, a quaint collection of curious dwellings has been built into the remains of the West Front, and the towering Norman gateway along with the medieval churches of St Mary and St James are all that remains. The greatness of Bury St Edmunds is preserved only in its history.

After the rustic charms of the East Anglian countryside, it made a pleasant change to be walking through the streets of the old market town on the River Lark. We strolled in the sunlight across the central square, past the Angel Hotel, made famous by Dickens as a regular haunt of Mr Pickwick, and through the fifteenth-century gatehouse. Inside, a relaxed haven of greenery led to the ruins of the Abbey, a very different place from the days when it held a shrine of rich magnificence. St Edmund's shrine was so encrusted with gold plates, crosses and jewelled works of art that when the King's men came to lay it waste, they found it very difficult to deface. They did, however, manage to carry away a number of cartloads of precious metals and rare jewels after their exertions.

We had half-expected to find a node in the remains of the abbey. Both the Michael and Mary currents led into the ruins, but how they performed when they met was very unusual. In the centre of the Choir, they came together, but did not cross. Rather, they 'kissed'. They joined briefly only to veer off on their respective routes. The point at which they fused was not dowseable as a node.

The Michael current proceeded along the axis of the abbey buildings, through the West Front with its picturesque cottages, and exactly through the most impressive of Bury's remaining buildings, the great Norman tower. Set into either side of this immense structure was a superb dragon's head, of a style that neither of us had come across before. They reminded us of Aztec or Mayan dragons rather than 12th century Norman. They seemed to have been put there specifically to mark the tower as a place of the dragon.

In Chequers Square, there was another surprise. The corner of a

One of the twin dragon heads on Bury's great Norman tower.

A half-hidden Masonic emblem at the lodge in Chequers Square, built in the flow of the St Michael energy.

modern building extended out into the flow of the current. Its lower windows were boarded or bricked-up. Stained-glass windows contained familiar symbols, of six-pointed stars, the square and compasses, the 'eye in the triangle'. It was a Masonic Lodge.

Other Masonic buildings were usually grand in design, yet this one seemed to be deliberately built to be as inconspicuous as possible. The boarded-up windows could mean only one thing—that it was within this room, directly in the influence of the Michael current which flowed through the imposing Norman tower, that Masonic rites were enacted.

'Mary' ran through the Abbey gardens and the 15th century gatehouse. This meant that both gatehouses marked the path of the currents. She continued across Angel Hill and up Abbeygate Street, passing through the Matthew Manning Centre, where one of the country's most famous spiritual healers is based. The gentle, healing energy of the Mary line was apparently being put to very good use.

THE OLD TRACK TO THE CAVE

'As he spoke: 'This is my palace' . . . a light began to glow and to pervade the cave, and to obliterate the stone walls and the antique hieroglyphics engraven thereon and to melt the earthen floor into itself like a fiery sun suddenly uprisen within the world, and there was everywhere a wandering ecstasy of sound; light and sound were one; light had a voice, and the music hung glittering in the air . . . 'I am Aengus; men call me the Young. I am the sunlight in the heart, the moonlight in the mind; I am the light at the end of every dream, the voice forever calling to come away; I am desire beyond joy or tears. Come with me . . . for my palace opens into the Garden of the Sun . . .'

A.E. (George Russell)

MARCH 25th, 1989. On the outskirts of Bury, the Michael current passed through both St Peter's Church and the nearby Westgate Chapel to leave the town at Glastonbury Road. A few miles away we found ourselves at Ickworth House, the grotesque creation of Frederick Harvey in the eighteenth century, with its domed rotunda and quite astonishing incongruity. We were pleased to discover that the line gave the house a very wide berth.

In the park, designed by Capability Brown, it went through the porch and tower of the gloomy and neglected private church belonging to the estate. We were very glad to get back to open country and discover the little church at Chedburgh, built on a raised mound, marking the route. Unfortunately, it was locked and we could not discover its dedication.

All Saints Church at Wickhambrook made up for this with its old oak porch, Saxon font and charming air of past glories. Norman heads looked down to the brook that flows past the disused 13th century door, and the Michael line ran through the tower, porch and Lady Altar. Two miles away was Stradishall Church, an ancient, moody place that looked as though it had been painstakingly prepared to feature in a Gothic horror film. Peeling plaster and cobwebs hung in the dusty sunlight and the pews had not smelt polish for at least a century. It was forgotten and deserted but beautiful in its decay, the Marie Celeste of country churches.

All Saint's at Great Thurlow was aligned on the flow, as was St Mary's at Withersfield, with its interesting collection of carved bench-ends that included St Michael and St George. Past a pub at Bartlow named *The Three Hills* after prominent local tumuli that marked the route, we came to Hadstock Church which was also aligned.

At Ickleton, the beautiful St Mary's Church, a former Benedictine Priory with its octagonal spire and impressive carvings, held many delights. The visitor is greeted on entering by the image of St Michael holding a balance, and St George in a window looks triumphantly down on his defeated dragon. As the eyes grow accustomed to the light, another dragon, this one double-headed, plus one of the most extraordinary collections of medieval wall-paintings in the country, begin to come to life. Every available space seems to be crammed with lively figures parading across the old walls, all in an excellent state of preservation. It must be the only church in Britain with the rather astonishing sight of a bare-breasted Mary Magdelane. A memorial plaque to Sir Robert George Wyndham Herbert recalls that, amongst other things, he was the chancellor of the Order of St Michael and St George. It is altogether a remarkable place. The day of our visit, there had been a service just an hour or so before, and the atmosphere was electric. It was Easter Sunday.

It occurred to us that the prefix 'Ick', as in Ickleton and, previously, Ickworth, might have some significance. Both of these places, each important in their own divergent ways, marked the route of the Michael current to the east of Bury St Edmunds, and it seemed interesting they both shared this common link. We were musing over this as we tracked the line through the Cambridgeshire countryside when we came across something that was to make us, for the time being at least, forget the landscape of Medieval, Norman or Saxon England. What we were to discover next was to take us right back to the earliest times of human existence, demonstrating that a sympathy with the terrestrial currents was indisputably central to prehistoric life.

As we drove down an insignificant country lane, we registered the Michael current passing through a crossroads. The old trackway down which it ran was cobbled, the stones worn smooth by use, and had a strong atmosphere. It was the Icknield Way, the ancient route along which countless thousands of people have passed from Paleolithic to Medieval times. Following the old track eventually leads into the Wiltshire countryside, to join with the Ridgeway, that other prehistoric path that terminates at Avebury.

We walked in the footsteps of those that had gone before, and found that the trackway almost exactly followed the course of the Michael current. At some points, it ran a few feet or yards to one side, then returned to join the path. There seemed little doubt that the wanderers of early times and the pilgrims of later days had followed the course of the Earth Spirit as it glided over the surface of the English countryside. They had continued a tradition that was rooted in another age as they had walked east or west to visit the old shrines, establishing a rapport with the secret rhythms and energies of the planet.

THE CAVE

Following the route of the Icknield Way leads the traveller to the Hertfordshire town of Royston. As you stand at the crossroads in the centre of town, all the

Tracking the St Michael current along the prehistoric Icknield Way.

bustle of modern life surrounds you, and traffic rumbles through oblivious to the immense antiquity of the place. A few feet away lies an ancient stone, the *Roy Stone*, which has been hollowed out to accept a Christian cross in later times and is thought to derive its name from some former connection with rites associated with royalty. It marks the crossing of two of the 'Royal Roads' of Britain, the Icknield Way and Ermine Street, which, according to the Welsh monk Geoffrey of Monmouth, were sacred highways built on the orders of the ancient British King Belinus.

Beneath a grating in the pavement, hidden from the eyes of passers-by, is a most remarkable monument to the one-time sanctity of the place. Royston Cave is of unknown origin, and was lost and forgotten until August, 1742, when workmen digging a hole came upon a millstone sunk into the ground. Beneath it was a cavity, into which were lowered a boy and then a man. It was the shaft of a cave, half-filled with earth and debris, which was enthusiastically excavated in the hope of finding treasure, mainly at night to avoid the unwelcome attentions of crowds of onlookers.

No treasure other than a few fragments of bone were found. What did reveal itself, though, was a unique subterranean chamber that has no parallel in western Europe. A bell-shaped chamber, 30 feet high and cut in the solid chalk, was covered in a series of strange carvings that many authorities agree may go back to prehistoric times. Among them is a *Sheela-na-Gig*, a pagan goddess of fertility. Many of the other carvings are symbolic representations of the Christian mysteries in a pageant of images that is a remarkable blend of both Pagan and Christian elements.

The first to make drawings of the carvings was William Stukeley, who received a badly written, ill spelt letter from local M.P. William Goodhall: 'You being a Person very Curious in Things of Antiquity, I thought it would Oblige you to give a short Account of a Place thought to be a very Grate Curiosity Latly discovered in the Town'. Stukeley immediately rode to Royston and recorded the sculpted reliefs, which include crucifixion scenes and figures of saints, the most prominent being St Catherine, holding a eight-spoked wheel. He was of the opinion that the cave had been a hermitage or oratory made by the Foundress of Royston, Lady Roisa de Vere.

Recently it has been shown that the Knights Templar had a connection with Royston, and attended the weekly market from their headquarters at Baldock nine miles away. It is very tempting to suggest that the Templars, with their blend of Pagan and Christian traditions, may have used the Cave for rites of initiation. There are also other indications of a strong esoteric background; the twelfth-century name for Royston was Crux Roasie, which could, like Stukeley's Foundress, be a memory of Rosicrucian/Templar mysteries enacted in the underground shrine. Also, Royston was, from the twelfth century, a centre of monastic life, and its Augustinian Priory continued without break for nearly four hundred years. Its regal connections seem to have been reinforced with royal visits by James I and later, Charles I, who spent a considerable time in the town.

Royston's Town Clerk was an enthusiastic champion of the Cave as well as a

The remarkable carvings in Royston Cave: Above, Pagan symbols, including a Sheela-na-gig *fertility figure, mingle with Christian images of early crucifixion scenes and St Catherine holding her wheel or sun-disk (below).*

keen morris dancer, who, we were delighted to discover, performed his rustic ritual on Mayday, echoing the ancient tradition. He immediately offered to close his office and unlock the old door that led down into the strange depths below the everyday world. Above, civilization carried on its frenzied activity. Below, we entered a world full of weird but powerful images. The sensory deprivation of everyday stimuli seemed to dissolve the centuries. Anybody standing in the uniquely magical atmosphere of the Cave cannot fail to experience its potency. Its shape, that of an inverted womb, and its images, predominently female, mark it as a place to honour the Earth Goddess. Directly in the centre of the Cave was a node. The Michael and Mary currents crossed, for the first time, in a chamber cut into the Earth itself. We had been led to the Cave via Royston Church, where the Michael energy had passed through the altar and changed direction at the 13th century font. One of the most interesting artefacts in the church had been a medieval statue of the Virgin Mary, *Our Lady of Royston*.

There was no doubt in our minds that Royston Cave was one of those mythical entrances into the Otherworld, situated at a place where the earth currents fuse to create energies that may be used to penetrate the veils of matter, traditionally a spot where illumination may be experienced. Now virtually forgotten, it is, in its way, as powerful a place of transformation as many of the more well-known structures that mark centres of transcendent change. Such a rare example of early rites, complete with its tapestry of magical images, emphasizes once more the crucial role of the Earth's energies in the prehistoric and early Christian religions. We were again led to wondering what other secrets the Earth may conceal directly beneath similar places where nodes existed.

KNIGHTS, QUEENS AND DRAGONS

On tracking the Mary current from Bury St Edmunds, we had found it winding through a pretty Victorian chapel in a cemetery to the west of the town centre. At Westley, it had missed a modern church by a few feet. However, hidden away in a field were the ruins of an ancient church, desolate and forgotten, but marking the flow precisely.

Little Saxham Church boasted a stained-glass window of St Mary above a crest bearing a serpent-entwined staff, besides its early round tower, reputed to be the finest in Suffolk. At the 13th century church of All Saints at Barrow, two medieval minstrels pranced about in the plasterwork above a brass plaque of St George.

At Ousden Church, with its intriguing fat, squat, Norman tower that marked the flow, sheep grazed in the churchyard and all seemed tranquil and serene, a picture of bucolic bliss. St Mary's at Lidgate was equally picturesque in its setting, this time built on a Norman motte and bailey. Inside, the air was sweet with damp mosses and perfumed flowers, all carefully arranged to transform the cold stone into a garden of delights. The charms of the English countryside were a sheer pleasure. But around the next corner was something of a surprise.

We were shaken out of our dreamy state by a startling sight, for out of nowhere, two fearsome dragons loomed up above us. Had the pleasant dream turned into a nightmare? We stared in disbelief at the images confronting us; ancient, eroded effigies of formidable presence. Their mouths leered lasciviously and their wings were very weathered. Each had a prominent erect phallus.

The Mary current ran within a few feet of the gateway they guarded. Beyond, a red-brick tower rose up above the old trees, and a short distance away was the isolated church of All Saints at Kirtling.

Inside, all seemed fairly ordinary, until, down by the altar, one of the most exquisite tomb memorials we had come across met our gaze. White stone columns lavishly decorated with mulberry, oak and vine leaves enclosed the

A seventeenth-century dragon guards the entrance to the site of Kirtling Manor.

effigy of Roger, 2nd Baron North, lying in state in full armour. Dragons crawled all over the decoration as if we had disturbed a hidden lair. The dignified figure of Sir Roger rested his feet on yet another dragon, its mouth shooting forth a forked iron tongue.

Sir Roger had been a powerful man. He was born at Kirtling, where his family had bought the manor, which had originally been Norman, in the 16th century. His father had been treasurer to Henry VIII during the dissolution of the monasteries. Later, he had supported Lady Jane Grey and Mary Tudor and had also found favour with Queen Elizabeth I, who, according to local tradition, was 'entertained' at Kirtling during her sister's reign. Roger had been a knight of the shire and entered the House of Commons and House of Lords. He had also been a diplomat who had intimate dealings with Catherine de Medici and Henry III of France. He entertained Elizabeth lavishly when she stayed at Kirtling, and she appointed him Treasurer of her household. He died in 1600, and, after a funeral service at St Paul's was buried in the magnificent tomb, complete with the protection of its brood of dragons.

The tower, all that now remains of the old manor house, is, along with its moat (the largest in Cambridgeshire), another indication of the one-time importance of this remote spot. It is difficult not to imagine some connection between the historical associations of such a place and the fact that it is built on a site through which flows the Mary energy. It is as if certain members of the British aristocracy knew all about such matters; one recalls the Hermetic statue at Somerleyton House, and the many other old estates and houses which are built on the terrestrial currents. The fondness of the North family for dragons may well have been an allusion to this, and the effigy of Sir Roger with his feet on a chained dragon could be symbolic of the taming of the raw Earth energy after the manner of the images of St Michael and St George.

The feet of Elizabethan treasurer Sir Roger North rest on a chained dragon in Kirtling Church.

THE HILL OF THE GIANTS

Four churches in quick succession followed Kirtling, those of Little Ditton, Stetchworth, Dullingham and Westley Waterless, the latter an interesting example with unusual 13th century sepulchral slabs. The church guide says it may have derived its dedication of St Mary the Less from *'St Mary in the Leys . . .'*

As 'Mary' crossed the countryside south-east of Cambridge, she led across the Gog Magog Hills to the site of Wandlebury Rings, an impressive 'hill-fort' of concentric earthworks that is now a country park and nature reserve. In the central enclosure, the current ran right through the middle of a dew-pond, an original prehistoric feature. Knowing Mary's predilection for water, this seemed particularly appropriate, although the pond was dry and treated more like a rubbish dump than an archaeological feature. The hill itself is the site of some most unusual chalk-cut figures located by the Cambridge archaeologist and dowser Tom Lethbridge, which he thought to represent the old Pagan Gods, Gog and Magog.

The churches of Great Shelford, Newton, Foxton and All Saints at Melbourn led us back to Royston, where, after passing through the cave, the Mary line ran through the old *Roy Stone* itself, with its hollowed basin full of rainwater. Royston's town clerk had explained to us how, until recently, it had been positioned on the opposite side of the crossroads, but the local people had felt it would be far better moved over to the other side. The intuition of Royston's inhabitants seemed to be fortuitous, for it had evidently been placed in precisely the right position.

ON THE TRAIL OF THE TEMPLARS

EASTER MONDAY, 1989. The Hertfordshire town of Baldock is Templar territory. The large church of St Mary's is situated at the junction of three ancient roads, and was rebuilt and served by chaplains of the Order of the Knights Templar when they were granted lands by the Church. As guardians of the pilgrim routes and protectors of travellers on their way to the shrines of Medieval Christendom, they could hardly have chosen a better position.

We had tracked the Michael current from Royston, along the Icknield Way, to the centre of town. It just scraped through a corner of the George and Dragon Pub to enter the church, where it ran diagonally through the tower and Lady Altar. The nature of the quest was changing, though. The pastoral pleasures of the East Anglian countryside seemed far behind; it was rapidly being replaced by the dubious delights of twentieth-century civilization.

The sprawling housing estates of Letchworth made following the current difficult. The whole landscape had been re-styled according to the plans of modern architects. Two churches were 'dead', with no dowseable energy connections. A third, however, called 'The Church on the Way', was right alongside the Icknield Way, and was situated on the flow. Disguised as a series of modern roads with all the paraphenalia of the townscape, the old route carried on regardless.

Just outside Letchworth was Ickleford, where, in the old days, the Icknield Way crossed the River Hiz. A bridge now supplanted the old ford, yet there was a special charm to the place. A 'green lane' (part of the old route) led directly to the church lych gate, and, following the current, aligned with the old church. It was a pagan sort of place, with Norman gargoyles and a 'Green Man' with holes in him like a colander where foliage was once inserted to bring the image to life. Right next door was a pub, 'The Green Man'. Concessions to Christianity were made by the church architecture and a stained-glass window of St Michael.

The old pilgrim route exactly marked the current for the next few miles, veering off to visit Deacon Hill and leaving the track as we approached the outskirts of Luton. Surely, we thought, there could be nothing left of ancient significance in such a ravaged landscape?

Dicing with death in the heavy traffic as we dowsed our way through the north of the town, we came upon a group of massive fourteen-storey tower blocks called 'Five Springs', a memory of the time when this place was open countryside where springs rose to the surface to form the source of the River Lea. From their lofty isolation, they peered down onto a most unexpected oasis of greenery, surrounded by trees. In the middle of the concrete jungle was an ancient earthwork, a place of magic and beauty, called Waulud's Bank, which some archaeologists, we were later to find, thought to be contemporary with Avebury.

The Michael current crossed at the junction of Henge Way and Waulud's Bank Road and ran through the earthwork to a mound on the southern side. It struck us as remarkable that a place such as this should have escaped the devastation of development when the landscape all around it had been sacrificed for industry and housing. Perhaps, we mused, the *genius loci* had adopted some form of magical protection . . .

Outside Luton, we followed the Icknield Way Path to the most famous religious establishment in Bedfordshire, the great monastic church of Dunstable Priory. Founded by Henry I in about 1131, it became a priory of Augustinian canons opposite his 'palace' of Kingsburie until a series of disasters in the year 1222. In June, the roof fell in and during a December storm the two western towers were brought down, demolishing the west front and the prior's house. From then until the spring of 1540, when an act of Parliament dissolved the great monasteries after a relentless campaign on the smaller houses, the great Priory was rebuilt in various stages. Situated on the main route between London and the Midlands, it was a sort of free hotel where all travellers could request hospitality, and by the Rule of the House, never be refused. It was the scene of many turbulent events, including the blasphemous Puritan baptism of a sheep at the font.

Despite the complex tapestry of the Priory's history and the destruction of much of its ancient remains, it is still a place of impressive grandeur. Its lofty arches and spacious doorways are built on the Michael current, although the only reference to any connection with the saint is that there was once an ancient altar of the Holy Cross and All Angels, perhaps an old memory of the archangel in the same way that churches often dedicated to All Saints or All Angels were once the domain of St Michael, leader of the heavenly hosts. As a final reminder, though, that the established Church was not the only one to inherit old sites situated on the channels of the terrestrial Spirit, we noticed that the large Methodist Church opposite the Priory also marked its route.

MARY AND THE KNIGHTS OF THE TEMPLE

It was time to head back to Templar territory, and we were to discover that they had not only situated their headquarters at Baldock on the Michael current, but had apparently achieved a suitably esoteric equilibrium by establishing themselves firmly on its counterpart as well. They have always been considered to be guardians of the Mysteries, and perhaps this helps to explain why nine poor knights founded a brotherhood that became so powerful that it threatened the Church of Rome. The greatest of the medieval romancers, Wolfram Von Eschenbach, conferred on them the most exalted status when he referred to them as the keepers of the Holy Grail in his epic romance, *Parzival*.

The first stop was St Mary's at Wallington, which boasts a memorial plaque to a certain Eric Blair, better known to the world as George Orwell. The beautiful little church of St Mary's at Clothall had all the atmosphere of a superb piece of geomancy. It was built on a mound next to a Roman Road, and the Mary current ran right down the centre of the building, through the font and altar. It also passed through Weston Church and the ruins of an ancient church to St Ethelreda near Graveley before visiting the site of a Templar Priory at Little Wymondley.

After tracking it through a huge rectangular earthwork at St Ippollitts we were led to what was once the large Templar Priory at Temple Dinsley, now a school. The distinctive Templar church of St Martin's at Preston was also on the energy flow, and had an unusual feeling that made the slanting evening sunlight that filtered through the old trees seem strangely mystical, like molten gold.

As we found the line going through St Mary's at King's Walden, we could see and hear the sprawl of Luton a few miles away and wondered whether we would have to spend another frustrating few hours following it through the heavily built-up area. We were lucky. 'Mary' travelled south, through the country park of Luton Hoo to a rather gloomy Victorian church built in 1892 on an ancient site. A similarly dismal place was St Mary's at Whipsnade. She then passed, for some inexplicable reason, through the entrance to Whipsnade Park Zoo!

THE BEACON

In the mid-18th century, a foreign visitor looked down from the top of the Ivinghoe hills and recorded that the vale below Ivinghoe Beacon was neatly laid out in meadows like well-kept gardens. These were the successors to the Celtic field strips which gave the English countryside so much charm in the old days; today, the scene is beautiful in a different way. The small hedged fields created by enclosing the land are reminiscent of the works of pastoral water-colourists.

Lying on the Icknield Way, close to the ancient British Roads of Akeman Street and Watling Street, the 'hill-fort' that crowns the Beacon was a centre for both Celts and Saxons, a focus for the fire-rituals that punctuated their annual cycle. It now belongs to the National Trust, and the 800 foot climb to its summit is rewarded by a panorama of the Chilterns, the Quainton Hills and the Dunstable Downs. It also lies directly in the path of the Mary current.

Ever since Royston Cave, 'Mary' had been running south of 'Michael', which had been following the route of Icknield Way. Now, a change had occurred. Michael had left the ancient pilgrim route at Dunstable, moving over to make way for Mary, who joined it at Ivinghoe Beacon. As if to emphasise some intangible difference, the route changes its name at this point to the *Lower Icknield Way*.

The charm of the countryside extends to St Mary's Church at Ivinghoe, where its roof is decorated with the outspread wings of carved angels, and its great timbers rest on grotesque heads of strange people and animals. It is aligned on the current, and, in a curious custom that seems to connect this place with distant Avebury, the villagers used, in former times, to hold a 'Fig Fair', a description of which was recorded in 1712: *'We have also a certain custom for the youth of this and neighbouring parishes to meet under Beacon Hill upon Palm Sunday to eat figs and drink ale brought thither for that purpose . . .'* In the same century, William Stukeley wrote of the Fig Fair at Avebury: *'The country people have an anniversary meeting on the top of Silbury Hill on every Palm Sunday, when they make merry with cakes, figs, sugar and water fetched from the swallowhead, or spring, of the Kennet.'* Such a connection seems particularly intriguing, as the Mary current links these places with its flowing energies. We could be looking at the memory of an archaic ritual that in some way celebrated this.

MARY AND THE PILGRIM ROUTE

For the next twenty or so miles, the Mary current coincided with the Lower Icknield Way occasionally leaving it to visit the following churches:

    All Saints at Marsworth
    All Saints at Buckland
    St Michael and All Saints at Aston Clinton
    St Mary the Virgin at Weston Turville
    St Nicholas at Great Kimble
    St Andrews at Chinnor
    St Peter and St Paul at Aston Rowant
    St Margarets at Lewknor
    St Leonards at Cuxham
    St Bartholemews at Brightwell Baldwin

Travelling through the Buckinghamshire countryside in early May was a sheer delight, with trees heavy with apple and cherry blossom that perfumed the air of sleepy villages with a heady aroma. It was almost as if we were caught up in a delicious dream, full of sensuous experiences. At St Andrews, Chinnor, a superbly carved pulpit showed the winding pilgrim route stretching over the verdant English countryside. At the point where the road disappeared into the horizon, the sun rose in great splendour. It was difficult not to see in this a profound symbolic representation of the old Icknield Way and its connection with the forces of the Earth and Sun. Other panels depicted similar scenes from lands far distant, all with the same powerful imagery. Just across the Oxfordshire border, we found the current passing through the gatehouse of Shirburn Castle.

St Michael And The Maharishi

MAY 4th 1989. Tracking the Michael current from Dunstable, we were led to the churches of St Giles at Totternhoe, St Mary at Eaton Bray and All Saints at Slapton. At Mentmore, St Mary's Church was perfectly aligned, and something nagged away at the back of our minds. The name of the place seemed to ring a bell. We talked to a lady in the churchyard and she admitted, with vague embarrassment, that the 'house' had been taken over by some rather strange characters who wandered about in robes. She was referring to the stately home of Mentmore Towers, situated in its expansive grounds behind the church. Then we remembered. The Maharishi Mahesh Yogi had recently bought it as a 'Centre of Enlightenment'.

This had intriguing implications. First, it looked as though the Maharishi, the founder of the world-wide Transcendental Meditation movement, was aware that Mentmore was situated on the St Michael current. Secondly, it seemed that he considered it an ideal place as a headquarters for the mind-expansion techniques that are the basis of 'TM', which could perhaps be enhanced by the terrestrial energies, and finally, with his aim to create 'World Enlightenment' through spiritual means, it appeared that he may be involved in stimulating the energies themselves in some way. Was one of his objectives to work with the energies of the St Michael Line to trigger a shift in human consciousness, as envisaged by other mystics who had also thought in terms of a 'St Michael' renaissance? The question of it all being a coincidence seemed to tax the imagination beyond the bounds of credulity. The fact that Mayer Rothschild, of the influential banking family, had bought Mentmore in 1850 also seemed to point to other tantalizing implications.

The magnificent medieval gem of All Saints at Hulcott was the next stop, with its village green glinting in the sunlight and its wooden belfry sheltering birds that seemed to sing louder than elsewhere. At Bierton, the church was aligned. Across the rich Buckinghamshire pastureland, the old market town of Aylesbury stood on its hill in the heart of the county, overlooking the Vale which stretches from the borders of Bedfordshire to those of Oxfordshire. We found ourselves at a pleasant cemetery on the outskirts, where two beautiful little Victorian chapels no more than fifty feet apart looked out over guardian stone angels and tranquil gardens. The current ran diagonally through them both and continued to another Victorian edifice, the Church of the Holy Trinity at Walton, a short distance away.

It then led through the grounds of Hartwell House, in fact precisely through the large ornamental gateway that is the main entrance. We discovered that Stone Church was aptly named; in front of the porch is a remarkable square monolith, a huge, powerful stone, hollowed out into a trough and planted with sweet peas and other plants. There can be no doubt that it is of immense antiquity, with its dark ironstone-coloured surface smothered with a tapestry of lichen and moss. The current flows right through it.

THE FOLLY

For a couple of miles, the Michael serpent virtually followed the main A418 road. Then, an interesting sight loomed. Half-hidden in a copse of old trees by the roadside was a ruined tower. Dinton Castle was a very romantic ruin, an ivy-draped octagonal structure incorporating many fossils, including trilobites and ammonites. There appeared to be little doubt that it had been built as a folly, for its eccentricities were typical of all the best idiosyncratic traditions of quaintness and curiosity. Later research showed it to have been constructed by John Vanhatten in 1769, evidently for his collection of fossils. However, he must have known, by intellect or intuition, exactly where to place it, for it lies directly in the path of the current.

The ruined folly of Dinton Castle.

At Haddenham, the church which marks the energy is on the edge of the village, flanked by ancient thatched cottages and a large duckpond. Those in search of dragons in such a picturesque setting may pause for refreshment at 'The Dragon' pub opposite, or explore the twisting lane called 'The Dragon's Tail', cautiously poking the undergrowth to arouse any fire-breathing beasts that may lurk within.

A few miles down the road, the beautiful Rycote Chapel was built aligned on the flow, a place of singular presence with an ancient gnarled Yew tree guarding it. At Cuddesdon church (All Saints), the line passed through an old stone cross, raised on a plinth near the porch. One of the loveliest of the Oxfordshire villages, its evocative church is built on a prominent mound and is of considerable size and antiquity. Until 1644 the Palace of the Bishops of Oxford was located here, when it, along with the manor house, was burnt down to prevent it falling into the hands of the Parliamentarians. Its history can be read in stone. The fine architecture of the 12th century building demonstrates its one-time importance, and inside, the place is full of memorials to forgotten bishops who ruled from this place. It seems strange that the powerful churchmen of a place such as Oxford should have chosen to have their headquarters at Cuddesdon. Perhaps they understood something about it that was not generally recognized.

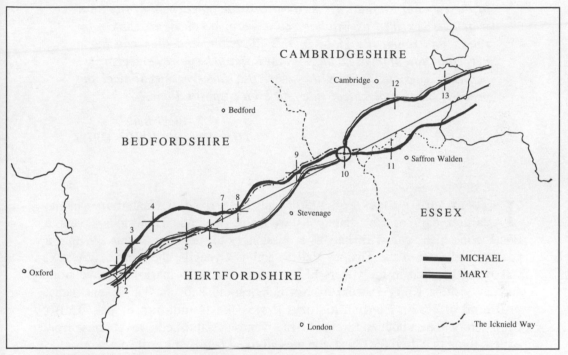

The Michael and Mary currents from Cambridgeshire to the Oxfordshire border: 1. Dinton; 2. Chinnor; 3. Aylesbury; 4. Mentmore; 5. Ivinghoe Beacon; 6. Whipsnade; 7. Dunstable; 8. Luton (Waulud's Bank); 9. Baldock; 10. Royston; 11. Ickleton; 12. Wandlebury Rings; 13. Kirtling.

Chapter Nine

WANDERING WESTWARDS

'The instrument of the spiritual activities in impelling the movements of the races of Man always westward, is the magnetism of the Sun, which is described as winding, as it were, a coil of invisible wire round and round the globe in this direction, and thus causing a perpetual flow of physical or, perhaps it would be more correct to say, aetheric, energies towards the west. But however mechanical the process, it has a psychical side and even a spiritual one.'

F. Bligh Bond
THE HILL OF VISION (1919)

THIRTY-EIGHT YEARS after St Augustine arrived at Canterbury, in the earliest days of Christianity as we know it, Pope Honorious I sent a Benedictine monk called Birinus as a missionary to the West Saxons. Within a year he had reached the Thames Valley, and as Cynegils, the King of Wessex, was being baptised in the waters of the River Thame to mark his conversion, another visiting King, Oswald of Northumbria, looked on. This event had a profound effect on English history: It was the foundation of post-Celtic Christianity in the south and west of Britain and it established a royal house from which, through Alfred the Great, the present royal family traces its descent.

The spot where this occurred was on the banks of the Thames at what is now Dorchester in Oxfordshire, a place that might well have become the capital of England if Fate had taken a slightly different turn. Even in prehistoric times Dorchester was a centre of great importance, and has been a place of continuous settlement for at least the last six thousand years. The site of a massive Henge known as the Big Rings, together with other remains of a Neolithic ritual complex were discovered in the summer of 1938, only to be destroyed later by gravel quarrying. The rescue excavations revealed one of the classic Neolithic sites of Britain, which included a great cursus, or long, straight earthwork stretching over the countryside, dated to 3,000 BC.

In the Iron and Bronze Ages it continued as a focal point, as the excavated artefacts testify. The Roman invasion overlaid the Ancient British traditions with different gods, and an altar to Jupiter has been found. Over a thousand years later, the country was Christianized, and new invaders, the Normans, built a remarkable abbey on the course of terrestrial force that wound through the valley, crossing the old Celtic River Goddess of the Thames or Isis to lead off to the magnificent 'fortress' on Sinodun (Castle) Hill. The Abbey, an exquisite 200-foot long building sitting astride the female Mary current is a reminder of the one-time significance of what looks today simply a small country village of great charm.

Its outstanding treasures are a superb Norman font of lead, one of the finest in England, with 12 graceful figures sitting beneath arches curling with greenery, and a stained-glass window recounting the history of St Mary between finely-carved tree branches of stone on which stand the original Norman figures. It is a place of great, but simple, dignity.

We had tracked the Michael current through St Mary's at Garsington, looking out from the side of its hill across the green countryside, to the most unusual church of St Peter's at Marsh Baldon, where its peculiar tower transforms itself from square to octagonal almost as if it had grown organically from the rich soil. Then, we had been led to one of the most beautiful of St Michael churches, at Clifton Hampden, built on an astonishingly steep mound and set in archetypally English countryside on the banks of the Thames. From the lower slopes, it looks like a place from a fairy tale. From its summit, one can see the ancient arched brick bridge spanning the river which snakes its way across the landscape. At the water's edge, young couples lay in the sun whilst others floated lazily by in punts and dinghies.

The inside of the church has great charm. A carved wooden St Michael glows deep brown in the rood-screen, with elaborate early designs decorating woodwork and polished brass, burnished with jewelled light from the windows. Not far away from the church on its conical hill, we found an odd stone pillar situated near the road, exactly in the centre of the current. Like a miniature Nelson's column, it stood enigmatically in a field beyond the trees.

St Mary's at Long Wittenham had its curiosities, too. It was built on the site of a wooden Saxon church, erected on a previously sacred spot. Dragons and griffins clamber over the choir stalls, on which men and women are bound together, apparently a symbolic representation of the perennial bondage of the sexes. An outstanding 12th century lead font had bishop-figures and spiral motifs cast and carved into it, and the ancient oak porch was brought from Lincoln Cathedral. In its own way, it was as quietly spectacular as the previous church.

Wittenham Clumps is a large earthwork of ten acres enclosed by a ditch and rampart, classified as a 'hillfort'. Commanding panoramic views of the Thames Valley, it also looks out to the Berkshire Downs, where a series of similar upland enclosures follow the line of the ancient Ridgeway. The Michael dragon line curves right through it to lead to an even more impressive prehistoric place: Sinodun Hill—'a regional administrative and political centre, performing the same functions as a medieval market town'. It has always been known as an influential place, and has survived the erosion of Nature and the destruction of Man despite their best attempts to change it. In the *Saturday Review* of July 2nd, 1870, an article reminds us that the loss of ancient countryside is not wholly a modern phenomenon:

'...the fortress at Dorchester and the fortress on Sinodun are among the most speaking monuments of the early history of our island, and till lately they were among its most perfect. But it is a grievous truth that while we are writing the dykes at Dorchester are being levelled. Hitherto the neighbouring ground has been grazed and the harmless sheep is no foe to history; but it has lately occurred to the owner of the ground that a few shillings more of yearly profit might be gained by turning pasture land into arable; and to such a sordid motive as this these precious antiquities are at this very moment being sacrificed.'

The lower earthworks were lost, but the farmer was eventually persuaded to leave the central enclosure. It was almost as if the Spirit of the place had to protect that particular area above everything else. Today it has the atmosphere of a hilltop Sacred Grove, with a ring of great trees growing within the earthen bank and ditch. It is another of those special, magical places that seem to preserve a rare glimpse of how the countryside once was, a sanctuary of ancient intimacy with Nature. In the spring, yellow cowslips glow in golden-green light filtering through the stained-glass leaves, and it is impossible not to recall that churches are built to echo such natural places of sanctuary; fluted columns imitate the old trees, whose branches entwine to form a canopy where nature spirits peer down like the gargoyles and grotesques in a country church. Ivy and creeping foliage that is often carved on fonts and bench-ends here decorates wood that is alive and pulsing with energy. Within the ring of trees is a node, a crossing point where the Michael current merges with the Mary, on its way from Dorchester Abbey across the Dyke Hills, which, together with Sinodun, form one of the most significant prehistoric centres in southern Britain. Between the branches, one can look out at Wittenham Clumps and the distant Abbey and visualize the two streams of energy flowing through the landscape to join in the twilight of the shady grove.

To the south of Sinodun Camp the Michael line looked as though it was heading for the church of All Saints at North Moreton, but in fact missed the building to go through a delightful 'Fairy Mound' next to it. It carried on through South Moreton, and another ancient mound, to continue to Blewburton Hill, a massive prehistoric earthwork on high ground, and a tumulus called Churn Knob. It crossed the Ridgeway to a place called Land's End and visited Farnborough Church, with two memorable stained-glass windows, one a memorial to Sir John Betjeman who lived at the rectory, the other a striking image of Christ with his feet on a writhing dragon, situated behind the altar. It then ran through two tumuli near South Fawley, where a stone roadside cross marked the centre, and we followed the route across the Hampshire countryside to Aldbourne, where its St Michael's Church, in the heart of the large village, stands in a commanding position. The Domesday Book records the presence of a landowning priest, one of only three in the whole diocese of Salisbury, which indicates its past importance. Its monuments and memorials also tell of its long history. Until the Reformation they included a chapel of considerable beauty built by the local Fraternity of the Blessed Virgin. In 1510, a bell was hung in the tower with the inscription, in

Latin, *'Mary, Star of the Seas, succour us'*. Mary was, in fact, the original dedication of the church, which was changed to St Michael and All Angels shortly afterwards. However, ancient traditions tend to persist, and the country people still keep St Mary's Day, 22nd July, as their annual Feast, while other remnants of the remote past remain, like the startling image of a *Green Man* with glaring eyes and leaves sprouting from the corners of his mouth. A touching gravestone reminds readers of their proper place within the scheme of things, however important their lives might appear:

> *'As you are now so once was I*
> *In Health & Strength: though now I lie*
> *As I am now so must you be,*
> *Therefore prepare to follow me'.*

THE VALE OF THE WHITE HORSE

Before the railway came, Didcot was a tiny village. Relics of its quiet past include some thatched cottages, but its church (All Saints, previously St Michael), with its magnificent 1300 year-old yew tree, now stands in the shadow of an electricity generating station. It was the first building the Mary line went through after leaving Sinodun Camp, and, like the next one at Harwell, was aligned on the current.

This was also the case at St Mary's, East Hendred, a spectacular Victorian edifice that seemed to be a power station of a different sort than the one which glowered on the horizon. Very close by and similarly aligned on the direction of flow was St Augustine's, which provided us with an unforgettable memory. On our arrival a few minutes before six o'clock, it was immediately assumed that we had come to witness the striking of the church's medieval clock, which still operates the bells. In a scene of frantic hilarity, without a moment to explain, we were ushered to climb the worn spiral staircase to the top of the tower, where an ancient, dusty room hid a blacksmith-made clock of some magnificence. Within a few seconds, a great whirring and clacking of early ironmongery filled the lofty chamber, and we were made to run to and fro around the clock to observe the frenetic movements of its machinery. There was no time to lose. From one angle could be observed the large cogs ticking the centuries away, its gears and springs in harmonious tension, about to trigger the striking mechanism. Then there was an explosion of activity as dowser, navigator and clock-keeper all rushed round the other side in unison to see the striker releasing its catches to ring the bells. It was a scene out of Dickens, or a pastiche of Chaplin and Laurel and Hardy. The whole tower shook and the bells were deafening as they pealed their thunderous music out over the countryside. It seemed to go on for an eternity before the metallic roar slowly faded. Standing hundreds of feet above the ground, with our ears still ringing and the medieval timbers still vibrating under our feet, was a memorable experience. It was as if the Gods were providing us with a little light musical divertissement for our labours. It was the dowser's birthday. ✓

We had seen many superb churches in exquisite settings, yet one can never tire of the discovery of hidden treasures. All Saints at the tiny hamlet of East Lockinge is another jewel; a wooden Saxon church once stood in a idyllic situation overlooking a slow, meandering bend in the river, which now comes within a few yards of the building. Tiny waterfalls cascade into rocky pools filled with waterweeds, shaded by old trees growing from the banks. It is a watery sort of spot. The font in the church was one of the biggest we had ever come across.

St Andrews at Letcombe Regis was not far away, followed by the Church of the Holy Cross at Sparsholt, a delapidated but delightful place. We were following the Mary line into the Vale of the White Horse, and from a tumulus marking the current, we could see Whitehorse Hill, with the prehistoric Uffington Castle above. But the hope that we would soon be surveying the Vale from the famous chalk-cut figure, or perhaps from the equally-famous Dragon Hill below, was only wishful thinking. We were led instead to the 'Cathedral of the Vale'—St Mary's at Uffington.

Surrounded by a great wealth of antiquities, it looks out to the Ridgeway which passes Uffington Castle and Wayland's Smithy, an atmospheric long-barrow ringed by trees. From the churchyard, the strange shape of the White Horse can be glimpsed, leaping across the sweeping curves of the downs. The hill below is said to be the site where St George killed the dragon, whose blood, spilt on the

Wayland's Smithy, one of a series of impressive prehistoric monuments around which the Mary current flows.

turf, has since prevented grass from growing on its summit. Across the fertile pasture to the west, a series of natural terraces known as the Giant's Stairs lead through a deep combe called the Manger.

Even in the fourteenth century, the White Horse was famous. A manuscript in Corpus Christi College, Cambridge, referred to it as one of the great wonders of ancient Britain, second only to Stonehenge, and early antiquarians, offended by its 'rude' and 'barbarous' character, later insisted on showing it as a fine Georgian stallion in their engravings. Today it is as striking as it ever was, but it has to be admitted that it is as likely to be the image of a dragon as that of a horse. A single flowing line runs from nose to tail, and the 360-foot-long figure has a peculiar beaked head, filled with a great round eye.

The church had a few dragons, too. St George stood on one in a niche and four other dragons' heads decorated the font. In the north transept was a chapel to St Michael. The map now revealed a curious feature. The current had left the Lower Icknield Way where it petered out on approaching the Thames valley. We had half-expected either it or its counterpart to join up with the Ridgeway leading to Avebury, but in fact Mary was running to the north, virually parallel to the old route, approximately a mile away. It was sweeping in a wide curve around Whitehorse Hill to head south to the large, impressively-built church at Bishopstone, before crossing the Ridgeway at Fox Hill. It then went through a

THE CHURCH OF ST MARY

U·F·F·L·N·G·T·O·N

Scripsit: Leonard N Gerber

long barrow, tumulus and two vanished ancient settlements called Upham and
Snap villages. The Mary current had swung right around the prehistoric centre
that included the White Horse, Uffington Castle, Dragon Hill and Wayland's
Smithy in the same manner that had been observed before at Avebury and other
special sites, as if to enclose it. It was now turning sharply to meet its opposite.
Somewhere in the next few miles we were going to discover another node.

THE MOUND OF THE DRAGON-KILLER

We were back in Wiltshire. The two currents were converging somewhere on
the outskirts of the village of Ogbourne St George. We drove up a narrow road,
got out and walked up a green lane.

The Mary current crossed a short way up and we poked our way through some
trees to see a quite remarkable sight. Standing in a field was a peculiarly-shaped
mound, a startling pointed earthwork over twenty feet high. It was like a great
cone of earth that once had a flat circular terrace all around, now eroded. It lies in
a field near the Roman Road and marks the crossing-point of the Michael and
Mary dragon lines leading deep into the Wiltshire countryside. For this reason we
assumed ancient provenance, but later, it was discovered that a local man had
built it during the Second World War. Such a strange labour raises many
questions. Was he inspired to continue the mound-building tradition by the
influence of this place? If so, was he aware of its peculiar significance? Perhaps
he knew something of the mystery of Ogbourne St George, the name being a

The conical mound in a field at Ogbourne St George.

fusion of Pagan and Christian elements – Og, the Celtic Solar giant and his Christian replacement St George.

The currents drew apart: Michael went through Ogbourne St George Church (one of the key points of the St Michael alignment) and Mary crossed the River Og. They then converged again in the churchyard at Ogbourne St Andrew a couple of miles away. There, a large prehistoric mound was, along with the church, located within a circular raised bank. In the middle of the mound was another node. Trees swayed and tall wildflowers whispered gently in the breeze in another of those secret magical places that understate their true significance. Mary ran directly along the axis of the church into the mound and disappeared off across the Marlborough Downs, through a tumulus on the golf course which has been conveniently converted to a tee. We had found two nodes within a couple of miles of each other, which was unique outside Glastonbury and Avebury, and both had been notable artificial earthen hills. But we were not yet finished with mounds. We were about to come across the largest prehistoric mound of earth in the country, second only to Silbury Hill.

MERLIN'S MOUND

The visitor to Marlborough can easily miss its most formidable ancient monument. Disguised by a thick tangle of trees and undergrowth, hidden behind the college chapel, is Marlborough Mound. Archaeologists now think it may be as old as Silbury itself, which makes it very special. Its legend makes it stand out also, for it is remembered in folklore as the very place where Merlin lies, asleep for aeons after his entanglement with a powerful sorceress. The Normans built a castle on its summit, and Marlborough's royal stature persisted when it later became a residence of King John, whose children were christened at the college.

It was here that John established one of the basic laws of the land in the Statutes of Marlborough, which laid down that no person can invade your property without a warrant, thus creating one of the foundations of civil liberties.

The legends, archaeology and situation of the mound give evidence of its pre-

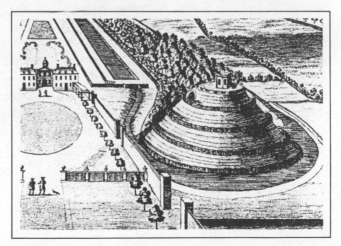

Stukeley's sketch of Marlborough Mound after its conversion into a terraced walk with a summerhouse on top.

historic importance. Red deer antlers, discovered a few feet inside the chalk, were dated to Neolithic times, and it stands near the banks of the River Kennet, which rises near its sister-mound, Silbury. Another spring fed a moat at its foot in Stukeley's time, whilst the smooth chalk sides were cut to create a spiral walk and a curious cave was dug into its side to form a grotto, ornamented with shells. The steep climb to the summit rewarded us with a fine view of the cast iron water tank at the top, a modern replacement for the summerhouse which once adorned it in the days when it was the haunt of eighteenth-century garden parties. We had to admit to a sense of disappointment on the discovery that the Michael current did not pass through it.

It ran very close, though. Within about fifty yards it passed, at a curious offset angle, through Marlborough College Chapel, a great abbey of a place with a carved and gilded interior of rich magnificence. A quartet was playing Greig, and a glance at the roll-call of old boys listed on the painted panelling revealed many famous names. It struck us as very curious that the mound was situated so close to the current, and yet appeared to have no connection. We wondered whether the serpent currents of the Earth could actually move. If they were organic, then there was every likelihood that they were also dynamic. Perhaps the path of the current had shifted at some stage in the past, and the College Chapel had become a later replacement for the spiritual use of the energy? There was a possibility that when the mound's significance had been lost, its Spirit had vacated the ancient hill to take up residence somewhere that was more attuned to its inspirational function.

Leaving Marlborough, we followed the Michael current along the valley of the River Kennet. It went through St George's Church at Preshute, a lovely, isolated place on the banks of the Kennet, to Manton, where, until the early nineteenth century, Michaelmas fairs were held every year. It ran along Lockeridge Dene, a beautiful valley bottom strewn with huge sarsen boulders and surrounded by trees and wild flowers. Some four thousand years ago, six hundred of the largest of these stones were carefully selected and transported to Avebury to build the greatest Temple in Europe. Another eighty or so may have been taken across Salisbury Plain to build Stonehenge. Since that time the stones were plundered for more secular purposes, until the prospect of their total disappearance led a local farmer in 1849 to vow that no more stones should be taken. Today it is still a place of gentle mystery, and one wonders how it must have appeared when the gigantic stones, sculpted into living shapes by Nature, inhabited it. One also wonders whether there could be any significance in the fact that the stones that were to form the two most notable prehistoric monuments of Britain were taken from this place, soaked in the emanations of the Michael current for so many millenia.

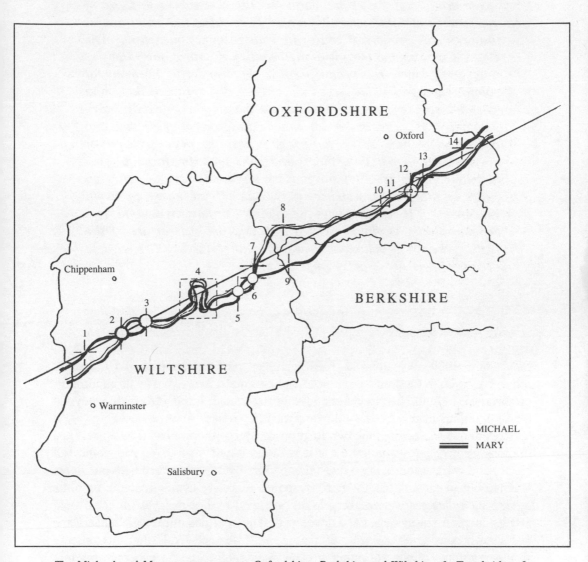

The Michael and Mary currents across Oxfordshire, Berkshire and Wiltshire: 1. Trowbridge; 2. Bowerhill; 3. Oliver's Castle; 4. The Avebury Complex; 5. Ogbourne St Andrew; 6. The mound at Ogbourne St George; 7. Ogbourne St George Church; 8. Uffington; 9. Aldbourne; 10. East Lockinge; 11. East Hendred; 12. Sinodun Hill; 13. Dorchester; 14. Cuddesdon.

RETURN TO THE SERPENT TEMPLE

'Everything that exists on earth is but the transient form of appearance of some celestial agency. Everything terrestrial has its prototype, its primordial cause, its ruling agency in heaven. The Chinese philosopher looking at the beauties of nature, the variety of hills and plains, rivers and oceans, the wonderful harmony of colour, light and shade, sees in it but the dim reflex of that more splendid scenery frescoed in ethereal beauty on heaven's starry firmament. He gazes at the sun, that dazzling regent of the day, and recognizes in him, as his terrestrial reflex, the male principle of creation, ruling everything that is under the sun. He lifts up his eyes to the moon, the beautiful queen of the night, and sees her reflex on earth in the female principle, pervading all sublunary forms of existence . . . He contemplates the spangled firmament at night, and compares with its dimly-reflected transcript on the surface of the earth, where the mountain peaks form the stars, the rivers and oceans answer to the milky way.'

> FENG-SHUI
> *The Science of Sacred Landscape in Old China*
> E.J. Eitel (1873)

MAY 5th, 1989. We stood at The Sanctuary on Overton Hill. To the west, Silbury glowed in mellow mood, aloof and enigmatic as ever. The large tumulus on distant Windmill Hill stood out on the horizon, and, hidden from view beyond the undulations of the Avebury downs, was the Henge.

Beneath our feet crossed the two currents of energy that we had tracked across a dragon-haunted landscape for the last two-and-a-half years. We had come full circle, and were at the end of a quest that had irrevocably changed both our lives. We had become aware that the Earth responds to an awakening recognition of its being. Such changes were detectable on one level by dowsing, as the local field and its currents strengthened and developed. The energies of the St Michael Line had grown considerably since we began, and it seemed likely that this process would continue, and even gather greater momentum, as more people became aware of them. The process is two-way: Human awareness affects the Earth and the Earth in its turn changes human awareness.

The places we had visited and the people we had met all seemed to link together like a jigsaw—the pieces, seen in isolation, were difficult to discern, yet when put together, a picture emerged that revealed history as entirely misunderstood. The people who built Avebury and Stonehenge possessed secrets of the vital Life Force that were once the foundation of civilized society. This civilization, working with the principles of natural science, had gone through a great transition at some remote time, yet the elements of its understanding had persisted in the form of esoteric religion and traditional mythology. The pieces of the jigsaw were still being discovered and fitted into place, but the image that was taking shape was of a landscape; a landscape of immense antiquity, obscured beneath the depredations of history and modern exploitation, but which is of vital significance if we are to re-establish a harmonious rapport with Nature. For hidden in the English countryside are secrets preserved for all time. In its monuments, hills and watercourses, the people of ancient times left clues to the unchanging nature of universal Laws which would outlast humanity itself. Perhaps they knew that one day people who had been deprived of their birthright to live according to these Laws would gaze upon this landscape and once again begin to sense its profound purpose.

For the present, the adventure was drawing to a close. There was, however, a final missing link. William Stukeley's vision of the Serpent Temple had shown a gigantic snake three miles in length laid out upon the Avebury countryside. We had discovered that the head of the serpent, where we stood at the Sanctuary, marked the crossing of the male and female currents, and that the solar, Michael energy exactly followed the course of the serpent's neck down the West Kennet stone avenue. At the Henge, it entered the great circle to merge with the lunar, Mary serpent flowing in from Silbury.

The massive ring of stones, with its two inner circles, was the vessel of fusion, the focus of rites of high magic at the moment of the Sun's appearance at Beltane. But the missing element was the Serpent's tail, the other enormous stone avenue that once led away to the west. Very little is known about the Beckhampton avenue, for it was already gone when John Aubrey came across Avebury in the 17th century. Since then it has largely been ignored, especially by those inhabiting heavily-upholstered armchairs who have seen the idea of a Serpent Temple as preposterous. Research shows, however, that many such structures once existed. At Shap, in Westmoreland, two stone circles were joined by a large avenue, with a smaller one leaving the main ring. Similar avenues formed a serpentine arrangement at many other sites, and the records of antiquarians frequently refer to the widespread existence of avenues leading to a sacred enclosure. In Scotland, serpent mounds have been found, like the one at Loch Nell: 'The head is a large cairn, and the body of the earthen reptile 300 feet long; and in the centre of the head there were evidences . . . of an altar having been placed there . . .'

The only remnants of the Beckhampton avenue still visible are the Long Stones at Avebury Trusloe, once part of the Beckhampton Cove, an arrangement of megaliths apparently in the avenue itself. Other than that, there is nothing except Stukeley's visionary sketch. It seemed a little remarkable, then, that we were about to come into contact with someone who had spent some years investigating the route of the avenue, and even tracking the energy that flowed down it in the same way as we had found at the West Kennet avenue. Another piece of the jigsaw was about to fall into place.

THE SERPENT'S TAIL

Brian Ashley is a dowser who is very much attuned to the Avebury landscape. Perhaps it is not surprising to find him in sympathy with its ancient purpose, for he lives at the heart of its mysteries, within the Henge. He also has some visionary ideas about its future; one of his dreams was to build a Neolithic-style timber 'sanctuary' across the road from the ancient site on Overton Hill. From there, it would have been possible to gaze out across the downs to Silbury, the stone avenue, Windmill Hill, West Kennet Long Barrow and other special places to see the landscape in its interconnected entirety, providing a centre for those who wished to explore the mysteries of the Avebury enigma. The thought of the great conical roofs extending almost to the ground, echoing the original prehistoric structures, seemed to us an inspired idea. Far better than the shabby transport café that currently occupies the site. But there has been much opposition from the planning authorities; perhaps it is an idea ahead of its time.

He had been tantalized by the idea of the Beckhampton stone avenue, and had discovered a current of energy running out from the west of the Henge, along the High Street, past the church and out into the fields of Manor Farm. It was very similar in dimensions to the Michael and Mary currents we had been tracking.

Various stones found incorporated into buildings and hedgerows led him to believe that he was following the 'Beckhampton serpent'—the Serpent's Tail of Stukeley's Temple. It led to the Long Stones, now isolated in the middle of a field, and on through the Longstones Barrow, a large mound near the Beckhampton roundabout. Eventually, it led along the old Bath Road to a most interesting place on Knoll Down.

The Serpent's Tail.

We stood in the shade of old trees, in what was once an earthwork of considerable size. It was wide at the entrance, with a path leading along its length, and as we walked through the dappled sunlight there was the impression that this was something very special. The atmosphere was uplifting. At the far end, it narrowed down dramatically, and the path split in two. So did the energy, which was flowing along the entire earthwork from the spot where two smaller currents merged to form the Beckhampton serpent. Each one issued from a large ram's-horn type spiral, one clockwise, the other anti-clockwise. They were male and female energy vortices, joining together to form the Serpent's Tail.

The female spiral was at the edge of an agricultural field. Standing on the male one, we were outside the trees of the earthwork and from the high position we could see Silbury to the south-east, with the Sanctuary beyond. It was obvious that the three sites were all of the same approximate elevation, and that they were in exact alignment. The Sanctuary was visible directly behind the flat top of the mound, so a dead straight line linked the head and tail of the Serpent, passing across the summit. Suddenly, we experienced a glimpse of one of the purposes of Silbury. The whole crux of the Beltane ritual was to do with timing and we had often wondered how great numbers of people, assembled for the Mayday rite, could be co-ordinated in the dark to arrive at the Henge at the correct time. Silbury was the answer. It was the communications centre.

From its flattened summit, both ends of the Serpent Temple were intervisible. It was a stage where the symbolic rites were performed, watched by all those who participated in a ritual spread over an entire sacred landscape. At the appropriate moment, signals could be given to the two extremities of the serpent's body, triggering a process that would fuse the energies from its tail to other, countrywide currents that linked sacred sites up and down the land. At a time determined by the cycles of the heavens, the energies of the Sun would stream down an alignment of shrines, positioned according to their function, to create an orgasmic coupling of male and female energies throughout the land.

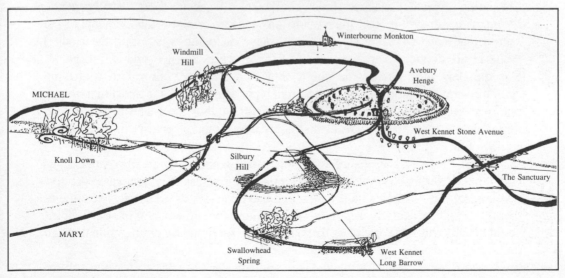

DAWN, MAY 6th, 1989. Sun at 15 degrees Taurus. A bright star shines overhead as we walk down the hill from the Sanctuary to join the stone avenue. The air is warm and the dark shapes play tricks on the eyes: They seem to move, like curious onlookers weary with waiting. As we silently pass between the lines of watching stones, we are aware that this slow procession marks the end of what has been, for us, a remarkable journey. It had taken us to many truly magical places and given us a glimpse of another reality. Slowly, we had come to appreciate the immense understanding that the people who built these monuments had of the natural world. They had perfected an art of living in harmony with the land which recognized the creative Life Force that animated it, and had participated in its manifestation. Their rites and festivals celebrated the key times when an alchemical fusion between the various energies, from earth and cosmos, took place according to the laws of universal rhythm. Their 'religion' had in reality been a natural science.

All the great monuments we had come across had been erected according to clearly defined principles, each place with its precise function. The crossing points of the male and female energies of the Earth were the sense organs of the land, receiving impulses of energy which were harmonized by the Earth itself. The special nature of these places, which often strike people as having a powerfully magical atmosphere, is also indicated by the energy field that is dowseable where the currents anchor themselves deep into the surface of the planet. In the early stages this had taken the form of various irregular pentagrams, but had suddenly changed in May 1988, at dawn in the Henge, to be replaced by three large 12-pointed stars, one within the other. Subsequently, this concentric formation had been found to have displaced the previous one at all node points checked. Yet again, we were merely performing the role of observers, unqualified to comment or speculate on the meaning of such changes.

Landscapes where these nodes occurred close together had been selected as centres of this ancient science of the dragon energies. At such places the serpentine currents changed their character, forsaking their usually gentle meanderings to assume coil-like contortions as if to 'contain' the elements of the sacred landscape. At Avebury, the main place of fusion was within the Henge, while at Glastonbury Tor, the course of the energies seemed uniquely organic. For the only time during the quest, they appeared to conform to a striking symbolic representation of how the archetypal forms of solar and lunar forces manifest. The male principle is a creative thrust into the material world; the female is the container, or Grail, that holds this explosive energy in harmonious equilibrium.

William Stukeley's vision of the ancient landscape covered in a stupendous collection of Serpent Temples, or Dracontia, the greatest of which was Avebury, was correct. Stone circles, many of which had once possessed avenues leading to them, marked particularly important places where the influence of the Earth Spirit could be concentrated, or channelled out into the surrounding countryside through its hidden network of veins and arteries.

Churches were serpent temples also, built on the old sites to use the refined spiritual energies under a different ethos. The dragon-slaying saints of Christianity were a graphic description of the underlying universal forces that are behind existence. The imagery is so apparent when the nature of the enigma is understood that such a realization seems suddenly quite obvious.

The elemental forces also play their part: The fire festivals throughout the ancient world seem to have been no empty rituals but actions to invigorate the system of flowing forces that permeate the planet. By the law of sympathetic resonance, the life-giving solar energy was drawn into beacon hills, mounds and elevated shrines at times when its qualities were especially potent. The element of earth was enshrined in the stones themselves as well as in the sanctified landscape. The flowing, airy element is responsible for the continuously mutable and mobile nature of the currents, reflecting the unseen realms of pure spirit from which they issue, whilst they also show an affinity for water, particularly the feminine, ruled as it is by the Moon.

The way the currents operate and their association with rocky outcrops had also led us to believe that, on a purely physical level, they were connected with geological fault lines in the Earth's crust. It seemed a remarkable coincidence that in the 13th century, the *same earthquake* had demolished two of the most important St Michael churches in southern Britain, at Glastonbury and St Michael's Mount, a hundred and fifty miles apart. St Michael's Church at Brentor was built on a volcanic mound, which also indicated that these energies might be issuing from deep within the planet, perhaps condensing as streams of bio-magnetic energy from the molten magma in the heart of the Earth. Their tendency to run along river valleys may be another facet of this. The sudden angular changes of direction that we had come across seemed to take place at what Guy Underwood called 'Blind Springs', spots where subterranean features produce a crossing of underground streams. Church fonts (in their original position) are invariably located over such crossings, which might explain how, for instance, the gargoyle font at Lostwithiel could affect the currents so dramatically.

The early Church had understood much of these matters, although the original operation of the system takes us back to very remote times. There has been a steady decline that has gradually eroded our relationship with Nature, a devolution, yet new ages have brought fresh evolutionary impulses. The earthly network, its old shrines often taken over as hill-forts as warlike tendencies became uppermost in the human spirit, needed to be re-dedicated to ideals of a higher order. Early Christianity provided the framework for a renaissance during an influx of new energies, and the religious revivals of Medieval times when the great cathedrals and churches were built was another example. Since then, much has been lost. The industrialization of the western world has progressively created a situation where humanity works against Nature instead of with it. The old knowledge has been driven underground, to survive only in secret societies and barely-audible tales of traditional folklore. Historically, though, it is impossible not to come face to face with evidence that many of the influential characters that shaped the fate of nations were privy to the secret workings of Nature; the Normans, the Benedictines, the Augustinian Canons, the Knights Templar, the

Freemasons, members of the Royal line and their supporters.

Today, we stand at the crossroads of evolution. To continue down a road that leads inevitably to an even greater alienation from Nature is clearly against the Laws of Creation. The remedy has been forced upon us: We must consider the Earth as a Mother who gives us Life, a treasurehouse of everyday, miraculous events, and nurtures all its creatures according to their own characteristics. This is a very ancient view. In coming to a conscious realization that the Earth and its inhabitants form a living whole, we will have transcended the barrier of time to link in spirit with those who lived their vision in another age. As another great cycle of Time draws to a close, the dawn of a new understanding illuminates the horizon: Humanity will assume its proper place in the scheme of things as co-creators of the world about us, a voluntary return to Divine Law. The memories that are now stirring within every individual are a response to new energies flooding into the Earth's field: It is for each person to become conscious of their role in this Great Work and participate in the process of evolution.

The three concentric 12-pointed stars found at node points.

THE GOLDEN DAWN

MAYDAY, AVEBURY, 2000 BC. In the darkness, flames leap from a hill behind Silbury, flickering in its watery moat and creating an image of a vast body, as invisible as infinite space, surrounded by living light. Figures appear, silhouetted against the glow, which begin to enact a sacred ritual on the great round stage elevated to just the correct position for its purpose. On the terrace below, hidden in the shade of the mound of the Goddess, others prepare for their part in the symbolic rite which is to represent in mime the secret workings of Nature.

From the head and tail of The Serpent, all eyes focus their gaze on the centre of the mystic ritual now in progress. Everyone is a part of the Great Rite which links them to their ancestors and the ordered rhythms of the Cosmos. Their emotions, energized by a joyous sense of unity, are suffused with a sacred fervour. They experience a deep and overwhelming love for all Creation. At the appropriate signal from the summit of the hill, certain individuals draw together to lead the procession down the great serpentine avenues, flanked on either side by lines of giant stones. Hundreds of others appear from the trees beyond to follow the wave of robed figures moving to the secret centre, hidden in the folds of the darkened landscape.

Suddenly, they come upon the Henge. Within, all is still. They cross the water-filled moat, glistening in the velvet black, to enter the holy of holies: The Sanctuary where the ultimate fusion takes place.

There is a hushed silence, broken abruptly by the dramatic chanting of deep, melodious invocations. The waters enclosing the vessel of change grow golden with the lightening sky. On the horizon, a star heralds the imminent appearance of the winged globe as its light is shed across the heavens, and the rings of stone glow with a power that spirals like a swirling vortex deep into the Earth and far out into the Heavens. The sense of individuality, of separateness, has vanished. Each being transcends to become fully conscious of the continuity of Nature, immersed in its all-encompassing splendour.

There is a burst of fire. A wave of rapture sweeps the land as the kiss of the Sun cascades over the Earth, drawn into its body by the great line of sacred fires sparked into life across country. There is an ecstatic orgasm between the winged secret flame of the Sun God and the coiled splendours of the Earth Goddess. The world is regenerated, and all its creatures rejoice.

The Spirit of the Earth knows that this will not always be so. There will come a time when humanity will choose to go against Nature, to exploit her bounteous gifts, causing a sickness across the planet. People will forget the ecstasies of communion, and life will become drab and colourless. In those coming dark ages, though, a deep sense of loss will cause the beginnings of a Great Return. They will look at the landscape and the old temples, built to withstand the cataclysms of millennia, and understand once again the sacred laws of Existence. When this day comes, humanity will have come of age. It will consciously acknowledge its role in the creative impulse that comes from the Sun, fertilizes the Earth, and calls forth the flame in the hearts of men and women to worship Life and the miraculous forces behind Creation.

The St

Michael

across

W
Oliver
Devil's Bed and Bol
Stoke St Michael
Glastonbury
St Michaels Othery
St Michaels Trull
Burrow Bridge
Sm
Holcombe Rogus
Creech St Mi
Corfe
Wellington Monument
Crediton
Cadbury Castle
Yes Tor
Lydford
Prestonbury Castle
Cheesewring
Spinsters Rock
The Hurlers
St Michaels Brentor
Roche Rock
Lostwithiel
Truro
Resugga Castle
Leedstown
Old Kea
Boscawen-un
Germoe
Carn Les Boal
St Michael's Mount

2-1-'87

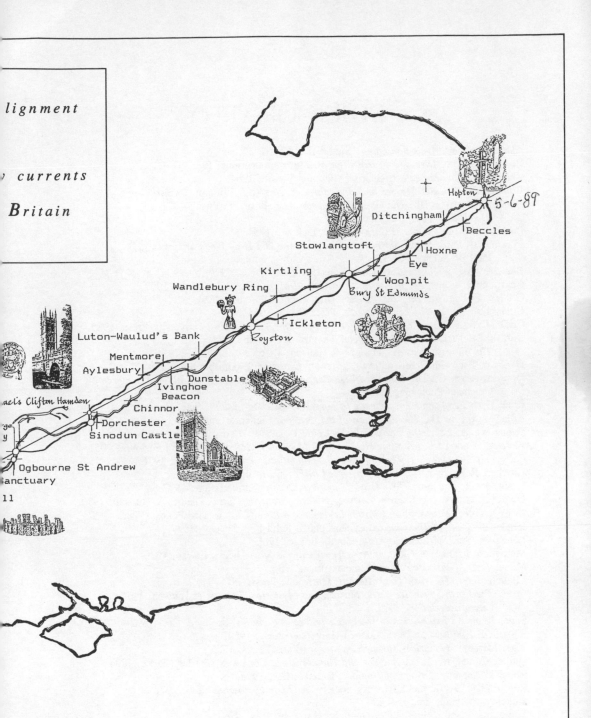

lignment

currents

Britain

Hopton 5-6-89

Ditchingham

Beccles

Stowlangtoft

Hoxne

Eye

Kirtling

Woolpit

Wandlebury Ring

Bury St Edmunds

Ickleton

Royston

Luton–Waulud's Bank

Mentmore

Aylesbury

Dunstable

Ivinghoe Beacon

...ael's Clifton Hamden

Chinnor

Dorchester

Sinodun Castle

...ge

...y

Ogbourne St Andrew

...anctuary

11

A series of maps (Ordnance Survey Landranger 1:50 000) is available with the earth currents associated with the St Michael Line marked as found during this quest. Details may be obtained (with SAE) from Pendragon Press, Box 888, Launceston, Cornwall, England PL15 7YH

BIBLIOGRAPHY

Ashe, Geoffrey, *Avalonian Quest*, Methuen & Co., 1982.

Bergamar, Kate, *Discovering Hill Figures*, Shire Publications, 1986.

Blake, William, *Jerusalem*, George Allen and Unwin, 1964.

Blight, J.T., *Ancient Crosses and Antiquities of Cornwall*, William Cornish, 1872.

Bond, Frederick Bligh, *The Gate of Remembrance*, Basil Blackwell, 1921.
    The Hill of Vision, 1919.

Borlase, W., *Antiquities of Cornwall*, W. Jackson, 1754.

Broadhurst, Paul, *Secret Shrines: In Search of the Old Holy Wells of Cornwall*,
    Paul Broadhurst, 1988.

Burl, Aubrey, *Prehistoric Avebury*, Yale University Press, 1979.

Charpentier, Louis, *Lés Mystéres de la Cathedral de Chartres*, Laffont, 1967.

Collins, Wilkie, *Rambles Beyond Railways*, Richard Bentley, 1851.

Colquhoun, Ithell, *The Living Stones*, Peter Owen, 1952.

Cook, J. with T. Rowley, *Dorchester Through the Ages*, Oxford University Press, 1985.

Dames, Michael, *The Avebury Cycle*, Thames & Hudson, 1977.
    The Silbury Treasure, Thames & Hudson, 1976.

Delgado, Pat, with Colin Andrews, *Circular Evidence*, Bloomsbury, 1989.

Dobson, Revd. C., *Did Our Lord Visit Britain As They Say In Cornwall And Somerset?*
    Covenant Publishing, 1936.

Eitel, E.J., *Feng-shui: The Science of Sacred Landscape in Old China*, Trubner & Co., 1873.

Elliot Smith, Sir G., *The Evolution of the Dragon*, Manchester University Press, 1919.

Evans-Wentz, J.D., *The Fairy Faith in Celtic Countries*, Henry Frowde, 1911.

Fletcher, Canon J.R., *A Short History of St Michael's Mount*, St Michael's Mount, 1951.

Graves, Tom, *Dowsing, Techniques and Applications*, Turnstone Books, 1976.

Hawker, R.S., *Footprints of Former Men in Far Cornwall*, 1870.

Hoult, Janet, *Dragons: Their History and Symbolism*, Gothic Image, 1987.

Huxley, Francis, *The Dragon, Spirit of Nature, Nature of Spirit*. Thames & Hudson, 1979.

Jeffrey, Peter, *East Anglian Ghosts, Legends and Lore*, Old Orchard Press, 1988.

Leadbeater, C.W., *The Chakras*, Theosophical Publishing Society, 1927.

Lonegren, Sig, *Spiritual Dowsing*, Gothic Image, 1986.

Maltwood, Katherine, *Glastonbury's Temple of the Stars*, James Clarke, 1929.

Mann, Nick, *Glastonbury Tor*, Annenterprise, 1986.

Michell, John, *The View Over Atlantis*, Garnstone Press, 1975.
    The Earth Spirit: Its Ways, Shrines and Mysteries, Thames & Hudson, 1975.
    City of Revelation, 1972.

Page, John, *An Exploration of Dartmoor and its Antiquities*, Seeley & Co., 1892.

Piggott, S., *William Stukeley*, Oxford University Press, 1950.

Pitts, Michael, *Footprints Through Avebury*, Michael Pitts, 1985.

Quiller Couch, M. & L., *Ancient and Holy Wells of Cornwall*, Charles Clarke, 1894.

Roberts, Anthony, *Sowers of Thunder*, Rider & Co., 1978.

Royston and District Local History Society, *A Guide to Royston Cave*, 1978.

Stukeley, William, *Abury*, 1743.

Tompkins, Peter, *The Magic of Obelisks*, Harper & Row, 1981.

Tudor Pole, Wellesley, *Michael, Prince of Heaven*, Watkins, 1951.

Underwood, Guy, *The Pattern of the Past*, Museum Press, 1969.

Watkins, Alfred, *The Old Straight Track*, Methuen & Co., 1925.

Weatherhill, Craig, *Belerion*, Alison Hodge, 1981.

Also: The French magazine *Atlantis* and the excellent church guides and histories available at churches from Land's End to East Anglia.

INDEX